POLITEXT 189

# The merchant vessel
# A sociologycal analysis

EDICIONS UPC

**POLITEXT**

Ricardo Rodríguez-Martos Dauer

# The merchant vessel
# A sociologycal analysis

EDICIONS UPC

English translation of the Spanish original:
El buque mercante. Un análisis sociológico.


First edition: September 2009


Cover design: Manuel Andreu


©      Ricardo Rodríguez-Martos Dauer, 2009

©      Edicions UPC, 2009
       Edicions de la Universitat Politècnica de Catalunya, SL
       Jordi Girona Salgado 1-3, 08034 Barcelona
       Tel.: 934 137 540   Fax: 934 137 541
       Edicions Virtuals: www.edicionsupc.es
       E-mail: edicions-upc@upc.edu

Production:   LIGHTNING SOURCE


Legal deposit: B-37679-2008
ISBN: 978-84-9880-366-2

This work may only be reproduced, distributed, publicly disclosed or transformed with permission from its
copyright holders, with the exception provided by the law. If you need to photocopy or scan a part of this
work, please contact CEDRO (Spanish Centre for Reprographic Rights) at www.cedro.org.

*To the memory of Alfredo Rubio,
my teacher.*

# index

| | |
|---|---|
| **Foreword** | 6 |
| **Preface** | 10 |
| **1 The merchant vessel as a form of total institution** | 14 |
| 1.1 The total institution: concept and elements | 15 |
| 1.2 Different types of total institutions: basic similarities and differences | 18 |
| 1.3 Structure and purpose of the merchant vessel, as a total institution | 19 |
| 1.4 Objections to application of the concept of total institution | 24 |
| 1.5 The vessel institution as socio-technical system | 25 |
| 1.6 Conclusion | 26 |
| **2 The inner life of the ship institution** | 30 |
| 2.1 Life aboard ship | 31 |
| 2.1.1 Introduction | 31 |
| 2.1.2 Hierarchically ordered life | 32 |
| 2.2 The ship's crew – a schematic view | 34 |
| 2.3 Roles | 34 |
| 2.3.1 The sociological sense of role | 34 |
| 2.3.2 Role performance | 37 |
| 2.3.3 Roles aboard a merchant vessel | 39 |
| 2.3.4 The enduring nature of shipboard roles | 48 |
| 2.4 Managing personnel and ratings: relations and differences | 49 |
| 2.5 The internal world of the crew | 54 |
| 2.5.1 Features | 54 |
| 2.5.2 Formal instrumental organisation | 56 |
| 2.5.3 Means of control: incentives and penalties | 58 |
| 2.5.4 Primary and secondary adjustments | 59 |
| 2.6 Links between the crew members | 67 |
| 2.6.1 Subgroups | 67 |
| 2.6.2 Tensions between subgroups | 69 |
| 2.6.3 Traditions, customs and attitudes | 74 |
| 2.7 The importance of a common system of life and a common language | 77 |
| 2.8 The crew in terms of ship type | 78 |
| 2.9 International crews | 82 |
| 2.9.1 Causes and factors explaining their appearance | 82 |
| 2.9.2 Sociocultural aspects to be borne in mind | 82 |

| | |
|---|---:|
| 2.9.3 How international crews affect ship safety | 84 |
| 2.10 Downsized crews | 87 |
| 2.10.1 Preliminary considerations | 87 |
| 2.10.2 Downsized crews and ship safety | 88 |
| 2.10.3 How life aboard is affected by smaller crews | 91 |
| 2.11 Flags of convenience | 92 |
| 2.11.1 General considerations | 92 |
| 2.11.2 The sociological implications | 93 |
| **3 The crew member** | **98** |
| 3.1 The crew member's world | 99 |
| 3.1.1 Seamen's awareness of themselves | 101 |
| 3.2 Reasons for becoming a seaman | 102 |
| 3.3 Recently embarked seamen | 108 |
| 3.4 Potential personal consequences of life on board ship | 113 |
| 3.4.1 Mutilation of the self | 114 |
| 3.4.2 Breakdown of the usual relationship between the acting individual and his acts | 116 |
| 3.4.3 Response of the crew member to his situation aboard ship | 119 |
| 3.5 Private space aboard ship | 121 |
| 3.6 The leisure time of the crew member | 123 |
| 3.7 Communication with other crew members: the importance of language | 128 |
| 3.8 The solitude of the seaman | 132 |
| 3.8.1 General factors relating to solitude amongst seamen | 132 |
| 3.8.2 Reduction of crews and increased solitude | 132 |
| 3.8.3 Boredom | 135 |
| 3.9 Stress and fatigue among seamen | 138 |
| 3.9.1 Stress | 138 |
| 3.9.2 Fatigue | 139 |
| 3.10 Women as professionals of the sea | 142 |
| 3.10.1 Introduction | 142 |
| 3.10.2 Integration into the crew | 143 |
| 3.10.3 Access to the labour market | 145 |
| 3.10.4 The potential influence of women on life aboard ship | 146 |
| 3.10.5 Women and the exercise of authority | 146 |
| 3.10.6 Family life and professional life | 147 |
| **4 The relations of crew members with the outside world** | **150** |
| 4.1 The relationship of the crew member with society in general | 151 |
| 4.1.1 Social identity of seafarers | 151 |
| 4.1.2 Information | 153 |
| 4.1.3 Social and political participation: associations and trade unions | 154 |
| 4.2 The ship in port | 155 |

| | |
|---|---|
| 4.2.1 The relationship of the seaman with people who come aboard | 157 |
| 4.2.2 The relationship of seamen with the port population: communication and fun | 158 |
| 4.3 Passenger ships and relations with the passengers | 160 |
| 4.4 The relationship of crew members with their families | 163 |
| 4.4.1 Seamen's family problems | 163 |
| 4.4.2 Family integration | 169 |
| 4.4.3 Communication with the family | 171 |
| 4.4.4 The family on board | 173 |
| 4.5 Rejoining family life: returning home | 175 |
| 4.6 Seamen rejoining society on land | 181 |
| 4.7 Seamen's welfare centres | 183 |
| **5 Crew recruitment and organisation criteria** | **186** |
| 5.1 Merchant ships as total institutions: the implications | 187 |
| 5.2 The personal and professional significance of good relations aboard ship | 188 |
| 5.3 Crew organisation, taking account of sociological and psychological aspects | 190 |
| 5.4 Recruitment schemes for future crews | 191 |
| 5.4.1 Prior considerations | 191 |
| 5.4.2 Admission tests for nautical studies | 192 |
| 5.5 The ship of the future | 205 |
| 5.5.1 Concerning technical progress | 205 |
| 5.5.2 The ideal crew on the ship of the future | 206 |
| 5.5.3 The viability of ships with downsized crews | 208 |
| 5.5.4 The crew member's relation with his own world | 211 |
| 5.6 The profile of the captain on ships in the immediate future | 212 |
| 5.7 The human factor at sea: research fields opening up | 213 |
| **6 Postscript** | **216** |
| **Bibliography** | **220** |
| Books, articles and talks/lectures | 221 |
| Studies and surveys | 226 |
| **Notes** | **228** |

# foreword

# foreword

A sociological study on living conditions aboard merchant ships: that is the main object of the pages of this book.

Carrying out a study of this kind involved combining two essential elements: a capacity for sociological analysis on the one hand, and direct experience of the sea on the other. Each of these elements can certainly be found separately, but only rarely are they found together in one person. Ricardo Rodríguez-Martos, however, has both types of knowledge, theoretical and practical: as a sociologist and as a merchant-marine captain. And he has succeeded in integrating both elements in his study, blending them skilfully.

The theoretical reference framework that the author adopts emerges as novel, pertinent and fruitful. Availing himself of the notion of the "total institution", as developed by the American sociologist Erwing Goffman in a work initially published in 1961, enables him to pursue an original approach, and a very solid one from the standpoint of sociological theory. Indeed Goffman himself alluded in his study to the life of a crew out at sea as a possible example for analysing the characteristics and specific functioning of a total institution. Yet what was there little more than an insinuation becomes, in Ricardo Rodríguez-Martos' book, the starting point for a coherent analysis and an outstanding application of the theoretical concept.

After defining the problems and explaining the analytical model upon which his work rests, the author offers us an objective, detailed panoramic view of the various factors at work in shaping the distinct life-style of the men –and occasionally the women– who make the sea their profession: the crews, the roles within the crew, and the kind of relations that arise between its various members; how these relations are influenced by the smaller size and international composition of the crews; what motivates sailors; the implications of life aboard in attempting to maintain a private sphere, in leisure activities, and in the dialectic between communication and solitude, between boredom and tension and fatigue.

This central part of the analysis is rounded off with an essential chapter on the social relations of the seafarer with the world outside, relations that are difficult precisely as a result of the character of life on board from a standpoint that sees the ship as a total institution. In addition to the situation of ships in ports and the particular case of passenger ships, the author places special emphasis on the issues of family relations, the problems sailors have in integrating into the family cell, and the problems arising from their return to family life, and to on-shore society in general.

In broad outline, these are the strictly sociological coordinates framing Ricardo Rodríguez-Martos' study. However, though without ever abandoning this scientific approach to his object of study, the author constantly goes beyond simply reporting the objective conditions of life on board and analysing its implications.

For indeed, underneath his entire approach, there is a twin concern born of his personal experience of life at sea.

First, there is his concern for the future outlook: concern over the consequences of the growing technical progress in ships, entailing a decrease in crew sizes with the crew being obliged to undertake work which is predominantly mechanical and, in many respects, dehumanising, with hardly anything to compensate for this because of the very isolation of the crew. And concern, accordingly, over how these crews should be organised, how their members should be selected, and over redefining to some extent the roles and modes of exercising authority on board.

Secondly and most importantly, concern over the human factor: the economic interests at play in the merchant marine world are considerable and legitimate. But behind and even above the necessary rationalism in work organisation, Ricardo Rodríguez-Martos sees the real protagonist of sea life when all is said and done: this protagonist is and should always be the human being, the seafarer as a person.

Joan Estruch
Professor of Sociology
Universitat Autònoma de Barcelona

# preface

# preface

Right from my first sea voyages I was struck by the importance of people getting on well on board, and the various factors that played a part in this. For that reason, along with my personal concern for the human factor, I have been gathering experience, information and academic studies over the course of seven years at sea, twenty years as a lecturer in what is now called the Faculty of Nautical Studies of Barcelona and 12 years in charge of the Apostleship of the Sea there, and all this bore fruit in the form of my doctoral thesis *El buque mercante como institución total* (The Merchant Ship as a Total Institution), submitted in June 1995 to the Faculty of Nautical Studies of the Polytechnic University of Barcelona, the thesis having been directed by Dr. Joan Estruch.

Having submitted the thesis, my wish for this work to serve as a reference book for seafarers, shipping companies and others and as a textbook for nautical students prompted me to make the adaptations needed to produce this book I am now presenting.

Since I had a great deal of material on the subject, I adopted as my work scheme that of the work *Assyliums* by Erwing Goffman, in which that sociologist gives a wide-ranging analysis of the nature of total institutions.

I believe that studying maritime sociology is indispensable in designing the ships of the future and also in managing them and organising life aboard them. The former task falls to the States, to labour regulations and to shipping companies or shipowners, while the latter will be of interest to all who are to live and work on board ships, particularly those who will be in positions of command responsibility on them.

It is clear to anyone who is or has been a seafarer that the greatest problems commonly arising on ships are related not so much to technical matters as to human relations.

There is a great deal of literature on the life of the sailor from the psychological and sociological standpoint, though the greater part of it is in the form of short articles concentrating on particular aspects. There are also a few books that attempt to portray the harsh reality of the seafarer's life through recording the accounts of seamen and the experiences of the author, such books being mines of individual experience but none too systematic for analytical purposes.

The aim of this work is thus to present an analysis of the sociological reality of seafarers and their environment.

For this purpose, it is divided into these five chapters:

1. **The merchant vessel as a form of total institution**: this first chapter gives a definition of a total institution, discusses the various types of such institutions, and goes on to specify how and why we can regard the merchant ship as a total institution.
2. **The inner life of the ship institution**: here the crew is studied as a social group, analysing the various roles found and their characteristics, the relations between officers and ratings, subgroups, international crews and downsized crews.
3. **The crew member**: this chapter approaches the study from the point of view of the individual inside the ship institution, considering his reasons for going aboard, his integration in the world of the crew, the identity of the sailor and his search for his own space.
4. **The relations of crew members with the outside world**: here we turn to how being a seafarer affects relations with society in general and with the family in particular - the sailor's attitude to people on shore, the typical problems of families in which the husband and father is a seaman, and the "crisis" of returning home.
5. **Crew recruitment and organisation criteria**: this last chapter seeks to summarise a number of basic points concerning life inside the ship institution and to use them in seeking valid criteria for designing crews in the current context of the merchant marine. For this purpose, a number of studies produced in various countries are drawn on, concerning the physical and psychological characteristics that a person intending to pursue the seafaring life should possess.

Hence this work is a study of the ship institution, its members and their relations with the world around them.

Ricardo Rodríguez-Martos Dauer
Barcelona, May 1996

# the merchant vessel as a form of total institution

## 1.1 The total institution: concept and elements

*A total institution can be defined as a place of residence and work in which a large number of individuals, all in the same situation and isolated from society for a significant period of time, share in their confinement a formally administered daily routine.*[1] We thus have an initial spatial factor, the place of residence and work, which acts as a framework for day-to-day life and the social relations of the group in question.

That place or space is not open: entry and departure are not free, the group members are in some way enclosed in it and isolated from the rest of society.

A factory or an office cannot be considered to be total institutions, despite having their own rules and although a close relationship is formed between those working in them, for all who work therein do so for only a limited number of hours, after which they resume their own private lives, in which they can engage in different activities. What is more, their members can leave their work posts if they have good reason to do so, and can in any case leave them physically even if they thereby break a rule.

As Nick Perry states[2], a basic characteristic of industrial societies is that for most of the populace it is both possible and probable for them to be associated with groups and organisations that have disparate aims, membership and behavioural expectations.

Perry further asserts that one way of differentiating totalitarian from democratic societies is (to take up a phrase of Goffman's) to analyse whether or not they are total institutions.

In a total institution, its members are set apart from outside life, they lack the chance to combine it with some other outside activity, to leave the place they are in and, anonymously or by adopting a different role, to join a much wider social setting. An inmate, on the other hand, cannot decide for himself when to leave. He comes to a place for a purpose, and the life he will lead there goes beyond his own purposes. The freedom of action and movement which characterise life outside the institution are lost here. There is a common purpose, a set of objectives standing above the interests of the individual. Its members, or most of them at least, have no choice regarding their behaviour and this is a source of conflict (another feature of total institutions).

The number of people is also of importance. One or two people can never form a total institution, given that there is no sense of group, of sacrificing many personal traits in favour of other common traits. There has to be a hierarchical structure, with a few individuals organising the life of the many. There must be a certain number of individuals, then, and they must furthermore be in a similar situation, that is, fully sharing daily life, with limitations more or less common to all members of the group.

Their "confinement" must also have a duration, so that the members of the institution have the chance to make a place for themselves in it and feel how it exercises enormous pressure upon them. Only these two conditions, of "isolation" and "confinement" together, give rise to the leading of an internal institutional life in which, in addition to the existence of an institutionalised hierarchy, other relationships and even power subgroups arise. Inmates are then obliged to find out where they fit within a complex interlocking mechanism, and to seek compensatory systems at group and individual level if they do not wish to be marginalised and have a bad time.

This group must, finally, have a "formally administered" pace of life, a routine. That is, the group has guidelines, laws or rules to which its members must adhere and which supersede its members' individual wills.

A large group of friends who decide to take a year off to sail round the world in a yacht, notwithstanding the fact that the voyage may involve isolation and even confinement, is not in principle a total institution, given that the friends have themselves freely decided to form the group for that purpose, and they themselves decide what to do at any particular time. Furthermore, if disputes and differences arise they can detach themselves from the group, cancel or alter the trip or do whatever they decide. There are no institutionalised rules, no social implications having repercussions for members wishing to abandon the expedition. Their very hierarchy, where such exists, is the fruit of an agreement amongst peers.

The formal administration of the life of the group is thus a basic factor in defining the nature of a total institution.

To return to Goffman[3]: *...Any institution absorbs part of the time and interest of its members and to an extent provides them with a world of its own: it has, in short, absorbing tendencies... The absorbing or totalising tendency is symbolised by the obstacles placed in the way of* *social interaction with the exterior and the exodus of its members, usually taking material form in locked doors, high walls, ditches, etc.*

Although in the course of the day inmates may have time of their own, in which they are in principle free to do what they wish within a framework of limitations, the institution always takes up part of the attention of its members, since it comes to form an inseparable part of their lives while they remain in it. Do what they might, the institution is always present.

And the confinement takes specific form in physical barriers which hinder, if not render impossible, departure from the institution.

*A basic element in the social ordering of modern society is that individuals tend to sleep, play and work in different places, with different companions, under different authorities and without a broad rational plan.*

The central characteristic of total institution can be described as a breaking down of the barriers which normally separate these three spheres of life.[4] Firstly, all aspects of life are conducted in the same place and under the same single authority. Secondly, each phase of the member's daily activity is carried on in the immediate company of a large batch of others, all of whom are treated alike and required to do the same thing together. Thirdly, all phases of the day's activities are tightly scheduled, with one activity leading at a prearranged time into the next, the whole sequence of activities being imposed from above by a system of explicit formal rulings and a body of officials whose job it is to see that they are complied with. Fourthly, the various enforced activities are brought together into a single rational plan purportedly designed to fulfil the institution's own aimes.

In the total institution, therefore, the variety of spheres in which individuals normally move, and which involve not only different centres or venues but also different roles, is broken. Citizens work, amuse themselves and rest in different places, with different people, and they also play different roles. A prisoner, even when playing football, remains prisoner number x, while an employee who goes to a sports centre to play football with his friends is no longer an employee but a member of that centre or of that group of friends.

In engaging in these activities in different places, the citizen referred to above also adapts to different sets of rules; where in one sphere he might be a subordinate, in the other he might be a leader. The change of sphere also involves a change of people, so that he can draw a completely clear dividing line between one group and another according to whether they are people imposed by a job or an activity, chosen individually or arising out of any other reasons of social relationships.

The sequence of life outside of a total institution leaves scope for individual's own organisation. Employees may have to eat in the works canteen at the time set for them, but they can later have their dinners where, when and with whom they wish.

Goffman also points to a control over that life, carried out by officials. But this does not have to be applicable strictly to all total institutions. We have to see, for example, if the so-called official forms part of the institution or only spends some time in it and does not therefore really form part of the institution.

There can be total institutions in which every single member is subject to a set of common rules, as in the case of a convent. However, somebody is always who exercise authority and have power to impose penalties, whether or not that somebody forms part of the institution.

Another important feature is that the rules are not improvised, but come from former times (have a history) and from above, so that even those with controlling functions have to comply with pre-established precepts.

Finally, and above all, there are objectives to be achieved, a purpose for which the institution was created and which inevitably marks the life of its inmates. The inmates are there for a purpose and in order to do something.

## 1.2 Different types of total institutions: basic similarities and differences

Goffman[5] establishes the following classification of total institutions:
- institutions for caring for incapable yet inoffensive persons (homes for the elderly, the blind, etc.;
- institutions to care for those who cannot take care of themselves and who constitute an involuntary danger to the community (psychiatric hospitals, hospices for lepers, etc.);
- institutions organised to protect the community against those who constitute a threat to it (prisons, concentration camps, etc.);
- institutions expressly designed for better performance of a particular job, and explicable only in terms of these instrumental purposes (army barracks, ships, work camps, etc.);
- institutions conceived as refuges from the world, often also serving as clerical training centres (monasteries, convents, etc.).

Without embarking upon study of the different types of total institutions, we could take a look at any similarities and differences there might be between the ones mentioned above.

These are institutions that inmates enter because they are forced to do so, as in the case of a psychiatric hospital, a prison, a concentration camp or even barracks for recruits who are to carry out military service, all institutions which inmates enter because they have no choice in the matter.

There are other institutions which inmates enter of their own accord: convents, barracks for professional soldiers, merchant vessels, etc., but this does not mean that inmates do not occasionally wish to leave and never return, or that if they do stay it is not due to reasons obliging them to do so.

There remains in any case a major difference: inmates do not enter on doctor's orders or because they are obliged to, and if they do so against their will it is because they are for some reason obliging themselves to do so or because some anomalous external factor induces them to enter.

Another difference is that in some institutions the purpose of the internment is purportedly rehabilitation (either of health or social behaviour), as in the case of psychiatric hospitals, prisons or reformatories.

In the case of seagoing vessels, barracks and convents, the purpose of the internment is simply to be able to carry out a particular personal or social project, which might involve exercising a profession, forming part of an effective army, achieving a deeper spiritual life, and so on.

In these last three examples, all are inmates, both the staff in authority and those obeying them, while in other cases a clear difference is discernible between those who control and direct and those who are really inmates.

### 1.3 Structure and purpose of the merchant vessel, as a total institution

Taking Goffman's[6] definition as a basis, we will now go on to see how a merchant vessel has the characteristics inherent to a total institution.[7]

*Place of residence and work*: This is not only a characteristic inherent to any total institution, but is indeed one of the aspects which best defines a seagoing vessel: a place of work and residence.

It is a place of work because the raison d'être of a vessel is maritime trade, from which the shipowner or shipping company hopes to make a profit. The vessel has been built for a specific type of shipping and a crew is recruited so that the vessel can accomplish its mission. But at the same time it is a place of residence, to some extent the crew's home for such time as they are aboard. The crew will work on the ship, seek their free-time leisure activities on the ship and sleep on the ship.

Nolan[8] speaks of a 24-hours society, *in which the routine of watches and work systems not only marks the system of work but also of meals, rest, leisure activities and social contacts.*

*A variable number of crew members*: Passenger liners can have crews of 500, 1000 or more (most of whom belong to the catering department). A freight vessel would traditionally have had a crew of 15 to 40 members, depending on its tonnage, with a crew of 30 being quite normal. As in all sectors of industry, there is nowadays a tendency to reduce the number of workers, so that due to automation vessels can now be found with less than half the former number of crew members. There are currently small vessels operating with crews of only 6 or 7 members.

What is more, not all crew members would be working together or on common tasks. Crew members on watch, on the bridge or in the machine room would be working alongside only one or two other crew members at most. Except for passenger ships, even in the kitchen there would only be two or three crew members working together, and sometimes only one. The crew members who work most as a team are the deck hands. It is nevertheless also true that a crew member, even when working alone, is doing so in a small area, so that there are other crew members not far away engaged in other tasks. Even while the others sleep, a crew member on watch functions comes to be as the eyes of the body at rest.

*Confinement and isolation for a significant period of time*: When the vessel is at sea, the crew have the physical obstacle of being surrounded by the sea. They cannot simply leave the ship as they wish. If there is any special event in their families, or any other occasion of social or cultural importance, they cannot simply travel freely. Except in an emergency, not even the captain is free to alter the course of the vessel.

A ship has a destination marked out by its assignment, a route drawn up by the shipowner or charterer, and nothing short of an emergency involving the vessel itself, an accident at sea or a situation which threatens the life of the crew can alter the course of the ship. To provide an example, a Spanish sailor on a trip from Vigo to Buenos Aires who receives news that a loved one is dying will note that the ship continues to carry him inexorably further from his family, and he may expect to be able to disembark only at the port of destination, where authorised to do so by the shipowner, from where he may take the first plane back to Spain, if he can afford it. In the meantime, he will spend a couple of weeks suffering, desperate from a feeling of powerlessness.

Even when a ship is in port it is not always feasible for the sailors to leave; permission will have to be sought from the captain, who would then normally consult the shipowner, and permission would then be needed from the competent authorities, who have to stamp a leave form. It is not infrequent for sailors who are awaiting their holidays or who have organised some family event to find that the relief crew is delayed or does not turn up and that they remain "tied" to the ship, unable to leave it. And the situation is more tricky still if disembarkation has to take place in a foreign port, for leaving the ship without the pertinent legal formalities would place the seafarers in an illegal situation.

Under such conditions the crew, "confined" on their ship, remain isolated for the days or weeks the voyage lasts. Furthermore, on board there is an authority with functions going beyond strict organisation of the work, so that crew members could be said to be subject to that authority twenty-four hours a day.

*Formal administration of the daily work*[9] through an authority is present.

The hierarchical structure of a vessel, even a merchant vessel, bears some similarity to the military world, from which it is indeed inherited. John A. Encandela[10] put it as follows: *A small group of managers imposes on a larger group a set of formal rules, regimented schedules, and the use of standard items of equipment such as dress, food, bedding, and the like.*

Uniforms are not normally worn on freight vessels, the crew wearing whatever they like. On passenger vessels, on the other hand, all crew members, depending on department and professional rank, will have to wear some kind of uniform.

Meals are of course arranged for the crew as a whole, although some distinctions can be made for members who have to carry out the physically toughest tasks or for any sufficiently numerous different group within the crew which might, for cultural or religious reasons, require special types of meals.

The cabins will all be the same within any particular professional rank; although less frequent nowadays, several crew members sometimes have to share crew quarters, especially on passenger vessels.

Forsyth and Bankston[11] feel that the division between supervisory staff (officers) and ratings is almost a caste structure, although both are equally controlled by the institution.

Encandela[12] considers that, on the basis of Goffman, many studies have been carried out to broaden the concept and make it more precise, though they always stress the differences which exist between the managers and the managed.

Both in institutions having the purpose of rehabilitation and protection of society (prisons, psychiatric hospitals, etc.) and those in which the purpose is simply caring for people (homes for the elderly), researchers have shown that a certain distancing between those with management and/or controlling functions and those who are managed and controlled is the basis on which such institutions can operate efficiently, even if at the expense of the quality of human relations[13].

Encandela[14] discusses his experiences in the summer of 1986 on a dredger of the Corps of Engineers of the United States army:*The ship's crew of 51 men ate, slept, recreated and worked on board for long periods of time without leaving its confines. The division of labor and formal social relations were established by a militarily defined hierarchy; however, in spite of this social arrangement, men of all ranks spoke of the ship's crew as a 'family' and 'community'. Many asserted that life at sea required all crew members, despite official rank, to share a set of experiences and emotions, drawing attention to camaraderie rather than social distance between managers and the managed.*

In various studies, such as those of Wiley[15], Hirschhorn[16], Weedfald[17] and other authors in the sixties and beginning of the seventies, the inhuman treatment often meted out in total institutions revealed a need to reduce the social distance between the managers and the managed. This gave rise to an egalitarian movement in American culture, which in turn involved a process of deinstitutionalisation (see Scull and Starr[18]) and a tendency to blur hierarchical lines. And for his part, Encandela[19] thinks that it is possible to create an atmosphere of camaraderie in daily life and work without altering the nature of the hierarchy.

As in any total institution, the authority factor and the hierarchical structure on a merchant vessel are in fact necessary to ensure that it runs well[20]. Another matter is looking at ways to prevent a hierarchical system degenerating into a despotic and inhuman regime. We will be returning to this subject when we discuss the internal life of the vessel institution, in the second chapter of this work.

*Routine*: the daily work on ships is notable for its large measure of routine. All watches and day work are always laid down in schedules. Tradition and custom have considerable weight on ships, so that the introduction of new systems or working instruments is often greeted with reticence.

Methods of carrying out and allocating work also fits in with notions of routine by which life on board is governed.

Each crew member occupies a place in this social structure and each member having a minimum of experience is perfectly well aware of his task 24 hours a day.

Even free time falls within a routine: resting, reading a novel, watching a film on video, and nowadays on some ships playing with a computer and the like. Routine sucks in individuals, and at sea it is easiest simply to follow a regular pattern of life, repeated from one day to the next.

In a study on human resources in the European shipping industry by M.B.A. Dyer-Smith and M. Stein[21], the authors gathered the following statements from crew members: *"Life at sea is dead time"*, *"On the bridge, you're on half a brain. Most of the time it's like being in a dream ... I don't need a brain anymore"*, *"When you're asleep the time passes quicker"*. Routine is not only accepted, but actually sought out, the idea being to have time pass as quickly as possible so as to get back home.

In his memoirs from his time as a stoker on the old coal-powered steamships in the 1930s, Karl Helbig[22] tells us how he kept his mind alive and at the same time fought boredom. Before starting his shift he would choose a theme –a book he had read, a film he had seen, the words of a song, an experience he'd had – and then, throughout his shift, he would go developing the plot in his mind, giving his imagination free rein.

*The objective*: The objective of the crew on a vessel is, firstly, that they fulfil their function in shipping, that is, that they transport goods or people in accordance with instructions issued from land, secondly that they see to it that once in port the operations relating to that shipping (such as loading or unloading) are carried out properly and, thirdly, to see that the ship is correctly maintained and safe. A ship is a business, and of course an attempt is made to operate it for the maximum possible profit. When a vessel is being built, factors relating to best output are the ones taken chiefly into account. Its outline, tonnage, distribution of holds, hull shape, equipment fitted, and so forth, serve the purpose of ensuring that the vessel is as profitable as possible.

One aspect remains: that of how and where to accommodate the crew. In this respect, advances have been made over the course of seafaring history, for we have moved from a situation in which the crew all slept packed together in an orlop deck to one in which the crew members of most vessels nowadays have cabins of their own. Despite this, and as we shall see later, factors such as the automation of vessels in recent years, smaller crews and short stays in ports have led to a poorer quality of life for the crew. As Dyer-Smith and M. Stein[23] note, *productivity has been increased with automation and the rationalisation of manpower. But these very efficiencies render the seafaring way of life even less attractive to young people, and severe difficulties are now encountered in crewing even the residual fleet of ships ... We believe a socio-technical redesign of the ship-crew system is required.*

It is only to be expected that the purpose for which a merchant vessel is built is to carry out an economic activity and that that activity must be as profitable as possible. But this must not lead to crew members being considered as mere parts of the vessel, without human needs; quite the contrary, for a vessel to operate well a number of the human needs of those running it must be satisfied.

## 1.4 Objections to application of the concept of total institution

Nick Perry[24] and other authors, however, question whether the concept of total institution should be applied to the merchant vessel, for they feel that the notion is no more than a first approximation which has informed the little social research done into shipboard behaviour in recent years.

Perry feels that too enthusiastic an acceptance of the idea of total institutions as a distinctive class of organisation leads to *a conceptual minefield for the unwary*. For him, Etzioni's[25] concept *of organisational scope* is more appropriate than Goffman's total institution. The argument is that organisational scope refers to all the activities in which an organisation's participants are jointly involved, without making assumptions as to how those activities are controlled, thereby recognising the possibility of considerable variations between one such organisation and another.

In the case of a ship, Perry considers that an important source of variation derives from its being an industrial unit, part of an economic enterprise. As determinants of shipboard conflict, we must look first to functional divisions deriving from the work structure.

Indeed, as noted in speaking of the various types of total institutions[26], there are major differences between a convent, a psychiatric institution, a barracks and a ship, to mention but a few.

It is further true that nowadays on some ships the crew consists of no more than seven or eight members, so that the numerous group notion becomes rather hazy, the crew member spending more time alone than in the company of others. And here the notion of total institution would become questionable. The very contractual aspect of the relationship of the crew member with the shipping company places the crew member in a position of less than the total obedience which holds in other total institutions.

However, and despite the fact that when it comes to taking factors from other total institutions for sociological analysis of the crew of a ship we often have to relativise them with significant distinctions, we can consider that, as explained in section 1.3, the concept of total institution is a very valid point of departure for analysis of the crew of a ship and their environment.

We must also bear in mind that there are major differences from one vessel to another. The internal situation of the crew of a ferry running the Barcelona-Palma de Mallorca route, with a journey time of eight hours and with most of crew also living in one of those two cities and therefore returning home every couple of days, even if only for a few hours, is totally different from that of the crew of a supertanker making 60-day voyages from Rotterdam to the Persian Gulf and practically not setting foot on land during the voyage, since the loading and unloading jetties are far from any city and the ship remains there for only a matter of hours.

A ship with a crew of forty is also different from one with a crew of eight, just as a ship on which all crew members are from one of the so-called developed countries differs from one in which the officers are from a developed country but the rest of the crew is from the "Third World".

The concept of total institution will, therefore, be not so much an instrument for unequivocally defining the vessel institution as a working tool which can assist a more thoroughgoing sociological study of the crew of a merchant vessel.

There is a further factor highly inherent to total institutions, which is that of the persistence of roles and the fact of living in the workplace. Lack of compensating release from the possible pressures or frustrations of a certain role, the need to find within the very working group a set of leisure companions, are aspects lying at the heart of total institutions and arising par excellence on a ship.

## 1.5 The vessel institution as socio-technical system

*Socio-technical systems are based on the theory that there is an interrelationship between technical conditions and social factors. There can be said to be interdependence between technology and social behaviour.*[27]

This means that the technical changes which arise, on a ship for example, have a direct influence on the social setting, while certain changes in the social system give rise to technical changes. The type of ship, its size and degree of automation imply differences in the life of the crew, in the training requirements for crew members, their number, and so forth.

Containerisation has led to a drastic reduction in the time a ship spends in port. Whereas formerly unloading general cargo with the ship's own derricks took three days, loads in containers now take less than one day. When corn was loaded in bags a ship spent days in port, whereas nowadays with elevators the ship can be loaded in a day. This factor of the considerable reduction of time spent in port has inevitably had a considerable repercussion on the social aspects of seamen's lives. During voyages nowadays there is often hardly any opportunity to set foot on land, whereas seamen would formerly have got to know the cities of call and their inhabitants. Furthermore, highly automated ships mean crew size can be cut by half or more, bringing still more isolation for the seaman, who then has fewer people to communicate with.

On the other hand, social factors have repercussions on the technical ones. One of the reasons underlying technical advances is a quest for lower labour costs. As wages and the frequency and duration of holidays in the merchant shipping industry increased, it became increasingly urgent to reduce crew sizes through automation, although a massive influx of Third World crew members on very low wages seems to have led to a certain slowdown in this process. The evolution of some notions of quality of life, too, has forced an improvement of the technical aspects of ships.

According to Nylehn[28], the first step in analysing a technical-social system is to describe the conditions of the group, the life of the crew in the case of a ship, the relationship between its members, communication, roles, and so forth. The second is to analyse the needs, motivations and attitudes of the individual as such.

## 1.6 Conclusion

Total institutions demand more complete and extensive role taking from their members than most other organisations.

The disparate types of total institutions have a long history. We might think of monastic life, which in the east has its roots in the 3rd century and in the west in the 5th century. The origins of military institutions have to be sought in the remotest antiquity, while ships too were to be found in antiquity plying the oceans and, whether they were warships or merchant vessels, a military discipline was imposed in which the captain had prerogatives which even included imposing the death penalty on a crew member.

*In every period total institutions have been strong organisations, legitimated by the cultural values of the society in which they operated*[29].

Indeed, the merchant vessel institution of nowadays has little to do with the institution holding sway on vessels when Columbus discovered America. The ships of First World countries, at least, have clearly been democratised, under labour relations in which each has his task and all receive their pay at the end of the month. In Spain, however, and well into the democratic period, there persisted what was called the "penal and disciplinary law of the merchant navy", which applied military criteria in laying down the rules of discipline on board. Nowadays, however, professional relations take place within the strict framework of contractual labour relations.

Having said this, the circumstances of being a living and working community which can spend weeks and months at sea means that legislation continues to confer upon captains prerogatives that managers of companies do not have, and ships with Third World crews are often in thrall to a very marked and even despotic authoritarianism.

Like any organisation pursuing certain purposes, total institutions endeavour to have recruits integrate as fully as possible, trading in their feelings of loneliness, uncertainty and uprootedness for feelings of belonging and even of pride.

We could say that the total institution arises out of a need to establish a structure and guidelines for behaviour and control of a human group so that the group offers the strongest assurance of achieving the proposed purpose.

When religious orders are founded, some time after a small group embarks upon a certain type of life, as new people join the group a need is felt to draw up regulations or rules, including vows or commitments. Homogeneity of attitudes within the group and reinforcement of the purpose which inspired creation of the group is achieved thereby, through a number of controls for preventing any departure from the founding idea.

In the military sphere, it was clear right from the very earliest times that the only way of approaching attack or defence was through iron discipline and perfect coordination of the troops. All the habits of life that officers endeavour to instil in a barracks, right down to what seems to be an absurd discipline and roles for losing the "bad habit" of thinking for oneself, point in the direction of perfect control of the troops so that they can be moved like pieces on a chess board.

The sense of total institution thus depends not so much on entry being against the will of the individual (psychiatric institutions, prisons, concentration camps, etc.) as on the fact that the group so formed, and isolated from the rest of society, has an internal organisation well-structured to permit carrying out of the purpose for which it was conceived, and even to ensure to the utmost extent that any personal sacrifice serves a common good.

It is, I feel, important to remember this aspect of common good lying behind the framework of the total institution definition. A total institution is not put in place in order to satisfy the needs of an individual who uses it to tyrannise a human group. Even the authoritarian and dictatorial regime of a prison is there for a society's more or less open defence of its common interests. Within a prison, taking such an institution in the civilised sense, once certain individuals have been interned in order to protect society from their conduct, life must be directed at providing inmates with a chance to find a social sense to their daily lives. The medieval dungeon would not come under this heading, for there was no life of a total institution as such: it was simply a matter of locking up in subhuman conditions people condemned to imprisonment for some crime.

Within the notion of ship institution, warships would be the one most clearly complying with the definition of total institution, above all because the human group is numerous and in each activity, whether work or leisure, the crew member is always in the company of others. And because the context is military, discipline reaches into the private sphere.

Except on passenger ships, with many crew members, on merchant vessels crew members carry out their work in small groups or even sometimes alone; leisure time, too, might find them shut up in their cabins or, even where cabins are shared, at least in a private domain. This does not mean that the crew member's role does not persist and that he remains "tied" to the work place, but he can undoubtedly experience greater privacy than on a warship. Subgroups will nevertheless be formed on merchant vessels, primary and secondary adjustments[30] will occur and the life of the institution as such will be created.

Finally, in order to analyse the merchant vessel as a total institution, we will undertake a study of three broad themes:
- The internal life of the institution, what characterises it and the sociological phenomena which develop within it.
- The crew member as an individual participating in this total institution.
- The relations of the crew member, as inmate of a total institution, with the world outside the institution.

Study of these aspects must serve to go more deeply into the sociological problems of crews on vessels, with a view to finding ways of making life aboard ship as humane as possible.

# 2

# the inner life of the ship institution

## 2.1 Life aboard ship

### 2.1.1 Introduction

Aboard a ship, exercising their professional functions, and also living together, sharing The merchant ship total institution consists, as we have seen, of a group of people meal times and rest times, isolated from the world ashore for however many days or weeks the trip takes, and far from their countries and their homes for weeks or even months on end.

These people all went aboard of their own free will, and are legally bound to the ship, or rather the shipowner, by employment contracts. However, since they spend long periods away at sea or outside the jurisdiction of their countries, prerogatives that may go beyond the normal provisions of employment contracts are acquired by personnel in command.

All these people fit into a hierarchical structure in which the personnel in command have considerable authority, an authority that covers not only the work to be done but also certain aspects of the private lives of the crew.

Thus the crew is not just a working team: it is also a human group whose members must be able to satisfy their private human needs and their basic needs for relating to others in human terms in the community around them.

This human group *is subject to the highly distinctive reciprocal actions that arise quite naturally when the ship sets sail, though not in other circumstances that might also be regarded as exceptional (when the ship is in harbour, being repaired, moored at a long-term anchoring berth or awaiting orders).*[31]

Routine is an important factor in the life and work of ships, as mentioned previously. Though often, and perhaps rightly, presented as a drawback of the seafaring way of life, it is also a highly valued treasure. Hence sailors often say, when setting off on a long run after a period at harbour, "so we're off to our health farm again".

The best atmosphere aboard ship is experienced on long runs: everybody settles into it, changing gear to make the best of it, and the crew-organisation arrangements work.

Naturally, everyone looks forward to arrival at port, particularly those who are homeward bound. However, in the life of the crew, something is lost. People get restless - to get home soon in the case of those who will be near their homes, and to enjoy the time off and break the monotony of it all for the others. Something in the organisation of life aboard ship goes downhill.

This is not to deny all the positive aspects of arriving at port, so eagerly awaited by seamen, but simply to point out that anything that upsets the routine that is inherent to life aboard has an influence on internal relations among the crew and the organisation of daily life aboard ship.

### 2.1.2 Hierarchically ordered life

The merchant ship is a highly hierarchical institution. This feature, as Hernández Izal[32] remarks, stems not only from legal provisions but also from atavism, as a hangover from past traditions.

The hardships of life at sea, the need for organised work with concise instructions admitting no argument, and the fact that at sea no recourse to any external authority is available, are all factors that have led to this highly hierarchical organisation. And this arrangement, as Hernández Izal also points out, is found both in free-market economies and in socialist countries.

Apart from its discipline and work-organisation purpose, this hierarchic approach also provides the terms of reference that are needed in socially organised life of any kind.

Though this does not necessarily imply that such hierarchical ordering should go beyond what is strictly required to organise a human group in social and labour terms, in fact we also find deformations with clearly military connotations, and in some cases even authoritarian excesses impinging on the private affairs of people, or even, in the worst cases, constituting an assault on the basic human dignity of those concerned.

Tony Lane[33] tells us that *Hierarchy touches almost every aspect of shipboard life. It is a subject which generates a lot of heat among seafarers, reveals deep-running social divisions and, in this respect at least, seems to offer a microcosm of society at large.*

Perhaps because the deck hands historically used to belong to the lowest social strata while the officers enjoyed some social standing, particularly when merchant fleets had close links with navies, the higher orders of the hierarchy have traditionally been at pains to maintain their status and keep tight control over their subordinates.

This mentality could have been relegated to history as the cultural level of ordinary seamen rose and as democratic models emerged in the industrially developed world, but instead it has become accentuated through the proliferation of ships with European officers and Asian or African ratings. Thus new barriers have appeared, leading to a further strengthening of the hierarchical order, at a time when ships with Spanish crews, for example, had witnessed a considerable attenuation of that order.

Another point to be taken into account here is that, as we have mentioned, a cargo vessel with a crew of 15 is very different from a passenger ship with a crew of 300.

We could wind up this section by saying that some degree of hierarchical ordering is necessary aboard ship on account of the great importance of an orderly and disciplined approach to the work for the safety of the ship and its crew. However, it is a different matter entirely when this hierarchical pattern takes over free time as well, with the crew feeling coerced 24 hours a day.

This arises when discriminatory treatment is adopted, of a kind more usually associated with master-and-servant relations than of relations of employment, or when matters that are important for the crew members as people are ignored.

Bernard Vincent, a French deacon who has spent many years aboard ships sailing under flags of convenience with international crews, records the case of a Muslim crew member: his religion prohibited eating pork, but this was disregarded, and he was faced with the choice of suffering pangs of hunger or pangs of conscience.

Even though the manner of issuing orders in the professional context, e.g. during manoeuvres, may well have some resemblance to military patterns, it should not be forgotten that the crew members are just as much employees of the shipping company as the officers, and that in fact the mission of the latter is not just to ensure that the jobs are done well but also to arrange things so that certain individual and collective human needs of the crew can be met.

## 2.2 The ship's crew – a schematic view

|  | Persons in command |  |
|---|---|---|
| Master / Captain | Chief Engineer |  |
| Chief Officer | First Engineer |  |
| Second Officer | Second Engineer | Radio officer |
| Third Officer | Third Engineer |  |
|  |  |  |
| Cadets | Cadets | Cadets |

|  | Petty Officers |  |
|---|---|---|
| (deck) | (engine room) | (catering) |
| Boatswain | Donkeyman | Chief Steward |
| Carpenter | Electrician | Cook |

|  | Ratings |  |
|---|---|---|
| AB Seamen | Greasers | Stewards |
| Ordinary Seaman |  | Galley boys |

By departments, the crew can be classified into:
- Deck department
- Engine department
- Catering department

We will now analyse in some detail the functions of each crew member, i.e. the role of each aboard ship. For this purpose, however, we will begin by setting down some prior considerations that are very important for our examination of what these roles, and more specifically the way they are enacted on a ship, signify from the sociological standpoint.

## 2.3 Roles

### 2.3.1 The sociological sense of role

The various actions performed in a society are for the most part classified, with such classification depending on them having some objective sense, and this in turn requiring linguistic objectification.

For example, a captain giving a manoeuvring order is doing something that is inherent to his role: giving orders. Anyone standing on the quay and seeing him doing that will assume that he is the captain. This action is called "giving orders", and is known as such.

When giving orders, the captain is fulfilling functions, he is "acting" in accordance with the role assigned to him, and he identifies with this action as one that comes with his job and his position of responsibility. This identification, however, is not complete: it does not encompass the entire "self" of the captain, just part of part of it.

Nevertheless, as Berger and Luckmann[34] explain, that part *is objectified, in line with socially available classifications. This segment is the real "social self", which is subjectively expressed as different from the "self" as a whole, and even opposed to it... The actor identifies in this way with the classifications of behaviour that are socially objectified in actu, but he distances himself from them when subsequently meditating on his behaviour.*

In other words, the captain can see himself as captain in the same way he sees himself as a husband, a father, a colleague etc., acting out in each case a socially classified function.

As a captain, there are a number of rules telling him how to act, what is expected of him, just as there are for him as husband or father.

People who enact different roles over a short period of time sometimes have the feeling that they are actors changing costume from act to act in order to play another part. In fact each role that a person acts out throughout his or her life amounts to a different role in the *theatre of life*.

*When enacting roles,* Berger and Luckmann assert, *individuals take part in a social world; when they internalise those roles, that same world becomes subjectively real for them.*

So people, through these functions or roles that are expected of them by society, recognise themselves as players of the roles concerned and accept them as their own.

The various roles are governed by social rules which have to be complied with if the person concerned wishes to avoid social reproof.

*Roles represent the institutional order... The enactment of the "role" represents the "role" itself... The role represents a complete institutional nexus of behaviour...*[35] Social order is structured in roles. A ship's crew is structured in roles: captain, chief engineer, boatswain, cook etc. Each has a framework of duties and rights which must be observed if the individual performing the role expects to be recognised in that role.

Hence each person comes to represent the role itself, i.e. the cook is no longer John Smith working as a cook: he objectifies himself as the cook, and everyone else, even if they do not know who he is or what his name is, knows what to expect of him as cook.

Secondly, the role of each of these crew members has a nexus with all the others within the *ship institution*, just as the latter fits into the higher set that is world shipping, within which there will also be a range of roles such as the manager of the shipping company, the head of personnel, the head of shipping movements, the shipper, the stevedore etc.

We can see from this how a person's activity can be specified as a series of roles learned by that person, and that the extent to which he fulfils the rules that socially govern that role will determine his rating of his own performance as captain or cook or whatever.

Society is generally structured through a role system, with the roles acting as terms of reference that enable individuals to get their bearings and know their place in that society, and that give society some assurance of proper functioning and continuity.

Anyone going aboard ship finds a crew-organisation system in place, in which everyone has a well defined mission, and thus the new member soon finds his place, since he is familiar with the posts before becoming acquainted with the particular people that are filling them on the ship. The captain is the captain, even though days may pass before he finds out that particular captain's name, and the same is true for the carpenter, the electrician, the greasers, the helmsmen and so on.

The person going aboard also knows straight away what role he is to fulfil, and as far as the rest of the crew are concerned he will be the new second officer, the new galley boy, the new steward or whatever.

As Berger and Luckmann put it[36], *The institution, with its set of programmed actions, is like the unwritten script of a theatre play. The performance of the play depends on the flesh-and-blood actors fulfilling their prescribed "roles" again and again. The actors personify the roles and act out the play by performing it on a certain stage. Neither the play nor the institution have any empirical existence outside this recurrent institution. Thus to say that the roles represent institutions is to say that they make it possible for the institutions to exist, again and again, as a real presence in the experience of specific individuals.*

Hence the crew does not exist without the crew members, without the various roles that each of them plays, and at the same time these roles find their meaning within the institution of the crew.

Though they are internationally defined, the various roles do vary somewhat from country to country, and even within a single country from shipowner to shipowner, or even at times from ship to ship. In some ships, for example, the third officer is allotted responsibility for the medicine chest, while in others it falls to the second officer.

Even so, there is a fundamental set of duties and attributes that are sufficiently well defined to let anyone going aboard know basically what will be expected of him and what he is entitled to.

If we are to find out how the crew society is structured, we must know what the roles performed in it are, and what the rules governing the crew society are.

The rules governing the basic functions of the various roles within a crew are set out in the internal rules of the shipping companies, in the trade legislation of the country concerned, and in various regulations and certain international conventions.

### 2.3.2 Role performance

We have already noted a role is a kind pattern guiding action. A role is what is expected of the person enacting it. Socially, what is expected of each role is so ingrained that a given person can display different, even contradictory, behaviour in fulfilling different roles. This can be seen perfectly well on land, with a given person being completely different in different spheres of life. An executive can be utterly scrupulous over discipline at work, and yet can become an anarchic driver at the wheel. A person can also be a meek employee at work and a tyrant when it comes to the education of his children.

In connection with such changes, psychology can clearly provide a great deal of information on compensations and frustrations. Here, however, we are not so much interested in that as in the influence certain models have on us. Somebody leading a group turns to a model that tells him that he must achieve efficiency in the work of the people under him, and that rules of discipline must be applied for that purpose.

Drivers intend to show that they are good drivers, which might be interpreted by a driver as being deft and confident at the wheel, displaying a level of skill that enables him to go faster than anyone else.

The meek employee will have learned that if he obeys his bosses' orders scrupulously, he will be well regarded by them, and this gives him confidence and satisfaction in his work.

A tyrannical father might have the idea that he must be tough with his children, as his parents were with him, since life is tough and they must be ready to fight.

A highly critical spirit is needed to realise that a person, when enacting a role, must have sufficient character and courage to create his own personality.

People who are capable of that stand out, and are usually respected, though they may be regarded as odd.

The Auschwitz prisoner Fr. Maximilian Kolbe broke the role-performance mould associated with concentration-camp prisoners when he offered his life in exchange for that of another prisoner who had a family. The role of prisoners would lead us to expect them to seek survival, not to volunteer for execution in place of another.

If we switch to the sphere of a merchant ship, we find that the variety of roles, as we have said, is very much reduced, since the role falling to the individual as a crew member almost takes over the person enacting it.

Even so, we can make the following points:
- As we will see when we come to primary and secondary adjustments[37], there are attitudes which, while not absolutely in line with the norm, are nonetheless normal enough in terms of what is to be expected of a crew member. For example, a crew member taking advantage of the ship's journeys to indulge in tourist activities may be deemed normal. And coming back aboard drunk in a port may also be deemed normal even though such behaviour is not officially condoned.
- The crew member learns how he is generally expected to enact his role, and this can become a tacit norm to the extent that even if what he does is reproachable it will not be criticised by his shipmates and it will be ignored if it falls within what is "normal".
- Within the hierarchical structure of the ship, and even though in theory the entire crew should aim for results as a team, some kinds of opposition or resistance arise in each post, the ultimate aim of these being to seek internal balance.

Thus the captain, as the representative of the shipowner and the law aboard ship, will soon forget the critical attitude he had as a ship's officer, and may be guilty of the same defects that he had criticised in the captains he had worked under. A crew member moved from deck service to the engine department will soon start criticising the deck crew, just as he had previously criticised the engine crew. It is all part of the process of becoming accepted.

Let us say, then, that the crew member will seek to enact the role assigned to him as can be expected of him.

### 2.3.3 Roles aboard a merchant vessel

We will now explain each of the basic roles encountered in the crew of a merchant ship.[38]

**The captain:**

The post that has drawn the most attention in legal terms is that of the captain or master, since he is ultimately responsible for the ship, and he is the representative of the shipping company before third parties and before the crew itself, the legal representative of the ship before the authorities, and can even be called upon to act, under certain circumstances, as a commissioner for oaths.

In addition to directing navigation, the captain also holds ultimate responsibility for the entire ship and all its departments. For that reason, there are certain decisions that only he can take.

This also gives him significant status and prerogatives. Historically, the captain had an almost omnipotent aura - in ancient Rome he was called the *magiseter navis*, while the English called him *master under God* and the French *maître après Dieu du navire*, with the Catalan book *Consulat de Mar* calling him *senyor de la nau*[39] (lord of the ship). In many cases, he was himself the owner or co-owner of the vessel.

All this has changed a great deal today. Firstly, the captain is an employee of the shipping company, and secondly, many decisions that formally fell to the captain are now taken on land and sent by fax, particularly decisions involving mercantile matters. In nautical terms, and as regards navigation and the safety and maintenance of the ship, the captain still has the last word, though the shipping company may sometimes put pressure on him in various ways.

It must however be remembered that within an institution roles undergo certain deformations which, though not intended in theory, do arise in practice, as part of the struggle of individuals and institutions to promote their own interests, even if standards of professionalism sometimes suffers as a result.

The captain is no doubt subject to many pressures, both from those seeking benefits and from those wishing to place the shipowner's interests above strictly professional interests. The captain's duties have two facets that frequently conflict.

In law, he has ultimate responsibility for the ship. If it puts to sea with some technical defect that he is aware of or should be aware of, and an accident occurs, he will have to answer for his conduct afterwards, and may be demoted or even face penal liability. This would be the case if a ship were to sail with a lifeboat in a state of disrepair and crew members then died for that reason following shipwreck.

On the other hand, a captain notifying his shipping company that the departure of the ship will be delayed for two days to repair the lifeboat, despite orders from the company to sail immediately, might be relegated to the post of chief officer on the next voyage, since the post of captain is at the discretion of the shipowner.

History gives us a case of these conflicting duties in the mythical shipwreck of the *Titanic*. The captain was aware that he was sailing through ice-ridden water, several ships in that region having stopped their engines until dawn for that very reason.

His duty as the one ultimately responsible for the ship might have been to do that, or to reduce speed. However, the ship had a set time for arrival in New York, with port services having been contracted for that purpose. Any delay would entail extra costs. Furthermore, the company hoped to win the *blue ribbon* on that voyage - the prize awarded to the ship having crossed the Atlantic in the shortest time. The presence aboard of the shipowner B. Ismay on that fateful voyage of the *Titanic* no doubt weighed heavily in the decision of captain E. Smith, though the shipowner declared, in the subsequent trial, that he had respected the nautical criteria of the captain at all times[40].

To this we must add that, as they say, "nothing ever happens". The *Titanic* could probable have covered the same route ten times under the same sea conditions without anything untoward happening... but that time something did. And that is often the case at sea. There are things on board that do not work as they should, and they do not matter because "nothing ever happens".

Hence many captains are reluctant to give the impression that they are excessively orthodox and unbending in responding to the mercantile criteria applied by the shipowner and the shipper. For indeed any sea journey involves considerable economic interests.

The shipper loading up the goods - who is thus the company paying for the journey and enabling the shipping company to make money - tries to impose his criteria. And goods arriving two days late can sometimes be worse for the owners of the goods than losing them altogether, since in the latter case *force majeure* would come into play, and moreover they would be covered by insurance. Consequently, the captain's role demands good judgement, character and a high level of professional expertise.

Turning to the captain's internal relations within the ship, his position will always be a solitary one to some extent since he is at the top, holding final responsibility on his own. Here too the difference between a good captain and a bad one can be seen: a good one will always have sufficient self-confidence and authority to enable him to have open, relaxed relations with the rest of the crew, while poor captains, showing insecurity and lacking the sense of authority, will seek to maintain their authority through a mistrustful attitude that generates stress.

Though he has his department chiefs, the captain also has the last word on personnel-related matters, and in general on the organisation of life aboard ship.

The role of the captain those requires wide-ranging involvement on the part of the person holding it. We said previously that the "professional self" does not take over the entire area of the "personal self", but rather just part of it. However, in ships, and particularly in the case of captains, very strong identification between the two can arise.

Aboard ships in general, as we will see in more detail later on, all the other roles that a person has on land (father, husband, friend, club member etc.) are driven into the background by the fact of spending days, weeks and sometimes months far from that private life he has left behind. Each crew member is in his role 24 hours a day while he is aboard ship.

This is even more true of the captain, since he is responsible for what happens on board even when he is asleep, in contrast with others who only have responsibility (and a shared one at that) when they are on duty. This having to be the captain at all times also means that he enjoys the prerogatives of his post at all times, and becomes used to his every word being obeyed.

This strong identification is revealed when the captain goes ashore. If he cannot be the boss at home, and generally feels that he is a nobody when not aboard ship, he will have problems adjusting to the new life ashore.

**The chief engineer:**

As his title indicates, he is the head of the engine department. In professional terms, he is comparable to the captain in his own special sphere. The difference is that the chief engineer's responsibility is limited to his department, while the captain's extends to cover the entire ship. The chief engineer also has continuous professional responsibility, at all times, for the engine department.

Even though he does not stand watch in person (though he usually does on small ships), he must look after the engines round the clock. His high rank aboard, similar to the captain's, also gives him the habit of authority, which can sometimes make it difficult for him to return to life ashore.

Precisely on account of this power, he will be subjected to pressures from people seeking his favour in return for services or personal advantages. Consequently, like the captain, he will need good professional and ethical sense to ensure that his actions are prompted only by professional considerations, not personal interest.

The chief engineer may also find himself having to choose between being scrupulous in professional matters, or giving preference to the ship's need for speed even at some risk to safety. However, this dilemma is not as acute as in the case of the captain, since when the captain has been informed of an engine-department problem, responsibility for the final decision rests with him, though without detriment to the share that technically falls to the chief engineer.

**The chief officer:**

He stands out from the other officers since he is charged with the loading and stowage arrangements for the ship, as well as being in charge of the deck department, organising the work of the seamen and covering the role of head of personnel aboard ship as well.

In addition to his responsibilities when keeping watch and to fulfilling the functions listed above, the chief officer also takes over the captain's functions if the captain is not aboard ship (in the harbour) or if he is ill.

Beyond his specific functions, during his time off, he is freed of responsibility in principle. However, any special situation arising, whatever the time, will oblige him to return to the full exercise of his professional duties.

On account of his powers regarding the loading and the general supervision of the ship, and of his role as the "second captain", he may often be "invited" to look the other way in professional matters for the sake of greater "commercial agility" for the ship, or to give way to pressures arising from various interests.

**The officers in general:**

They have responsibility in fulfilling their professional tasks: watchkeeping, maintenance, safety, the medicine chest etc.

The first engineer officer is comparable to the chief bridge officer, though with the difference we saw between the captain and the chief officer - i.e. that the attributes of the first engineer officer are limited to the engine department, though there he acts as the second in command and will have general responsibilities over and above watchkeeping, or the additional mission of directing the work of the engine-room staff.

Aside from these aspects, the officers have lesser responsibility, and thus a degree of authority that differs significantly from those described above. Their role is thus easier to live with, although they too may also find themselves in a quandary when they are aware of some defect in the ship and perhaps the negligence of their superiors regarding it, but nonetheless choose to keep quiet about it and take the easy way out.

Indeed, who the captain is can have a significant effect on the officers' roles. A captain who puts his professionalism first, and who thus demands and backs a responsible attitude among his officers, will make it much easier for them to carry out their functions, while a captain who pursues his own personal interest and gives way to internal or external pressures will sometimes undermine the authority of his officers and make it difficult for them to exercise their functions.

The officers have direct authority over those under them in their departments, and a certain general authority over any subordinate.

The radio officer - a role that seems to be on the way out - is in charge of the ship's radiotelegraphy and is responsible for the ship's radio station. Complete discretion is expected of him regarding the official or private messages he sends out or receives.

Lastly, the cadets go through their official work experience to get their qualifications as officers. They have no responsibility and their mission aboard ship is to learn.

**The petty officers:**

This group takes in the boatswain and the carpenter (deck department), the donkeyman and the electrician (engine-room), and the steward and cook (catering).

**The boatswain:**

He acts as the seamen's boss. Taking orders from the chief officer, he directs the work of the seamen. He is usually a veteran of the sea, with a good practical knowledge of his trade. This post normally goes to most highly experienced seamen, there not being any specific academic requirement.

As a veteran seafarer, he sometimes gives young officers a hard time, trying to prove that experience teaches more than books. He normally has some natural ascendancy over the seamen.

It is a post of confidence, and the man holding it knows it. This often puts a distance between him and the other deck hands, prompting him to seek personal relations rather with other petty officers.

Since he is the immediate authority on deck, he directs the seamen, and acts as a liaison between the chief officer and the deck hands. On account of his rank as a petty officer, he has a certain degree of authority over any other subordinate.

**The carpenter:**

He is also sometimes known as the "planker", and is quite independent in his work. As a carpenter, it is his job to keep everything made of wood in good condition (there are usually a lot of wooden items on ships), and to look after the upkeep of ship interiors, etc.

He is also charged with measuring the water levels in the bilges and holds, and with some safety functions. His responsibility is quite limited, and he works at the orders of the chief officer.

As a petty officer, he too has some authority over the other subordinates.

**The donkeyman:**

All that was said regarding the boatswain goes for him too, though in connection with the engine room - i.e. he directs, under the orders of the chief engineer officer or the first engineer officer, the work of the greasers. He is usually a greaser promoted to donkeyman after years of experience.

As in the case of the boatswain, the subordinates in his department respect and obey him.

He is given a better cabin than the greasers, and has his meals with the other petty officers.

**The electrician:**

As the word indicates, he is in charge of the proper functioning of the electrical equipment aboard, and works under the orders of the first engineer officer. He works with considerable independence, and only exercises authority with engine-room staff assigned to him to help out with some particular job, though he also holds a certain general authority over subordinates since he is a petty officer.

**The chief steward:**

Nowadays, particularly in ships with cut-down crews, this is a post that is on the way to extinction. However, it was a very important one in days gone by, and even today, on some large ships and passenger ships, the chief steward has a very significant function aboard ship.

The mission of the chief steward is to direct the catering staff and, in particular, to look after food provisions. On ships with a chief steward, he is the one who buys all necessary provisions in port, plans the menus and administers the funds provided by the shipping company for these purposes.

He also buys the tobacco and drinks, and is generally given charge of what is known in marine parlance as the *entrepôt* - all the goods (basically tobacco and alcoholic drinks) that ships on international runs can take aboard duty-free for consumption at sea. He also looks after the bed linen, table linen, tableware etc. His chief responsibility is to handle those functions well.

When he has the role of administering the funds provided by the shipowner for the crew's maintenance, he is also responsible for the proper use of those funds. The degree of integrity and professionalism shown by this crew member has a considerable influence on the general atmosphere aboard ship.

Ships spend a lot of money on provisions. The suppliers know this, and try to get on good terms with whoever has the power to decide how much is to be bought and from whom. Hence the chief steward has to deal with offers of gifts and favours, which are tempting. From straightforward commission payments to drawing up inflated invoices and sharing out the gains afterwards, there is a whole range of temptations beckoning this member of the crew.

A dishonest chief steward will try to gain more room for manoeuvre by drawing the captain in to take a share in his gains, and sometimes the chief engineer and the first officer too. Eventually, this can end up undermining the power structure aboard ship, with this crew member, who is after all a subordinate, though in charge of other subordinates, taking real control of the ship in practical terms and for many purposes.

On smaller ships, it is usually the captain that administers the money for buying provisions. Working under the orders of the chief steward are the cook, the galley boys and the assistant stewards.

**The cook:**

His job is to prepare the meals and, along with the chief steward, to draw up the menus, do the stock-keeping and make lists of items to be purchased. Working under him are the galley boys or cook's assistants. His responsibility is restricted to his kitchen functions.

He works under the chief steward, though under the first officer too since the latter is head of personnel. His work is, however, quite independent.

**Ratings:**

This group takes in the deck hands and the engine and catering department assistants.

**The deck hands:**

This group comprises the able-bodied seamen and the ordinary seamen. There are different ranks within it, for example the able-bodied seamen, who are the veteran seamen who are usually given the job of helmsman during manoeuvres. Even so, no distinction is made in terms of responsibility, only in terms of the work they do. They usually work daytime hours in their deck work, with rests at meal times, and the day's work coming to an end in the early evening. They are directly under the orders of the boatswain. When needed on the bridge, they work under sea-watch conditions (2 hours at the helm and 4 hours' rest) at the orders of the officer of the watch. Otherwise they are engaged in deck maintenance work.

During manoeuvres they are given posts on the bridge or on the fore and poop decks.

**The engine-room crewmen:**

They are usually called greasers or oilers, and their work is to look after the maintenance of the engine and some repair work undertaken aboard. They normally work under sea-watch conditions (4 hours' watch and 8 hours' rest), though some may have daytime shifts for certain jobs.

They are under the orders of the donkeyman, the watch officer and the first engineer officer. Their responsibility is restricted to doing what they are asked to do, responsibility as such falling to their superiors.

**The catering crewmen:**

*The messmen or stewards and the galley boys:* On cargo vessels, the messmen are there to serve the officers (make the beds, clean the cabins and the mess room, serve at table etc.).

They are under the orders of the officers they serve and the chief steward.

On passenger vessels, the stewards form a large group, since they have to attend to however many passengers the ship may have to take, which can be hundreds - in which case they will usually be under the orders of the *purser*.

The galley boys are the kitchen assistants. On many ships they serve at the petty officers' table. Their working hours are similar to the cook's. When the bread is made aboard, they usually get up earlier to make it. They are under the orders of the chief steward and the cook.

The catering staff as such have the least impact on navigation, but they play an important role in everyday life aboard ship.

So far we have looked at a standard outline of the crew of a cargo vessel. In the case of an oil tanker, for example, we would have to add the *pumpman*, who is in charge of the tanks and of loading and unloading the oil. On passenger vessels, there are various levels of stewards, a *maître*, a *purser* etc., the latter being perhaps worthy of special mention.

*The purser:* If he is a fully qualified officer he will belong to the officer class, otherwise to the petty officers, even though in fact his place is somewhere between the two. On a passenger vessel, the purser could be seen as a kind of "hotel manager". He has to organise all the services laid on for the passengers. In theory, a fully qualified officer should hold this post, as mentioned, though this is not the case on many passenger ships. The job of the purser is similar to that of the chief steward in that both are in charge of provisions and both have the direct power to administer a great deal of money.

We noted in connection with the chief steward that he could end up holding significant *de facto* power in a cargo vessel; if we turn to a passenger vessel with one or more pursers and a chief steward, we can appreciate that they could form a really strong body on board.

We have given a general description of the various professional roles that a ship's crew members perform, without seeking to be exhaustive or to provide a technical or legal analysis of the crew structure, which is not the aim here.

We have merely sought to take stock of the various posts on a ship, bearing in mind that we are studying the various roles of crew members from a sociological point of view, and that these various posts held by the crew will be referred to again and again throughout this book.

### 2.3.4 The enduring nature of shipboard roles

We have said that roles are like the parts played by individuals in the great "theatre of life". In the same way, the various roles we have been looking at are played out in the great "theatre of the ship". Some of these roles identify the person to such an extent that the person can hardly be distinguished from the role.

General speaking, we can say that on ships the identification of individuals with their roles is greater than it is on land, since a person goes on being a captain, or a greaser, galley boy or whatever, all the time he is aboard ship. Indeed there will probably even be a little sign on his cabin door stating his position.

He will have his meals in whichever messroom is appointed for his professional rank. On many ships there is one messroom for the officers (sometimes even one for the bridge and another for the engine department), another for the petty officers and another for the crewmen in general.

The post, the role, stays with the individual at all times during his time aboard. Even when the ship is in port, crew members are often required to show a pass or identity document stating their professional level aboard when they wish to go ashore or return to ship.

It is also frequently the case that the post becomes the crew member's nickname. Thus the boatswain on Spanish ships is called the *nostromo* (an old word meaning "our master"), the carpenter is usually called *maestro* (or "chips" in English-speaking crews), the electrician *chispas*, meaning sparks, and so on. And when people call out to them, they customarily use those expressions rather than John or Joe or whatever the man's real name is.

On passenger ships, the officers always wear their uniforms, and the seamen and deckhands generally wear the associated working clothes at all times.

At any time and in any place aboard ship, the post occupied by each aboard conditions his relations with others, particularly in terms of the vertical levels in the hierarchy, though also horizontally to some extent, owing to the influence of professional affinity within inter-personal relations aboard ship.

Thus a merchant ship is a highly institutionalised social nucleus.

### 2.4 Managing personnel and ratings: relations and differences

The hierarchical structure of a merchant ship, as we have said, has a determining influence on the relationship between crew members.

We have seen that, in broad outline, there are the levels of captain and chief engineer, the officers, the petty officers and the crew members.

In the day-to-day work, the petty officers will exert clear authority over the crew, the latter to some extent demanding such direction since it enables them to fulfil their duties properly.

Overall, as explained above, the first officer is in charge of general discipline aboard, though in the case of the engine department the first engineer will normally take care of that.

The captain will intervene in certain special cases, or when officers are involved.

The chief engineer behaves likewise with his officers, even though in fact the engine room is also under the captain's jurisdiction, he being the captain of the entire ship.

The captain usually keeps his distance from all the rest of the crew, except the chief engineer and sometimes an officer or two - though on occasions, the chief steward may become part of the captain's small circle of friends if he comes from the same part of the world or for reasons of his *de facto* powers.

In social terms, there are two fundamental groups, set apart by technical skills and social strata: the captain, chief engineer and officers on the one hand, and the petty officers and crew on the other.

In traditional ships with crews of 15 or more, this divide is seen particularly in terms of cabins, messrooms and day rooms.

This special status for the officers forms a considerable barrier, one which manifests itself in Spanish ships by the use of the term of address *Don* and in English ships by *Sir*, while ratings will be addressed initially by their first names and thereafter, in Spanish, using the familiar *tú* form of the verb. This differential treatment does not arise on German ships, for example, where officers and crew alike are addressed by the equivalent of Mr. plus the surname.

The ratings form one large group which includes the petty officers because, amongst other reasons, they are often promoted crew members, and in any case their distinction lies in their skills (e.g. as electrician). The cultural level of this large group is fairly even, and generally low. They have a plainer messroom, and normally serve themselves. The petty officers sometimes have their own messrooms and have their meals served for them.

This varies according to the nationality of the ship, and naturally in ships sailing under flags of convenience, many variant arrangements may be encountered - as in the case of the European captain and first officer making a Filipino officer have his meals with the Filipino crew members.

The cabins for the crew are on a lower deck, and are smaller; sometimes they are shared, particularly on passenger ships where several crew members may sleep in one cabin to make the most of the space inside the ship.

Counteracting this hierarchical structure are the power groups we referred to earlier, and their influence may result in modifications to this scheme in practice.

Yet the relation between officers and crew, which is in some ways comparable to the relation between the staff and the inmates in other total institutions, is offset by the fact that everybody from the captain down to the humblest seaman all suffer isolation, solitude, danger, longer spells away from home and the feeling of being forgotten to some extent by society as a whole.

Crews on ships making long trips, as we have said, usually generate a feeling of forming a single group, a family. Under such conditions, the ship takes on connotations of one big home. Hence when a crew member has spent a few hours ashore at a foreign port, he has the feeling on coming back on board that he is coming home, back to his point of reference, the group of people he knows, and so on.

Calendar high points such as Christmas or the New Year provide grounds on some ships for everybody's common status as a human being to take precedence for a few hours over the hierarchy - and although the latter never entirely disappears, it may be attenuated by a few drinks together or a few songs sung by all. In addition to the authority and responsibility held by each, professional status has other general implications, such as:

**Access to information:**

Information on the port of destination, a change of line or of any other kind concerning decisions of the shipowner or freighter is received in different ways depending on one's position aboard ship.

The first to receive such news is the captain, who may inform the entire crew immediately, or inform just the officers, or keep it to himself for whatever time he sees fit. In point of fact, when the ship is at sea, the telegraph operator is the first to receive that information, on account of his job of transmitting and receiving radiotelegraphic messages. However, as we have said, he is not supposed to make any use of it. Moreover, news or instructions that are regarded as delicate may reach the captain by post or by some other means when the ship is in a port.

Be that as it may, the ordinary crew members are usually the last to hear about it.

In what ways is information important?

A ship may be assigned to a line that is more or less regular, or it may be what is knows as a "tramp", meaning that when it is heading for one port, the one after that is not known.

Even so, when a crew member goes aboard, he will want to know the route ahead so that his family or friends can write to him at the ports of call along the way.

Moreover, when a ship puts into home ports quite frequently, there will always be attempts to calculate when it will be in this or that port, since this will enable wives, for example, to travel to that port to meet up with the husband, or to go aboard with him.

The crewmen always has their ears pinned for news on route changes, particularly when such changes might interfere with some personal or family project.

That is why unofficial news and rumours abound - what is known on land as the "grapevine" and at sea as the "scuttlebutt".

The captain, then, is always the first to receive the information, which is sometimes in the form of mere projects. For example, it might be that the shipping company is considering the possibility of undertaking a new freight-line, and instructs the captain to report on the suitability of the ship for that line, or to find out which navigation charts might be needed. At this stage it is no more than just a possibility, and he may keep it secret. A change in route may also be kept secret until, for example, the ship has left Spanish waters to avoid having to deal with crew members wishing to disembark upon learning of the new route.

All this means that the crew member often feels as if he were being treated like just another piece of equipment on the ship, his status as a person being ignored. In the last analysis, however, the captain is just another crew member too, and his personal interests will not be taken into account either.

So we can say that no real schism arises in the crew on a ship in the way it can in a prison institution where there is a clear distinction of roles and situations as between the staff and the inmates. Aboard ship, everybody is an inmate.

As noted when we first broached this matter of information, a distinction can be made in this sense between the shipping company (including the shipowner, freighter, broker, shipagent, etc.) and the crew. It is the shipping company that decides where the ship will be going, what cargo it will take, when it needs to be unloaded in 8 hours, and when it is better to lie at anchor rather than to dock for the sake of cutting costs.

**Favours:**

There are people on a ship whose position on board enables them to grant certain favours. This could be the captain, as the ultimate source of authority on board, since the person in charge in any human group always has some opportunities for favouritism.

Yet aboard ship there are (or can be) other positions holding *de facto* powers. One example is the chief steward, as we have said, who is responsible for provisions in ships having a chief steward, and who thus deals with suppliers in ports and handles a lot of money.

His position is open to arranging gifts for people he wants to be on good terms with. Such gifts may take the form simply of sharing any favours or commissions he receives with those other people, since he buys a lot and since each supplier will try to win him over as a purchaser.

On some ships, particularly passenger ships, extraordinary power aboard ship may be associated with the post of chief steward. Anybody in his good books may stand to gain a lot.

The cook is another person whose favour can bring benefits, or even the officers' messman, not so much because they hold any direct power, but rather because being on good terms with someone who performs a service for you can lead to better service. In the case of the messman, this would not be on account of his position as such, but because he could be a protégé of the chief steward or maybe even the captain.

These unofficial powers may go as far as seriously undermining the authority of an officer at times, who in such cases will stick to his professional work and keep away from trouble in other aspects of life aboard the ship.

This possibility of attaining certain positions of power in rather unorthodox ways is in line with what Goffman calls "secondary adjustments"[41], through which residents of a total institution may attain some control over that institution.

**Solidarity:**

One of the reactions arising in the face of this life of isolation, and sometimes of discrimination, is solidarity.

It comes in various degrees. In ships engaged on long trips particularly, with a single group of men spending a long time away from their private worlds, the whole crew tends to develop a sense of fraternity making them feel united despite any differences or disputes arising.

On shorter trips, this feeling is less likely to develop, since each chance a crew member has to return to his own world, even if only for a few hours, heightens his sense of aversion at having to go back into the closed world of that group.

Another more close-knit degree of solidarity is sometimes found within subgroups. It might be the deckhands uniting against a despotic boatswain, or a group of people from one country banding together in relation to people from another country, and so on.

As we will see later on, various subgroups can clearly be discerned within the crew as a whole. Whenever a subgroup of this kind is faced with what it regards as unfair or abusive action by another dominant subgroup, it develops a strong sense of solidarity and fights back by means of complaints, strikes etc.

At sea the sense of solidarity is traditional. This can be seen in the way ships help each other in situations of danger.

In ports too, sailors from different ships and different countries have a certain feeling of being united by something over and above nationality: they are seafarers all.

There is a saying that goes, "the seafarer shows solidarity at sea but is an individualist ashore", he needing the others at sea but not in his home country.

## 2.5 The internal world of the crew

### 2.5.1 Features

*Among the inmates of many total institutions, there is a feeling that all the time spent there is time lost, wasted or robbed from one's life.*[42] This feeling may manifest itself among crew members on a merchant vessel in various ways.

In the case of a person who was not moved to go to sea by any vocation or special interest, who just turned to it through some circumstance or other, it may be that time spent aboard ship strikes him as something that must be put up with, particularly when the ship is at sea. From day one of each trip, he will be counting the approximate number of days left before he will be able to disembark again.

Indeed, many crew members (including those who became sailors because they liked the profession), upon returning to the sea after a period of holidays, would like to be able to close their eyes and to find when they opened them again that they were back at home once more. However, as the days go by, they start rediscovering certain good things about life aboard ship, which is after all, in a way, the world they are used to.

This feeling is heavily influenced by how long it has been since their last contact with their homes, their families etc.. For that very reason it has been pointed out on a number of occasions that ship crews on longer trips are usually better humoured than the crews of ships that frequently put into ports that are the home towns of some of the crew members. In the latter case, there will always be some grumpy seaman who was at home the day before, calculating that he has twenty days to get through before going back home again.

This could be compared to the Monday blues or the return-to-work syndrome after the holidays. What an effort it is to get up on Monday to go to work, and how one's mood has improved by mid-week! In the same way, September is a tough month for landlubbers after their summer holidays in August, though after the first few weeks they start seeing the bright side of everyday life again.

On ships, as soon as a person gets it into his head that he is going to have to spend a long time away from his family or friends, he finds it easier to appreciate the good things around him, and so the time passes more agreeably.

Even so, there are people who merely doze the time away, or "kill time" in the full sense of the expression, when their working hours are over. Here, though, the atmosphere aboard ship has a decisive influence.

A crew member who comes across others with whom he can develop some kind of friendship, who can meet up with them and interact with them, will find a bright side to life on board much more easily. In this way, the games of cards, or the dominoes or board games that are often played after evening meals, or even conversations at meal times, can all help to make a crew member feel more part of a family of a kind.

At Christmas on the high seas, when people's minds have returned from their home thoughts, then, if a party is organised on board, if the messroom is decorated, if a special meal is served, if the crew makes an effort to have a little celebration, the feeling of solitude might disappear.

On the other hand, on ships with crew members of different nationalities, with only small numbers in each professional group (and with each group eating separately), and maybe with flexible meal times[43], a crew member can live in appalling solitude, feeling that the only attitude left to take is to think "I have x months left to get some money together and then get back home."

To overcome this feeling, it is very important, among other things, for there always to be several crew members from each nationality represented, and where possible for there not to be too many nationalities and languages aboard, as too many can add to the sense of isolation. A sailor should have access to other colleagues and be able to feel a team atmosphere and camaraderie, with the chance to enjoy things for a while now and then too.

The chance to pursue games, sports, cultural activities etc. is important - including reading, films (quite possible for everybody these days with the video), suitable rooms for getting together, table games, some sports activity such as table tennis etc.

Another thing that is important is the chance to go ashore when the ship is in port, or the availability of launches when the ship is at anchor; excursions ashore can be arranged to get to know new places (port districts are similar the world over).

On land, people can pursue hobbies, do sports etc., and this enables them to switch off from other worries. This is necessary at sea too.

*The links that join the individual to social entities of various kinds have common characteristics. The individual's participation in the entity, whether it be an ideology, a country, a trade, a family, a person or simply a dialogue, will have the same general features. This will create obligations for that individual: some quite tough, in that they entail making choices, working or performing services, or investing time or money; others softer and more warming, requiring him to feel part of the entity, to identify with it and to express emotional adhesion. Participation in a social entity implies commitment and adhesion at the same time.*[44]

Life as a crew member demands certain attitudes from the individual, such as being available whenever he is needed, accepting hierarchical norms and social norms aboard ship, etc.

On the other hand, the crew member retains the right to some privacy, to some rest time, and also the fundamental consideration set down in the contract binding him to the shipowner: his pay.

Crew members are expected to carry out their duties responsibly and to take part in life aboard ship in general, not just doing the work assigned to them but also taking part in some way in leisure activities.

People who keep themselves to themselves, keeping out of the conversations or recreational activities of the others, arouse suspicions, and end up being marginalised by the rest of the crew.

As far as work is concerned, each crew member is of course expected to carry out his tasks, yet there are certain failings that are particularly shunned, such as oversleeping and turning up late to manoeuvres, or repeatedly taking over watches late, even if only by a few minutes.

### 2.5.2 Formal instrumental organisation

Goffman[45] defines *formal instrumental organisation* as a deliberately coordinated system of activities aimed at achieving some explicit general ends.

Many forms of such organisations may arise.

We will focus on formal instrumental organisations based in a single unit which is to some extent isolated from the world outside - organisations which can also be called establishments, institutions or social organisations.

In the case of a ship's crew, which is a variant of what Goffman calls a "walled organisation", the individual is obliged to immerse himself in an extra-individual activity, which is seen as the symbol of his commitment and adhesion.

Each member of the crew must contribute a useful activity, which is more or less prescribed in advance, partly through labour legislation, shipping-company regulations or ship rules, and partly because it is inherent to the life and work of a ship in general.

Following Goffman's criterion identifying an organisation with its authorities, the Anglo-American graphic scheme for marking out these boundaries could perhaps be applied to a ship in this way:

*One:* For the duration of his stay aboard, the crew member is assured certain welfare conditions, the level depending on the type of ship, the country it belongs to and the initiative of the shipowner. In practice, the aim is to cover the minimum required so that the people concerned can perform their work with at least the minimum level of motivation.

The welfare conditions will relate to comfort, health and safety.

The crew member will be entitled to rest periods, annual holidays, professional recognition in accordance with his rank, and in general respect for his human dignity.

These welfare conditions pre-suppose that the crew member is, as a human being, rather more than just a crew member.

Naturally, these conditions, as we have said, will vary widely depending on the type of ship, the flag it is sailing under, etc.

For example, many Third-World seamen are hired for a shipboard period of 9 or 10 months in exchange for an all-inclusive salary. Thus when they go ashore for their "holidays", what is really happening is that their contract has ended and they are going home with what they have earned, and will not be paid any more while they are ashore. Each crew member will then decide when he needs to earn some more money and thus bring his "holidays" to an end.

*Two:* There must be an element of "voluntary collaboration", i.e. convergent interests between the organisation (the shipping company) and the subject (the crew member). Normally the convergent interest will be economic: the shipping company needs the crew member to enable it to run its maritime business, and the crew member needs the shipping company to obtain a salary and thus earn his living.

However, there are other sources of motivation for the crew member, which may be as powerful or even more powerful than his economic motivation, though he will try not to make them too obvious in order to put the greatest possible pressure on the company management when negotiating money matters or other benefits.

Among these sources of motivation are vocation, the spirit of adventure, the desire to see the world etc. Even though the economic aspect is fundamental, and even though seafarers traditionally curse their profession, the sense of vocation is a motive that must not be underrated[46].

We can wind up this section by saying that the organisation aboard ship must lead to the pursuit of effective, safe action and to achieving a collective spirit and daily living conditions that are conducive to a good atmosphere on board.

### 2.5.3 Means of control: incentives and penalties

Formal instrumental organisations accept that resorting to incentives and/or penalties is sometimes needed.

Both are found on merchant ships.

Financial incentives are not customary as personal incentives, though they may be offered as a general bonus for the crew. The captain can be an exception, since he sometimes receives personal bonuses, though in general the extra payments will be standard, stipulated ones.

Perhaps the most important incentive is promotion. The ordinary seaman may be promoted to petty officer. The officer may make his way up to become captain or chief engineer. Sometimes, however, crew members let promotion opportunities go by in order to avoid taking greater responsibility, particularly when they conclude that the extra money does not make up for the heavier workload or the increase in responsibility.

Another incentive, a spontaneous one, is what Hernández Izal[47] calls "accentuated solidarity", i.e. when a crew member is rewarded by his shipmates with special approval, or expressions of solidarity, that go beyond what is usual.

As for penalties, these are the ones associated with work discipline, though they are particularly strict on account of the circumstances.

In fact, the Merchant Marine's discipline has historically been quite close to military discipline.

In the same work Hernández Izal quotes the *Costums marítims de Barcelona* (Maritime Customs of Barcelona) as saying that there were penalties such as *the beheading of coastal pilots evincing ignorance of the stretch of coast with which they profess acqaintance; or tossing into the sea, without subsequent recovery, any lookout man who repeatedly falls asleep when on watch.*

Hernández Izal also tells that the legislation in force from 1930 to 1950 contained the penalty of depriving sailors of their wine ration for variable periods of time.

However that may be, the "Ley Penal y Disciplinaria de la Marina Mercante" (Merchant Marine's penal and disciplinary code), which was in force up to a few years ago, set down a system for classifying offences as minor, serious and major, each with their associated penalties.

Penalties for minor offences ranged from verbal reprimands to the loss of a day's pay. Serious offences could entail debarment from promotion for a certain length of time, the loss of up to one seventh of a month's pay etc. Major offences could be penalised with suspension of employment and pay for a certain length of time, or even dismissal.

The legislation currently applying in Spain is "Ley 27/1992 de Puertos del Estado y de la Marina Mercante" (Statute 27/1992 on Ports of the State and the Merchant Marine), which refers to the provisions of law - penal, labour, administrative etc. as applicable - regarding the penalties available.

We might add that just as there might be a spontaneous "reward" for crew members from other crew members in the form of special solidarity, there could also be a spontaneous sanction from shipmates for a crew member showing disregard for the collective good, such sanctioning taking the form of marginalising and cold-shouldering the offender.

### 2.5.4 Primary and secondary adjustments

In our society in general, and also within an institution such as the crew of a ship, individuals are not only expected to carry out a certain activity, but also to observe general patterns of behaviour. Goffman[48] says: *There is thus at the very heart of the social provisions of an organisation an integrated concept of the member, not only as such but also as a human being.*

To be a sailor is not not merely to exercise a profession, to do a job. The sailor, by the fact of living aboard ship and being part of a temporarily isolated community on the move, takes on special traits. When a person goes aboard ship for the first time, in addition to learning a trade (helmsman, greaser etc.) or applying theoretical studies that he has completed (as in the case of officers), he will also have to learn how to live on a ship and how to take his place in a highly structured community with various subgroups, a community which will have a range of habits that form a sub-culture alongside the official labour regulations.

From the sociological standpoint, a man is like an actor playing a part assigned to him, or that perhaps he himself chose, in the great theatre of life[49]. But the fact is that he is also expected to play the part in a certain way.

Hence both the shipowner and any crewman expect everybody on board to behave like "seamen" in the usual sense of the term.

It is assumed that he is always ready to go into action, even if he is not on watch, if the circumstances require or if a superior deems it advisable (within certain natural limits) - and this even during his time off. It is assumed that when he goes ashore at port, he will come back in time for his watch, and when the time comes for the ship to leave, he will be back on board again, and so on.

Informally, it is taken for granted that any crew member would leave the sea if he had a good offer of employment on land.

These attitudes in the individual that are part of what is expected of him in the organisation are what Goffman calls primary adjustments.

Louis A. Zurcher[50], in his study of the warship as a total institution, following up Goffman's study on interns, includes among these primary adjustments what he calls the informal organisation, which is a wide-ranging set of customs, rites, traditions and habits that develop on board and that make the crew member identify with his ship and his shipmates, thus achieving higher efficiency from all aboard.

Thus, to turn back to the merchant marine, we could include among these primary adjustments certain rites of initiation, featuring practical jokes - for example, the classic joke on Spanish ships of sending a student on work experience to fetch the "wrench for the master compass", which usually turns out to be the heaviest tool in the engine room. Another joke is the baptism that is arranged when a newcomer goes over the equator for the first time, often consisting of emptying a bucket of water over the head of the novice when he is not expecting it. The effect of these rites on a novice is that, after some time, he begins to feel a veteran, and plays the same jokes on new entrants.

The news coming via the "scuttlebutt" grapevine give advance un-official warning to the crew, and mean that when the official news comes, the crew are already in the know... In this way, rumours begin to circulate regarding the port of destination (on a tramp ship) before it is officially announced.

Zuercher takes the view that all behaviour patterns and attitudes that are beyond the bounds of the official ones or those envisaged in the terms of employment, but which nevertheless contribute to the aim of any maritime voyage (efficient, safe shipping) can be deemed *primary adjustments*.

Similarly, he terms *secondary adjustments* all such behaviour patterns which, under the guise of doing what is expected of a crew member, are in fact geared towards ends or activities that deviate from his role, serving only the interest of an individual or group, and even running counter to the general interest.

Here there is a discrepancy between Zurcher and Goffman, since for the latter these secondary adjustments do not necessarily have to feature this element of deceit, or running counter to the general interest: for the latter they may be mechanisms serving balance, even when private interests are entailed aside from the common good. For our part, we will follow Goffman's criterion in this.

A sailor who indulges in smuggling is using the ship for a purpose other than its intended purpose, and is taking advantage of his role on board to seek private profit.

The shipping company might have a shrewd idea that a group of crew members is up to business of that kind, and may even benefit from it in the sense that these crew members will perhaps be content with a low salary on a route offering rich pickings from smuggling.

To take one example, this happened quite a lot on Spanish ships, particularly after the Spanish Civil War on the South American routes, and until well into the seventies on the routes between mainland Spain and the Canary Islands.

However, the fact that the shipping company may stand to gain to some extent in terms of paying lower wages does not make this crew activity a primary adjustment, since the contraband may cause problems for the ship on putting into port, or may give rise to penalties, and may even, depending on how it is concealed, endanger the cargo. Smuggling can also be a cause of squabbling among the crew, thus spoiling good relations aboard ship.

Also to be included under this heading are favours of all kinds that can be offered or exchanged. Without going into details, let it suffice to refer to the sections in which we spoke of the *de facto* power of certain crew members, which may give rise to Mafioso-style groups.

In the 1950s, there were also some who signed up for a ship bound for the United States with the sole intention of absconding in some port over there. The frequency of these attempts at illegal entry into the country prompted, for many years in the past and even today as well, highly stringent controls by the American immigration authorities as regards ship arrivals and departures.

Purchasing provisions for the ship, particularly with respect to food for the crew, has traditionally led to the person in charge of it seeking to make money by spending less than the sum allocated by the shipping company for the purpose, using doctored invoices, or simply accepting commissions.

These fraudulent actions, such as smuggling and misappropriating money intended for feeding the crew, are often suspected if not actually known by the shipping company, the latter turning a blind eye to them. Even the inspectors of the company may be taking a cut in those activities. If this happens, it will have a profoundly negative effect on order and on everyday life, and may thoroughly distort the hierarchical scheme on board.

This phenomenon is particularly prevalent on passenger ships[51]. On such ships, the catering department might amount to 60% of the total crew, and comprises one or more pursers, a chief steward, kitchen staff and a great many assistant stewards. The amount of food eaten by 700 or 1,000 passengers involves handling large sums of money, and even though most payments are made directly by the shipping company, great interests are at stake.

Even the assistant stewards have a splendid opportunity to indulge in private business (little "souvenirs", tokens of appreciation and so on) among the passengers themselves. It cannot be said that this is common practice, but it is, or has been, more frequent than one would wish.

Goffman also points out that members of organisations may also show excessive zeal in performing their duties. This may be regarded as negative by the shipping company when it entails, for example, incurring expenses regarded as unnecessary, or ship-time lost, through over-insistence on the ship not putting to sea until all the life-saving and safety gear is in perfect condition.

The officer in charge of the lifeboats, for example, is supposed to report their condition to the captain, as well as whether any of the provisions, equipment, flares etc. kept on the lifeboats need replacing. The captain, for his part, will have to come to decisions on this if everything is not quite as it should be.

In any case, the officer, in his capacity as crew member aware of a shortfall, can and should report it directly (if necessary) to the port authorities so that it can be remedied before the ship leaves. However, bringing the lifeboats or their equipment up to standard may be expensive and may sometimes involve keeping the ship at a standstill for several days. A dim view may be taken by the shipping company of such excessive zeal, and a captain showing such meticulousness in what is in fact his duty may find himself demoted to first officer on some other pretext.[52]

Naturally, how these attitudes are regarded in general will depend on the time and on the mentality of the crew members and the managers of the shipping company: an attitude that meets with approval in one organisation may be reproved in another.

Goffman tells us that in the North American navy in the nineteenth century, a daily ration of alcohol was granted to each crew member (a matter that would be viewed as coming under secondary adjustments nowadays), while recreational games such as the game known as checkers in the States and draughts in Britain was regarded as a special privilege. In our own day, it is quite usual for the shipping company to provide not only table games but also video films and video games too for crew relaxation purposes.

On Spanish ships, having moderate amounts of alcoholic drinks is regarded as perfectly normal, even a sailor's right. Drunkenness, though, is thoroughly disapproved of, and is penalised during navigation, and particularly when on duty. In port, if the ship's work is not affected, finding a crew member coming back on board a little "tipsy" may be regarded as tolerable, or even normal.

Secondary adjustments, Goffman tells us, contribute to institutional stability.

Secondary adjustments may be divided into two types: violent adjustments and repressed adjustments.[53] *Violent adjustments are those of participants who, with the specific intention of leaving the organisation or altering its structure radically, interrupt its normal functioning in either case.*

*Repressed adjustments are, like primary ones, in line with existing institutional structures, introducing no pressure aimed at radical change, and indeed sometimes fulfil the obvious function of channelling strains that would otherwise be destructive. The most well established, stable parts of the "underground" life of an organisation thus tend to be made up primarily of repressed rather than violent adjustments.*

Let us try to examine the secondary adjustments in a ship's crew. These adjustments will arise in various ways depending on the hierarchical levels involved.

Before starting, however, we must bear in mind that on ships many factors are involved in making distinctions between hierarchical levels.

One notion is, no doubt, the post held on board, thus putting the captain right at the top, followed by the chief engineer and the first officer, and then further down the other officers, thus giving a hierarchical ordering.

Thereafter, as we have said, we will find the petty officers, and finally the ratings.

Viewing it simply, we could say that the people at the top level have inherent motivation - primary adjustment - that comes from their degree of commitment and emotional adhesion to the organisation for various reasons: because they are there, initially at least, by vocation, and because the authority of their posts implies responsibility before the shipping company and indeed before the Law.

If we wish to hunt out secondary adjustments, we will no doubt find them. Some will be the prerogative of this level, or rather of some people on this level. Other secondary adjustments, however, will be the same as for the rest of the crew, with the difference that some will have a better chance to apply them than others, though they would also clash with the greater ethical standards associated with posts concerned.

In other words:

A secondary adjustment that is exclusive to certain individuals on this level would be the special treatment often received by the captain and sometimes the first officer and chief engineer in ports, whether in the form of gifts from companies that are unrelated to the shipping company but are involved in shipping, or in the form of an invitation to a good restaurant, or to go on an excursion etc.

As for greater facilities for availing themselves of other secondary adjustments, we could refer to the business we have already mentioned of parallel gains that can be made on some ships running on some lines through smuggling.

No doubt, and particularly for the captain though also for the officers in general, such practices have serious professional, legal and ethical connotations, which act as a strong dissuasion, or at least a brake. Nevertheless, if somebody at this level decides to take part in such an operation, or even to organise one, he will find it all the easier the higher his post is, on account of the prerogatives of the post.

At this hierarchical level -those in charge- we must also bear in mind a factor that is very important in assessing the possibilities for secondary adjustments: length of service. This is a factor which is not exclusive to this level, and which forms and intersecting group involving the various groups we have singled out. A crew member, whatever his group or level, who has been working for the shipping company for many years, will have that extra degree of commitment and emotional adhesion to the organisation that we referred to earlier.

Even so, even though we have been talking about a top hierarchical level that includes the captain and the officers, it is important to realise that the captain is to be seen as a level apart, because he stands head and shoulders above the rest of the crew in terms of authority and responsibility. This makes his post a post of trust for the shipping company, and thus that the captain has particularly strong links with the company. The shipping company expects more than just professional competence: it expects clear loyalty and vigilance in defending the interests of the company.

Within the level of those in charge, however, we also find young officers who have just come aboard. They will not have the links born of length of service, unless they have a clear wish to make their careers in the company concerned. And their level of authority, which is also rather limited, will not give them much access to secondary adjustments requiring influence.

On the other hand -and forming a further intersection group with other crew members of any level with no length-of-service links to defend- these young officers may also have fewer scruples than others when it comes to seeking personal profit, even if that runs counter to the interests of the shipping company.

Naturally, when discussing these possibilities, we are discussing exactly that: possibilities; we are not pre-judging the ethics of any crew member. As in any social context, there are honest people and dishonest people.

Let us now turn to an intermediate level in our theoretical levels, the petty officers, whom we have referred to previously. In this group, the length-of-service and loyalty factor carries special weight, particularly in the cases of the boatswain, the donkeyman and the chief steward, these being posts which are normally reached through length of service. The carpenter, the electrician and the cook are professional workers who can join the ship directly for those roles.

This classification is valid for ships staffed mostly by permanent staff, but will not be equally valid for some small companies, particularly those using flags of convenience, who cover their staffing requirements as they go. If we leave aside the figure of the chief steward, and sometimes the cook, the rest of the group will perhaps have the fewest opportunities for secondary adjustments. They have a strong professional interest, tied to length of service, they do not normally have access to external rewards, and they will tend to avoid endangering their jobs.

When there is one aboard, the chief steward, of whom we have had occasion to speak previously, is a figure inherently representing a *de facto* power on ships. In terms of power, he may even establish an intersection group with the captain himself. Like the captain, he will enjoy secondary adjustments that are specifically associated with his post[54]. How strong he can become on the ship depends on how much the captain, and sometimes the shipping company itself, are prepared to countenance.

And so we arrive at the lowest level in the hierarchy, the ratings. These will have few work-related opportunities for secondary adjustments, with the exception of catering staff in general, since these will have quite a lot of scope either through their relations with the chief steward or through being in contact with the passengers on passenger ships.

The bridge and engine-room hands, who are in fact the real professionals of the sea among the ratings, will have little potential for such secondary adjustments other than small advantages or favours they may arrange between themselves, or cooperating in some secondary adjustment with crew members from other levels or departments.

Escapist activities are a special kind of secondary adjustment. As we have seen, these should be regarded as primary adjustments, if we follow Zurcher[55]. Games of cards or dominoes, board games or videos and so on, offering the crew a chance to get away from it all, contribute towards a good atmosphere aboard, helping people to become relaxed, and thus they help to get things running smoothly aboard ship.

Stop-offs in ports also have recreational potential.

There are crews, particularly young ones, who take to the sea because they enjoy roaming here and there, getting to know different countries.

Then there are secondary adjustments that allow individuals to rebel without overstepping the mark: for example, gestures of contempt, muttered cheeky replies, or even exaggerated shows of respect that in fact mask sneering when carrying out orders.

A smug grin may serve to show defiance with regard to a superior who is perhaps not too sure of himself.

It is indeed common among some crew members, particularly ones who have considerable experience behind them, to subject superiors to a kind of thinly veiled war of nerves that serves as a test to find out the real extent of their authority.

Another special feature within secondary adjustments is the tendency to reserve a private space for oneself[56], however small.

Here too Zurcher would see a primary adjustment, since this makes the crew work better. This private space would consist of the individual's cabin, posters, stickers, decorations, plants and even the small pets that crew members sometimes keep in their cabins. That is their world, and small belongings that would have no special significance at home - just a photo in a frame or whatever - become veritable treasures aboard a ship. The same goes for pennant flags, ashtrays and so on.

We will also find the bragging of the sailor with the biggest transistor, or a huge radiocassettee, or fine-looking shoes, or a leather jacket he bought in this or that city. Crew members often go to great trouble to get showily dressed up when going ashore in ports.

Within the social institutions that ships are, the crew member, who as we know is living out his role 24 hours a day, will do everything he can to safeguard his self-identity, wishing to make it clear that there is more to him than his post.

## 2.6 Links between the crew members

### 2.6.1 Subgroups

The feeling of solitude is the strongest feeling weighing on the seafarer. When somebody goes aboard for the first time, he finds himself in strange surroundings, governed by unfamiliar rules of conduct, relations, customs and even language.

This prompts crew members to form smaller groups in which they can talk about their private aspirations or worries, since everybody needs to get such things out.

This happens in every social context, be it an office, a school, a university faculty or among young people doing their military service. The greater need felt by the individual for it, the stronger this trend will be. In an office, where only a few hours are spent together, this phenomenon is not so essential, though individuals will always get on better with some than with others. But when people feel exposed to some extent, there will be a stronger drive to create these subgroups.

A child going to school initially finds himself alone amongst people he does not know, and the easiest way to get over that feeling will be to establish relations of trust and mutual support with one or two other children. He will then start talking about "my friend" or "my friends", and when he arrives at school each day he will seek out that friend or friends. As time passes, that circle will normally grow bigger, and he will feel gradually more self-confident within the class group. Later on he will even begin to feel integrated in the school as a whole.

This process, albeit with the natural differences arising from being older, arises whenever a person finds himself outside his familiar or usual surroundings. The young man turning up for military service, for example, will immediately join a group of people from his own town or region, or at his own sociocultural level, and so on.

After a while, as he finds his place in what had been new surroundings for him, his contact with the people who were his first friends may fall off as he gradually gets to know the other recruits.

Much the same applies aboard ships. People need to form affective bonds, and it is always easier to do that with one or two people than with a lot of people all at once. There are always points of contact and points of divergence between people.

At the subgroup level, it is easier to come to a tacit, reciprocal agreement on emphasising things we have in common rather than things that separate us. The longer a crew spends together, the greater the chances for a stable relation to emerge through patterns of harmony and discord in their relations. Nevertheless, that is not always so:
- there are problems of personal chemistry which can get worse rather than better with time,
- different ways of reacting to adverse circumstances and to prolonged isolation can spoil a relation that had started out well,
- the various subgroups that form can find themselves increasingly fighting against each other,
- crew members being transferred to other ships upsets the structure of these subgroups; this is beneficial when it breaks up groups that were causing problems on the ship, and negative when it destroys friendly relations aboard.

These subgroups are normally formed within a particular hierarchical level, with other factors such as place of origin, age, cultural level also exerting an influence.

If we bear in mind how crews are organised[57], we can appreciate that both its hierarchical structure and its various departments split the total human group up into subgroups right from the outset. If we then add in a need for personal affinities, we can see that the chances of establishing any close personal relations are rather slight.

This can also be seen in ports, when off-duty crew members usually go ashore in small groups.

A crew member who is in the habit of going ashore alone comes to be seen as someone not be wholly trusted.

Another obstacle to the creation of close links is, among other things, the fact that the crew members do not always end up on the same ship, and then if they come from different places they will not be able to carry on with any friendship that might have arisen. Even if they do live in the same town, it is sometimes the case that they will not wish to see each other during their holidays so as not to be reminded of the ship.

The English refer to "Board of Trade acquaintances"[58], thus pointing to the personal interest in what is anyway a relation born of need. For all these reasons, few lasting friendships are formed among crew members. Nevertheless, while the trip lasts, particularly on ships doing long runs, a strong spirit of solidarity is created, and so the crew member can feel supported as part of a kind of family.

This being part of a family, in a broad sense, not just of a particular ship but rather of the marine family in general, is reflected in oddities of behaviour, habits and expressions which form what we could call a subculture of seafaring people, one which characterises them, and one which they are in some way proud of.

### 2.6.2 Tensions between subgroups

Taking the various hierarchical levels and the departmental divisions as our starting point, let us look at what tensions may arise.

The deck and the engine-room hands perform functions with a direct bearing on the efficiency and safety of the ship.

Falling to the deck crew are navigation, the general maintenance of the ship (the hull, the decks, the rigging etc.), the job of preparing, taking aboard and stowing the cargo and then unloading it again at the end, the ship's stability as a safety factor in sailing, and in general the legal, labour, administrative and commercial relations that are the particular incumbency of the first officer and the captain.

As for the engine-room staff, they are in control of the ship's propulsion system, the generator, and all the electrical and mechanical engines and fittings. If the ship's engines do not work, the ship cannot go anywhere, and most of its other work cannot be performed either. This staff department first appeared on ships when steam engines came in replacing sails.

The fact that both these departments have people in positions of authority (the captain and officers for the deck department, and the chief engineer and engineer officers for the engine department) means that rivalry arises to see how has most power aboard. The saying "oil and water don't mix"[59] dates back to the times of steam ships.

As we have already said, absolute command aboard ship rests with the captain, who thus has authority over all the crew members, including the chief engineer. The captain[60] looks after communication with the shipping company and takes decisions affecting the entire ship. The engineer officers, for their part, can make the ship go slower or faster. It is up to them to get the generators to produce a healthy supply of electricity and to look after many other things.

Nick Perry[61] studied two tankers and, in connection with these tensions between the deck and the engine departments, tells us, for example, that on one of the ships, the water that came out of the sinks in the deck officers' washroom was rather murky, whereas it was crystal clear in the engineer officers' washroom. Or again that the air conditioning in the deck officers' mess room and cabins did not work, though it worked just fine in the engineer officers' rooms.

Authoritarianism is another breeder of tensions. In fact this aspect has changed a lot in our day since criteria of employment contracts have come in. Nevertheless, the captain still has significant prerogatives.

It must also be borne in mind that a large part of the world's shipping fleet works with international crews, with the senior staff from one country and the rest of the crew from other countries. Hence the crew on many such ships, who are only tenuously protected by vague legislation and are anyway subject to the fear of losing their jobs, see the captain as a powerful man to be feared and obeyed.

Even aside from this, on account of the very nature of navigation, all legal provisions grant the captain powers that go way beyond what would be expected merely from a labour-law standpoint. Respect for officers is also far higher on a ship with an international crew than on one sailing under an European flag.

Strikes in the marine fleet are viewed very differently from strikes in factories on land. What is involved when a ship is immobilised - with goods that belong to another company or other companies, with very high and varying economic interests at stake - means that strikes are taken extremely seriously. As an example, we can cite a case that arises again and again: crew members from a Third World country go on strike over wages that have not been paid to them, though without notifying the court in the port as they should. The captain, having access to much better legal advice, accuses them of sedition, and brings the local police on board to remove the crew members from the ship for repatriation. When they get back to their country, they will have no way of seeking redress against this injustice.

In terms of tension, this authoritarian framework often makes some fearful of losing their authority and makes others take a defensive stance against what they see as a dictatorship.

Behind a despotic captain there often lurks an insecure person: being unable to inspire respect, he resorts to exercising his command in a dehumanised way. And it is also the case that defiant reactions by subordinates are often prompted by social resentment - the feeling that they have to be subordinate even in their free time.

Merchant vessels also feature the separation we have mentioned between the area set aside for officers and the one for the crew. On passenger ships, this distinction is very sharp, and is accentuated by uniforms. On such ships, the officers, even though they have only restricted access to the passenger areas, do in fact strike up relations with the passengers, while this is usually forbidden for the ratings outside their work context.

On small ships whose crew members are all from the same country, relations are usually much more easy-going, and visible differences between the two sides are scarcely to be seen. On ships with international crews, a sharper divide reappears, reminiscent of bygone times.

In the Spanish merchant marine down to the early 1970s, the image of captains and officers was closely bound up with giving orders in a style that was more military than civil. Nowadays this has changed quite a lot, particularly on European and North American ships.

As is usually the case, the differences between levels are felt more keenly by ratings than by officers, since the former have fewer comforts aboard ship and often find that, despite being older and with more years at sea behind them, they have to take orders from somebody younger with less sea experience.

With international crews, the strain inherent in the differences of status between officers and crew are heightened by a sense of a deeper divide - between peoples of nations, or sometimes between races.

In a small space shared by people with different levels of rank and amenities, in which some are concerned with exerting authority and the others with resisting excessive authoritarianism, it is inevitable that tensions will arise, yet such strains will be far more likely when "national categories" are added to the barrier of professional categories.

This bias based on race and nationality is still unfortunately a reality. In this, it would be much better if, in crews made up of various nationalities, each nationality were represented on all the hierarchical levels, to avoid the divide of professional rank being deepened by national differences.

According to Nick Perry[62] again, there are tensions that stem from two principles that act simultaneously: the hierarchy principle and the solidarity principle.

Everybody on board knows that whatever a person's rank, he will suffer as much as anyone else from feeling alone, from being far from home, from the dangers of the sea and the rough ride through storms, and that consequently what unites them is more than what divides them when they are out in the middle of the ocean. Seafaring people tend to have a highly developed sense of solidarity, at least as regards the shared aspects of life aboard.

Moreover, as Nick Perry also points out, tensions between officers and ratings are sharper in the deck department than in the engine department, since engine officers usually do heavier work, and get covered in oil and grease almost as much as any other crew member of that department.

There is certainly some truth in this, since sailors feel closer to an officer who gets drenched just like them when a downpour comes along when they are in the middle of mooring manoeuvres, or who has to put up with the dust and noise just as they do in loading and unloading operations. On the other hand, for a sailor soaked in sweat and with his hands aching, the sight of a spotless officer up on the bridge will not usually inspire admiration.

Tensions also arise in the struggle for professional promotion. Crew members circulate among the various ships of a company, and the holidays or illness of one may be a promotion opportunity for another.

These tensions are experienced differently from post to post aboard ship. The captain is obliged first and foremost to earn the approval of the shipping company, and this may lead him to do things or give orders that are detrimental to the crew - for example, making a saving by cutting out the motor-launch service to take sailors ashore when the ship is lying at anchor, thereby thwarting the crew's desire to go ashore but perhaps winning points with the shipping company on account of the money saved. The merits of the other crew members will usually be assessed by the captain, who reports on them.

In the case of the other crew members, even though they may have direct relations with the shipping company, their promotion prospects will depend particularly on the reports of their superiors. These can give rise to tensions, of a similar kind to those arising in any human activity, though here once more the circumstances compound matters.

P.G. Herbst[63] presents a diagram showing the various factors that are conducive to distance-keeping within a crew:

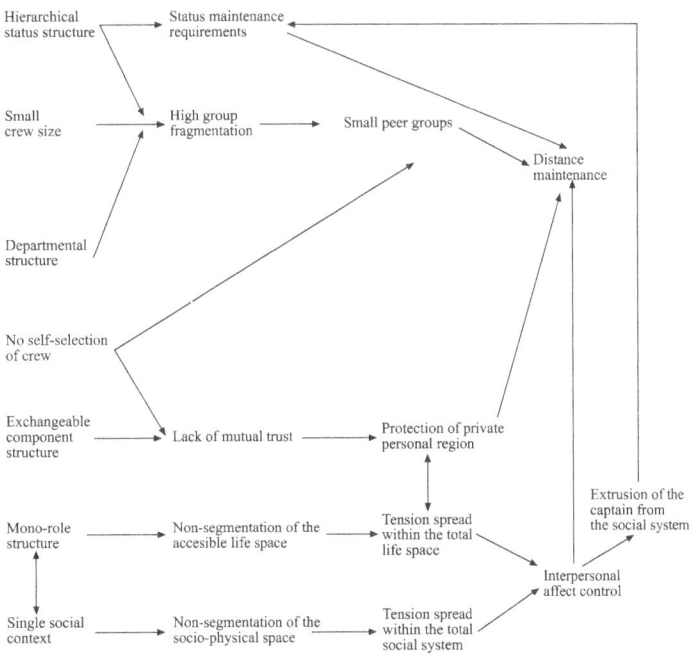

Fig. 1. Organisational conditions which contribute to distance maintenance. P.G. Herbst

To begin with the hierarchical structure, this is based on respect for authority, and consequently officers will tend to keep their distance from the rest of the crew.

The captain stands wholly aloof[64], condemned to solitude in order to preserve respect for this post.

This hierarchical structure substantially fragments the crew as a social group.

In ships with a small crew, additional fragmentation occurs in that several small groups appear on similar levels. The closer contact that comes through having fewer people on board requires greater efforts to maintain distances.

The departmental structure is also a factor behind fragmentation, as explained, since it also encourages certain distances to be maintained between people.

Crews are not formed by bringing people together on the basis of coherent criteria: a group of professionals is simply brought together with no account being taken of their personal traits or whether they will get on well together. Herbst[65] says that *At the interpersonal level the crew has more the characteristics of an aggregate than that of a structured community.*

This factor, together with the possibility that any crew member may be transferred to another ship at any time, causes a mutual lack of trust, and this in its turn, following Herbst's diagram, encourages the instinctive protection of one's private space, which in turn reinforces this keeping of distances.

Furthermore, tensions are created that affect the entire social system on board since the crew is a structure in which each member has just one role, which is his 24 hours a day, there being no segmentation of the life space that might enable him to "switch off" since there is insufficient physical segmentation to mark social separations.

This in its turn leads to a certain control in interpersonal treatment that further reinforces the keeping of distances.

### 2.6.3 Traditions, customs and attitudes

As we saw in chapter one, all total institutions are governed by a number of norms that seek to ensure the attainment of the objective set. Sometimes these norms are rules or written regulations, and other times they are customs or traditions that have become a fundamental part of the life system even though they are not laid down anywhere.

The more closed an institution is, the sharper the inmutability of its customs. A ship is an open institution in the sense that it moves from port to port, its crew come into contact with all kinds of people, and moreover they themselves come from different towns or cities. Nor must it be forgotten that crews change owing to substitutions for holidays.

Yet at the same time it is a closed institution in the sense that, in professional and social terms, the general rootlessness of seafarers makes them disinclined to make changes in their traditional patterns of life and work aboard ship.

Even so it must also be noted that this situation has been changing over recent decades. Before, over many many years, navigation evolved only very slowly, and sailors could maintain throughout their professional lives fairly fixed patterns that they had learned and perfected over the years, exhibiting a wary attitude towards any innovation.

Nowadays, as we have said, this has changed quite a lot, for various reasons. For one thing, technical progress, particularly through computers, has developed at a dizzying pace and has imposed major changes in all systems for navigating, loading and unloading, and work on board in general. For another, steady improvements in the training of crews have also led to greater adaptability to new techniques and systems.

Nonetheless, the fact remains that traditions, customs and rites continue to be cultivated on ships to an extent that landlubbers find astonishing.

A familiar story is a young officer coming aboard brimming with modern technical knowledge only to come up against an old captain who goes out his way to show him that his studies are practically worthless and that all that counts is the way things have always been done.

Although the features of life and work aboard ship have been explained in the various sections of this book, we might still briefly recall some of the more important points in this context:

Let us recall that that it is rare to find a hierarchical order like a ship's in any other sphere of civil activity. The captain and the officers form a veritable caste apart. On Spanish ships, the use of the respectful term of address "Don" by subordinates when addressing an officer is a clear manifestation of this status. At the same time, it is quite normal for the officer to use the familiar form *"tú"* (you) when addressing subordinates, even when they are older than him. It is also noticeable that many subordinates are grateful for that manner of treatment, regarding officers who use the polite form *"usted"* (you) to them as more distant.

A similar relation frequently arises between the captain and the chief engineer on the one side and the other officers on the other.

These ranks have prerogatives that result in a difference in the size and amenities of cabins, messrooms and day rooms, and in the officers having their cabins cleaned and their meals served for them when the others do not, among other tokens of status.

And even in the officers' messroom, nobody can start eating until the captain arrives, and he will be served first.

On a different level, there are also considerations of status among the crew members. The petty officers, as we have said, stand on their privileges with regard to those under them, and among those subordinates, the veteran will keep a distance from novices.

In fact, though not so obviously, there are expectations regarding the behaviour of each member in any social establishment, even when no specific work is assigned to the members.

As Goffman says, among the people in any society there are *contact rules which simultaneously serve as identification, a guide to ideal behaviour and a basis for solidarity and division at the same time.*[66] In a ship's crew, each person has a role, a very specific mission, with its attendant rights and duties, and these set his working hours and rest time, and the spaces allotted for each work, rest or recreation activity.

This set-up is a matter or routine, and for that reason it serves to give support and confidence to crew members in dealing with personal problems, solitude and rootlessness, as well as with the dangers that the sea inherently poses.

Nicknames are also common on ships: *Paws* (this was given to a sailor with enormous hands); *Big Bonce* (a captain with rather a large head); *Sozzle* (an officer who was frequently under the influence). The nicknames are often related to place of origin as well.

Customs and traditions differ from one type of ship to another, and across nationalities too, though even so there are a number of common aspects, and this enables us to talk about what Hernández Izal calls "the seafarer's subculture"[67], with reference to a range of traits that are common to most sailors, and which he summarizes as follows:
- a lack of prospects within the profession itself, which makes him think of leaving the sea if he has other aspirations;
- a certain sense of resignation regarding his situation as a crew member;
- a sensation of security aboard ship, as compared with insecurity when dealing with wider surroundings;
- adaptability to people, climates, other countries etc.;
- the demand for a private space of his own;

- versatility and aptitude for fulfilling various posts and for dealing with new situations;
- a strong sense of community, in response to the contingency situation that arises at sea;
- a highly critical attitude towards outsiders involved with the ship (shipping-company employees, brokers etc.).

Lastly, we could pick out a number of attitudes that are typical among seafarers, such as the instinctive tendency to fasten down objects left on tables or shelves (even when ashore), orderly living habits, shaped by a timetable that is the same day after day, wanting to have money when getting into port, the habit of smoking expensive cigarettes and drinking good whiskies (which are cheaper on board ships), scheduling time in terms of port arrivals and departures rather than by working days and Sundays (since the latter do not mean much aboard), and so on.

## 2.7 The importance of a common system of life and a common language

Goffman tells us[68] that members of total institutions recover their personal stability when they learn the institutional system.

In section 3.3, when dealing with crew members, we will discuss the problems of the newcomer to the sea, coming from an atmosphere, or at times a culture of his own, that have nothing to do with those of the other crew members. There we have an adaptation problem right from the outset.

Here, however, we will look at the importance for the crew as a whole of having a common pattern of life and language.

People need to feel part of some human group. Even if we become solitary to some extent during our lives, there is still always something that serves as a basis to support us, to give us confidence and to help us identify ourselves.

Louis A. Zurcher[69] in his work on the U.S. navy produced studies taking Goffman's analysis of Total Institutions as his starting point, and when speaking of new recruits ("boots") he tells us that:... *the boots attend daily classes in Naval tradition and customs, gunnery, first aid, seamanship, Naval history, military conduct, and shipboard organization. ... They learn Naval argot ... the floor is a "deck" ... (and) it is not right and left but "starboard and port"...* He also tells us that *The routine use of obscene expressions is all part of wanting to belong, since the words become part of the language of a social group.*

A total institution needs to give its members an identity. The crew of a ship, apart from being made up of very different people, also has one very important thing in common: they are all embarking on the same adventure.

Being acquainted with the historical background, even if it might seem irrelevant, helps to integrate the crew. This notion of history refers not so much to what the navy did in the sixteenth century as to everything in the most immediate past - the everyday experiences of the sailors on service at the time. Thus on ships belonging to the same company, anecdotes are told concerning this man and that, since most of the men know each other. If a stranger turns up on board, he may have a certain feeling of being an outsider until he becomes sufficiently acquainted with the people being talked about.

And then there is the common professional lexicon. No person (whether a lawyer, doctor, bricklayer, farmer or anything else) can regard himself as a member of his group if he has not mastered the associated professional language, by which we mean not just the technical vocabulary in the strict sense, but also the casual, colloquial language employed.

Some of these expressions make no sense to people outside the profession. For example, Spanish sailors commonly use the English word "beachcomber" to refer not just to tramps who search beaches for flotsam and jetsam, but to any pitiful person.

The pronunciation of the word on Spanish ships has degenerated to *pichicoma*, and is basically used in connection with the people who come aboard in ports to bring documents or on some other business. It is clearly pejorative, and is sometimes used among sailors as an insult. Sailors new to the sea and joining the profession will quickly adopt this and other expressions. Using them will make them feel more integrated in the profession.

## 2.8 The crew in terms of ship type

When discussing the various roles, reference has already been made on some occasions to the various kinds of ship and how this affects the crew. In broaching this subject, we can make distinctions between the following kinds of ships:

**Passenger ships**, with crew members running into the hundreds (*Queen Mary II* - 1,253 crew members). These ships have a complex social structure. They are highly hierarchical, and the various departments are like sealed units, with little inter-relation between the crew members.

The subgroups we referred to in section 2.6 become particularly significant in such ships, and all the circumstances favour internal tensions and primary and secondary adjustments.

The great complexity of such a crew is due to the fact that there can be several thousand passengers aboard, adding up to a true "floating city", with some people working so that others can get from one port to another, or simply enjoy a holiday for a few days or weeks.

However, life aboard a passenger ship is organised in a most orderly fashion, even for the passengers: what with their sustenance, their recreational, sporting and cultural activities, the schedule of arrivals and departures in ports and their tourist outings, their time is all fully organised.

This floating city is equipped with everything required for a society to work:

There is a higher authority, the captain, to whom all owe allegiance, with standards and rules for conduct. There are other people - officers and pursers - whose functions include certain policing and controlling roles.

There are services to meet the needs of the "city's inhabitants": the kitchen, the bakery, the room service, a sick bay with medical facilities, premises for hair-dressing and laundry services, shops, bars, dining rooms, a chapel with one or more chaplains when there are passengers of different faiths, communications services (telephone, telegraph, fax etc.), a photographer, a printing service, an internal daily newspaper, a gymnasium, a swimming pool, carpenters, plumbers, electricians...

All these services are laid on for commercial reasons, to make the passengers' stay on board more attractive, thus persuading people to come aboard that particular ship and go on that particular cruise.

Yet there are still two groups in this "floating city", two groups that can scarcely be lumped together from a sociological perspective: the crew and the passengers. There are indeed interactions between certain crew members and the passengers: the captain has a special significance for the passengers, as do the officers, since they are people in uniform who complete the glamorous backdrop; and the cabin stewards count too, since they have direct relations with the passengers, and then the other crew members have at least an anecdotal presence.

For the crew, the passengers are on the one hand "the cargo to be transported" and on the other they provide a chance for contact with people who, though not crew members, are nonetheless voyaging with them. The connotations of such contact, however, will vary widely depending on the posts of the crew members.

For the captain and the officers, apart from the professional view of the passengers as being there to be transported and looked after, those same passengers also provide opportunities for striking up relations, and in a way that works to the advantage of the captain and officers in that they are admired by the passengers.

For the cabin stewards, the passengers may be seen as a source of good tips, or as a chance to observe various types of people and behaviour patterns, though they may also bring the humiliation of having to be deferential or sometimes even of having to put up with disdainful treatment (the Asian or Central American stewards on luxury cruisers in the Caribbean come to mind).

Everything we have said so far about the crew remains valid here, though with very complex additional ramifications. The crew retains all the sociological characteristics of the merchant marine, but the contact with the passengers - which means contact with, not blending with - has repercussions on the life of the crew that can run very deep.

**Ferries:** these are passenger ships, but covering short runs only, often lasting only a few hours, and though the passengers have most of the services listed for passenger ships, particularly medical services, shops and bars, the short duration of the crossings means that the passengers never gel into a group: they are together only as people are thrown together briefly on a bus, with very little interaction between them.

As for the crew, whose relations with the passengers will be minimal except for the cabin stewards, they never really come to be a total institution since the ship usually puts into port every day - and always the same ports - and so crew life as such scarcely exists, apart from the small groups that live and work together.

Here the connotation of performing the same role day and night disappears, and the crew member can go ashore almost every day even if only for a short time. Even when the stop-offs in ports are so short that the crew members often do not bother to go ashore, these continual stop-offs in ports, particularly when most of the crew live in those same ports, completely annul the need to seek out links over and above professional links, such link-formation being essential if we are to study a ship's crew as a total institution.

**Large cargo ships**, bulk carriers, oil tankers and large container vessels: these ships usually have crews of 20 to 30 members. Their voyages are usually long, and the ship as a total institution is fully developed aboard them.

These ships are usually well fitted out, with good comfort for the crew: good cabins, good day rooms, and air conditioning. The crew maintains a hierarchical structure, with clear distinctions between departments and professional categories.

However, since they are usually on long runs, certain links tend to be created among crew members, even across ranks and posts.

Such ships are the ones that best fit what we could call the standard scheme for a total institution.

**Small tramps and coasters:** these are usually small ships with small crews: 6 to 10 people. Though there are a few modern, well-equipped ones, it is in this group that we tend to find old, uncomfortable and neglected vessels. Aside from the state of the ship, the classic crew scheme is greatly affected by the small size of the crew.

The hierarchical structure is much reduced, and is restricted virtually to professional distinctions. When a newcomer arrives aboard, he never knows the post of any crew member he comes across. Life is free of formalities, there is often just one messroom for all, and everything is done rather casually, the poor state of the vessel itself often encouraging a lax attitude.

However, this does not mean that the crew are all buddies on such ships, that rank is irrelevant - it just means that relations depend mainly on the particular people involved more than on norms or rules. Thus the captain will make it quite clear that he is the boss, and may even be despotic, especially if he is European and the others are from a Third World country. The officers themselves will base their authority more on strength of character than on pre-established rules of respect. Roles on such ships are not so clearly pre-defined, and crew members must shape their role aboard in accordance with their own personality rather than with a written organisation chart.

We could indeed analyse the various kinds of ship in greater detail, and that would no doubt be worthwhile. However, we will let the foregoing suffice to make it clear that there are significant differences between different kinds of ships, and accordingly a sailor may well feel more integrated in some types than in others, depending on his navigational role, his own character, and of course the kind of people he encounters.

## 2.9 International crews

### 2.9.1 Causes and factors explaining their appearance

The internationalisation of crews was prompted by two main sets of circumstances:
- The difficulties experienced by shipping companies in industrially developed countries in the 1960s and early 70s in finding crews from their own country. Hence German, Norwegian, and Swedish shipping companies, for example, would hire some of the crew in their own country, and others from poorer European countries, such as Spain.
- The economic crisis affecting shipping in the 1970s, which obliged shipowners to cut costs drastically. The chance to sign on citizens of Asia or Africa then came along, they working for cheaper rates than even the cheapest Europeans.

Later, the internationalisation process has coincided with a progressive drop in the offer of seafarers in developed countries and with an increase of seafarers in developing countries. According to the BIMCO/ISF Manpower 2005 update, 71% of the approximately 466.000 officers and 76% of the approximately 721.000 ratings worldwide come from developing countries.

Given the lower standard of living in these countries, this has resulted in a reduction of the crew wages as a crew's desired salary is usually in accordance with their country's standard of living.

Often, a shipowner looks for a captain of his same nationality in order to keep control of the vessel and then employs ratings and part of the officers from any developing country, through a manning agency, so as to get cheap manpower. That is the reason why he will hoist a flag of convenience, to benefit from a tax reduction and from the possibility to have foreign crew members.

A ship registered with a flag of convenience will be ruled by the law of a country which is different from the one of the shipowner.

### 2.9.2 Sociocultural aspects to be borne in mind

It is well known that the problems that arise when people of different nationalities live and work together are not limited to speaking or understanding a particular language: a much greater problem is the lack of understanding with regard to cultural differences, social customs, religious beliefs and practices etc.

When we go off on a tourist trip spending a few days or weeks exploring a country and enjoying its food and drink, however much we may like the cuisine, we will always be pleased to reunited with our own bowl of soup with its homely style.

When sailing on a ship with a crew from one's own country, one copes with the travelling around, the times at sea and the times in ports here and there, with the feeling that what is travelling is a chunk of one's own land. The food on board is roughly the same as at home, one knows the songs that are sung, one discusses news of common interest, and one celebrates the festivities of the common country of origin. There may be personal differences, or even differences arising from the various regions or communities of origin within the country, yet deep down everyone will enjoy a status that, professional rank aside, is held in common: the status conferred by nationality.

On a ship with an international crew, in addition to the fragmentation that may be caused by the classical structure of any crew[70], there will be another source of fragmentation - the various nationalities - which can easily lead to misapprehensions and misunderstandings, or worse to instances of disdain and resentment.

Here we come across a significant issue in connection with international crews: is it better to make the national divides match the hierarchical divides, or match the departmental divides, or to mix nationalities across those divides?

If, for example, the officers are from one country and the crew from another country or from various other countries, this will mean that the divide between the two levels will be sharper than usual, which could facilitate abuse on the one side and boycotts on the other.

If, to take another example, the deck crew is from one country, and the engine crew from another, this will add to the problems of relation between those two departments, relations which are prone to tension in any case.

If a mixing policy is employed, for example with Asian officers and subordinates co-existing with British officers and subordinates, then the situation will be more conducive to a more democratic life together, within the ship's hierarchical order.

The problem comes in that when each of these professional groups is small anyway, then adding in the factor of differences in nationality will make it harder to find a group of colleagues whose circumstances and rank are similar to one's own for the purpose of enjoying a more relaxed relation unfettered by the frequently tense formal treatment associated with maintaining order and discipline.

In terms of human solidarity, I believe that the system that best ensures the greatest respect for human dignity is the system of mixing nationalities across the various hierarchical levels, in order to achieve a certain balance that makes life aboard a little fairer.

In any event, the captain will always remain an isolated member of the crew, whatever his nationality, although as we have explained he will usually be of the same nationality as the shipowner.

### 2.9.3 How international crews affect ship safety

E. González Pino[71] tells us *that Communication problems among multiracial crews can be very serious. On some ships, notes and orders are written in the language of the subordinates, and the officers carry plastic-coated copies to enable them to deal with the rest of the crew (P. Roberts). This would not seem to be the best way of arranging this, particularly in emergencies.*

*We fully agree with captain Roberts that if the personnel on board do not understand the language used by the officer, it would be advisable to regard the ship as unfit to sail.*

*It is usual for multiracial crews to appoint a leader, usually the boatswain, to act as interpreter between the chief officer and the crew. This gives rise to a number of problems.*

*Firstly, if some serious incident arises, acting swiftly is of the utmost importance, and if the boatswain is involved and is thus unable to act as interpreter, the consequences could be very serious.*

Communication among crew members is important for the functioning of the crew and for the way if affects the daily life of each crew member.[72]

From the standpoint of the crew as a whole, as a total institution, we can see that with international crews a further and important source of division - language - is added to the circumstances of isolation and having to share a daily routine.

Moreover, when analysing total institutions, reference is always made to the distinction between the personnel of the institution and the inmates.

In the case of ships, it must be made clear that the staff taking on functions of command and organisation are also inmates, and that from the captain down to the galley boy, all are employees of the shipping company and all are subject to the problems of a life lived in common.[73] This relation between those in charge and their subordinates can have a strong element of camaraderie - in some cases as when the crew are all of the same nationality - but it can also be highly discriminatory and tense when the main officers are deeply divided from the rest of the crew by disdain and mistrust on the one side, and bitterness and a feeling of marginalisation on the other, with general difficulties of understanding on both sides.

In this type of crew, instead of the traditional subgroups based on professional levels and departments and certain power-based subgroups, we find other subgroups based on nationality. Hence a dispute between two crew members of differing nationality might split the crew, with the nationality factor weighing more heavily in the balance than considerations of hierarchy or department.

For work and life to run smoothly on board, for the ship to be safe and to perform its allotted task without risk, good relations aboard and good mutual understanding are necessary. When the crew members have difficulty in understanding each other, the crew cannot act as a team.

Difficulties in understanding, as we have read in the quotation from González Pino, put the ship's safety in danger when the crew members fail to understand each other.

This has already been ascertained in accidents involving passenger ships, when such ships were carrying European or North American passengers and had hired Asian stewards with no foreign language skills other than a rudimentary knowledge of the English associated with their work. In cases of emergency, particularly when the stewards had to convey instructions to the passengers, serious problems have been recorded.

Difficulty in understanding also has other negative repercussions, such as mistrust, misunderstandings, and the isolation of the subgroups. It is not only a drawback for subordinates, by giving rise to exploitation and ill treatment; for the officers too, having a large group of people of another nationality, and frequently of another culture as well (Asian, African etc.), can prompt feelings of fear and thus give rise to an extra-rigid attitude. As we have remarked before, a despotic attitude in an officer often stems from a feeling of insecurity.

Paul Chapman[74] tells us that *Conflicts are inevitable when people from a variety of cultures are brought together in the same workplace. But when officers or managers deliberately take unfair advantage of these workers' economic or social vulnerability, because they are from other cultures, it is exploitation - a form of violence.*

*... In 1984 ... a Filipino bosun, Willi Sanchez struck and killed his Norwegian first mate. Sanchez had been aboard the ship for the previous nine months and had shown no signs of a violent temper. He appeared*

*to be cooperative and pleasant, despite palpable tensions on board, which a chaplain in Brooklyn, New York, had noticed the previous month.*

*In the trial that followed, witnesses attested that the first mate had incessantly taunted Sanchez but, consistent with his upbringing, the seafarer had ignored the provocations. Finally he had lost control under the pressure and struck the chief mate. The cultural difference between the two men is important. Two people from the same culture may have been able to find a way of reconciling their differences.*

In developed countries, labour regulations for the merchant marine are based on civil employment models: each crew member has rights and duties, and everybody must respect everybody else while still observing shipboard discipline.

On German ships, officers and crew address each other as *Herr...* (Mr...) as a sign of respect for the individual, without detriment to the sense of authority. It should be added, however, that when there are non-European crew members on board, the treatment is not the same, even assuming that some respect is still shown.

On Spanish ships, the attributes of those in charge are generally restricted to labour matters, along with any extensions needed for organising and leading a community of people that are cut off for some time from any other source of authority.

This is the case, as we have said, in marines of developed countries, The surprising thing is that officers from those countries, when faced with a crew from a country in the so-called Third World, frequently forget their democratic principles and treat the crew despotically, or at least with some measure of disdain.

The rules on such ships are clear: "if you don't like it, you can leave", or "if you complain too much, you'll be sent home and you won't be taken aboard again". Since these crew members do not have suitable legal protection in their own countries and sign on for service through agencies, they have little scope for insisting on rights or for making protest.

When a crew turns to a trade union in a port, such as the ITF (International Transport Federation) or to a mission like Apostleship of the Sea or a Centre for Seafarers' Rights, and succeeds in bringing and winning an action, its members often find that, though their demands have been met, they may never be recruited again, since the shipping company or recruitment agency concerned will make sure that they are never offered work again. Consequently it is no exaggeration to say that we have now returned to a situation where people are exploited at sea.

Evidently, this does nothing to enhance the safety of ships or the quality of the work they do, though it does offer, in the short term, cheap and submissive labour.

On ships with international crews, the problem of food will also be accentuated. Customs vary widely, and the ship's cook will have a hard time trying to keep everyone happy.

## 2.10 Downsized crews

### 2.10.1 Preliminary considerations

Dr. Hernández Izal[75] examines the consequences, from a sociological point of view, of reducing the number of crew members on a ship. He studied a supertanker, *Ionnis Colocotronis*, whose crew was to be reduced from 38 to 15 members.

In his study he says that *The reciprocal isolation rate (a parameter that cannot be overlooked) goes up by a factor of 2.53 for the smaller crew (reduced from 38 to 15), since each crew member comes across two others when he used to come across five. The fundamentals for the study are always rootlessness and space anxiety.*

Downsizing crews thus entails in all cases increasing the rootlessness of the marine profession regarding the social setting and, in the case of shrinking the crew on ships designed for larger numbers, the appearance of space anxiety.[76] P.G. Herbst [77], when studying the effects of gradually reducing crew numbers on merchant vessels, along with fragmentation by departments and roles, stresses the following points:
- most of the crew members become isolated;
- the chances for collective interaction, whether in work or in leisure activities, become extremely limited;
- however large the ship is, it is divided into work areas and private areas, and so the separation between the few remaining crew members becomes accentuated.

Furthermore, Herbst also tells us that as crew size is reduced, each remaining member feels more visible to the others, and thus finds it more difficult to maintain distance as a member of the group. This will probably make him feel physically more isolated from the group and will heighten his sense of solitude.

### 2.10.2 Downsized crews and ship safety

If we survey the tasks to be performed at sea, the time available for each crew member and the potential for versatility, then it is no doubt possible to arrange a mathematical reduction of the number of crew members, and this is indeed done. However, it is once again striking how little attention is usually paid to the psychological and sociological repercussions, and the major knock-on effects for shipping in general. As we have already remarked, in the context of airline pilots or astronauts, nobody entertains any doubts about the importance of fatigue, psychic balance, etc., and yet in the context of the sea...

González Pino[78] tells us that *Downsizing crews without the necessary restructuring of watches and other tasks aboard can have an impact on the safety of the ship. There are a number of parameters to be taken into account:*

*Stress, strain and fatigue: if the downsizing entails increasing the duties, the watch time and the workload of the surviving crew members, it may have a negative impact on the safety of the ship.*
- *Stress is the sum of aggressions coming from the environment, the work conditions and the workload. It is an objective value, and is thus quantifiable.*
- *Strain is an individual's response to stress, and is therefore a subjective value.*
- *Fatigue can be described as the degradation of human performance, the slowing down of physical and mental reflexes, and/or the impairment of the ability to make rational decisions.*

*In the world of shipping, higher levels of these risks are accepted than in the worlds of air or road transport.*

When talking about fatigue we must include not just the physical tiredness arising from worker longer hours or from working under tougher conditions, but also the mental tiredness that comes from isolation, the lack of stimuli and proper communication, and also from boredom and increasing apathy.

All these factors can lead to a loss of physical and mental reflexes, and thus to lower safety for the ship. When the aspect of fatigue aboard ships and its role in accidents are studied, these factors turn up again and again.

Efraim Marcovitz[79] puts it like this: *The tendency to minimise crew costs by all means seems at times hard to understand - even when looking at it only from the pure economical point of view.*

> *... The following examples suggest some of the common causes for fatigue on board modern ships and their possible consequences:*
> 1. *Insufficient number of officers/undertrained officers: The master has to take over sea watches while at sea and has to personally attend to many of the responsibilities that should have been looked after by an officer when leaving or entering port. Especially where the sea traffic is dense, fatigue is practically inevitable.*
> 2. *Overworked crew and officers - apart from not fulfilling their respective jobs properly - are more likely to get themselves involved in personal accidents on board the ship, especially when in port.*
> 3. *Inadequate safety standards on board the ship ... exert extra mental strain on the master - and consequently on his officers and crew - leading to fatigue.*
>
> *The fatigue factor, like any other contributor to maritime casualties, should be eliminated - as far as possible - by combined efforts of all the maritime community.*

This account is concerned chiefly with the work-efficiency aspect rather than the aspects of isolation or poor motivation. It is, however, an approach that helps us to see the problem of downsized crews from another viewpoint.

In the case of the captain and the officers in a standard crew, there is an officer on duty for each of the three watches (3 shifts of 4 hours each every 12 hours). But there are small ships with only a captain and a chief officer aboard, and these take turns to do 6 hours on watch followed by 6 hours' rest - in theory, though in practice we must also take account of meal times and all the other jobs to be done aboard in connection with maintenance, control and administration.

Furthermore, many of these ships sail in waters like the English Channel in which the density of sea traffic and the prevalence of fog mean that the captain, whatever his theoretical watch hours, has to stay on the bridge, either directing navigation or resting on a sofa to be ready for action at all times, and so he may have to spend a couple of days without being able to sleep properly, just taking little naps now and then.

And on top of this, when he can finally get to bed, the ship will be nearing port, and he will then have to look after the docking manoeuvres and then all the formalities associated with arrival in port.

Thus the chief officer will have to look after the loading and unloading tasks from beginning to end, and since the ships usually spend only a short time in port (a matter of hours, or with luck one or two days), the ship will soon be putting to sea again with no chance for any resting.

The rest of the crew will have to cover various functions at sea. Four or five subordinate crew members working in a versatile way can between them look after the jobs of the deck, engine and catering departments.

When they arrive in port, there will be repairs to be done, and attention to be paid to the loading and unloading operations, and thus scarcely any time for resting or getting away from it all.

Projects for downsizing crews take account, on paper, of the possibility of using land-based work teams to look after operations when the ship comes into port, with the crew thus getting time off. In fact over 20 years ago, there were some German shipping companies that had "Relief Crews" that looked after the ship when it returned to its base port, and covered all the loading and unloading operations. In the meantime, the crew members of that ship would have a couple of days off. Another attractive feature of this was that the working year for all sailors would include shipboard time, relief-crew time (without going to sea) and holiday time.

That was the scene at a time when labour for ships was in short supply, and the shipping companies were all striving to offer the best living, working and wage conditions so that their ships would be adequately manned. They were times when sailors were a scarce commodity, particularly in the north of Europe, and were thus in a position to be demanding.

Over recent years, the drastic cheapening of labour, due among other things to the abundant supply from Third World countries, together with the phenomenon of flags of convenience which we will discuss later on, have meant that many shipping companies have ceased to feel concerned about the living and working conditions of the sailors on board their ships, their only concern being that the ships complete the runs assigned to them. After all, whatever the crew size and whatever level of fatigue or competence in the crew, the ship always arrives - except when it doesn't ... but then there's always the insurance...

Marcovitz[80] concludes: *Despite the work of the ILO and IMO, it should be noted that there are no binding instruments which set hours of work limits or which require mandatory rest periods. ... The seafarers believe that the only way the fatigue issue will be addressed is through the formulation of mandatory requirements with regard to maximum hours of work and minimum mandatory rest periods and their strict enforcement, by both flag and port states.*

Regarding the risk of fire, Ricard Marí[81] singles out the human factor as a growing cause of fires aboard ship. In his doctoral thesis, he refers to a statistic from the USCG (U.S. Coast Guard) which tells us that fires aboard ship caused by human factors amounted to 35.1% in 1983 and 46.5% in 1987.

Prominent among the causes of fire in both years was carelessness and poor maintenance. However, while operator failures were much higher in 1983 than in 1987, fires due to insufficient safety measures were much higher in 1987 than in 1983.

The main point of interest here is the fact that somewhere between 35 and 50% of fires in recent years were due to the human factor. Various causes attributable to the crew can be considered in this context, such as lack of skills, lack of personnel (with its twin effects of maintenance work not getting done and fatigue diminishing the quality of work that does get done), negligence, language problems etc.

Marí has this to say regarding the number of crew members:

*The ship must have a sufficient number of competent crew members to cover maximum-activity situations and conditions, taking account of the total hours' service aboard and the rest periods that should be assigned to any seaman.*

What number of crew members constitutes a "sufficient number" is governed by regulations, though the figures are based on considerations of tonnage in the case of the deck crew and the power rating of the engine for the engine crew. No doubt a calculation can in theory be produced for the number of crew members needed to cover the shipping duties assigned, but account ought to be taken of the negative factors of stress and fatigue, particularly when emergency conditions arise and a handful of sailors have to take on a workload that might prove too much for them, even aside from the demotivating isolation involved.

When discussing downsized crews, reference is often made to automation, enabling a few skilled people to control a ship perfectly well.

However, when we take a look at ships sailing with small crews these days, we find that in most cases the cut-back was made without any improvement to the ships technical endowment, and with crews no more highly skilled than before.

Consequently, we are driven to conclude that in fact all that is sought in many cases is staff-cutting pure and simple.

### 2.10.3 How life aboard is affected by smaller crews

As we said in section 2.5 a seaman, like anybody else, needs to feel integrated into a group, and backed by it. He can then refer, in a manner of speaking, to "his family aboard". He may also want to be alone at some times, and accordingly we stressed the importance of a private space in section 3.5.

However, the pleasure of that voluntary isolation, lasting for just a while or maybe for a few hours, will be backed by the knowledge that not far away there is a group of people he can rejoin when he wishes. In this context, meal times are a good chance for gratifying meetings with other shipmates. The joking there, and even some arguments, will help to make him feel accompanied.

On ships with 7 crew members, everybody will be either working or sleeping; and then if they are from two or three different nationalities, the solitude borne by the crew member can become acute.

On a ship with 30 crew members, the boatswain rounds up 7 or 8 men on deck and shares out the work to be done in accordance with the work scheme set by the chief officer. On a ship with a crew of 7, the boatswain may have only one seaman available.

It should also be borne in mind that with so few people aboard, the hierarchical order largely disappears, and a friendlier atmosphere reigns. This, however, will depend to a great extent on the character and approach taken by each member, and thus cannot be counted on.

## 2.11 Flags of convenience

### 2.11.1 General considerations

Since ships sailing under flags of convenience have been frequently mentioned, let us turn our attention for a while to this phenomenon which has so greatly influenced maritime sociology.

The entire maritime world has been turned upside down by flags of convenience - which are also referred to under the term "tax havens" since they make shipowners practically exempt from taxes. Countries such as Panama and Liberia, to name the two best known examples, already had a merchant fleet before the Second World War, but it was in the 1950s that the practice of using these flags began to take off and to extend to other flags such as Cyprus, Singapore, Bahamas etc.

As from the 1970s, the world began to experience the phenomenon of shipowners from countries with long merchant-marine traditions rushing en masse to de-register from the original registries of their ships and to re-register them in these countries "of convenience". Hernández Izal[82] provides us with the following figures: in 1948 ships sailing under flags of convenience amounted to 3.75% of the world tonnage; in 1959 they amounted to 13.5%, in 1974 to 24.3%, and by the mid 1980s the figure was put at around 30%.

According to recent data, the current tonnage of ships sailing under flags of convenience amounts to 54.15%[83] of the total world tonnage.

The benefits for ships sailing under these flags are not limited to being practically exempt from taxes: the ships are also governed by less stringent regulations on safety, crew qualifications and working conditions.

Naturally, there are differences between the various flags of convenience, as there are between shipowners resorting to them. Thus we can find ultra-modern ships with highly competent crews sailing under these flags, and we can also find ships in a deplorable state with crews having low skills and lower wages. Reference should also be made to the second registers, a formula used by developed countries that permit ship owners to profit from fiscal advantages, as well as from contracting foreign crew, within certain limits, without having to resort to a flag of convenience. In Spain, the second register is that of the Canary Islands.

### 2.11.2 The sociological implications

The following implications can be noted:
1. Growing unemployment among seafarers from developed countries.
2. A general drop in wage levels and in welfare gains.
3. Encroachment in the profession.
4. Falling safety standards.
5. Increasing solitude.
6. Corruption and illicit self-enrichment are boosted.

This list does not seek to be exhaustive, but merely to illustrate the strong repercussions this flagging-out has in the world of the sea. And when we look at those implications, we find these consequences:
1. At centres for seafarer's welfare, such as the Apostleship of the Sea, one reproach is often heard:
   *You do everything you can to help sailors from the Third World, but they are the very ones that are taking our jobs away from us (i.e. local sailors).* Spanish sailors, to take just one example, see the shipowners hauling down the Spanish flag and hauling up in its place the Panamanian one or some other flag of convenience. Initially, to honour existing commitments, they may keep on the same crew - sometimes, but not always. However, as time goes by, that crew will be replaced by Asian or African crew members, with the captain and perhaps the chief engineer and chief officer still being retained as

Spanish members. The remainder of the crew will be foreign. The Spanish merchant fleet is well on the way to extinction, and unemployment is growing incessantly among the merchant marine.
2. Unemployment boosts the supply of labour, and this leads to lower pay. For when all is said and done, there will always be someone hungry enough to accept anything on offer. In the early 1970s, shipping companies went to extraordinary lengths to entice sailors into joining their company, so that they could have their ships manned and ready to sail. It was at that time that two months' holiday for every five months spent aboard became the norm in Spain - and that was only the beginning: under traditional flags nowadays, the holidays come every 4 months, and sometimes less.

Under such arrangements, a shipowner has to have more than one crew per ship, depending on the type of ship and the type of work it does. Hence the average ratio in British ships on high-sea routes is currently 1.8 crews per ship, and for ferries running between Calais and Dover, 4.8 crews per ferry.[84]

The same shipowner, if he registers the ship under a free registry (or flag of convenience), has the option of hiring full crews from the Third World through agencies, and then he will only need one crew per ship, since the salary total to be paid (which will anyway be much lower than in the case of using European sailors) will only need to cover the time the crew is aboard ship. When the crew goes ashore for their "holidays", what is really happening is that their contract has been terminated, and the shipowner will have no further dealings with them unless he hires them again later for another trip.
3. Encroachments in the profession arise in this context when the administrative authorities in some of these countries of convenience issue qualifications for officers and captains too readily; there are cases of some agents or consulates abroad issuing certificates to people who have never studied at all, and who thus have lower salary expectations. This means that the posts of captain or officers on some of these ships are held by people who are not qualified for those roles - while all the time there are qualified officers unemployed.
4. One result of this encroachment is lower safety standards. A person in command on a ship but not duly qualified for that role is a potential hazard for the ship itself, for the crew, for navigation, for the cargo and for the environment as a whole. Accidents at sea usually have serious implications.

In fact, many shipping companies have realised that having skilled personnel is a good investment for running a business-like, responsible shipping service. Others, however, running decrepit ships, do not seem so concerned about that. Perhaps this is because if the ship goes down, another can be bought with the insurance money, and if need be another company can be formed...

5. The subject of increasing solitude is dealt with in section 3.8.1, and so here we will merely say that it can stem from long trips, and from using small, international crews with very low pay and thus little scope for telephoning home.
6. Flags of convenience create the conditions for downright abuse and exploitation. This potential stems from the extremely precarious living conditions that prevail over much of our planet.

Paul Chapman[85] transcribes the following text from a letter received at the New York Center for Seafarers' Rights in 1986:

*We are three Tanzanians, three Sri Lankans and three Indians on a Greek ship with an otherwise all Greek crew. Our contract papers are totally false - we have not signed articles, and we are not listed in the crew's logbook. Technically we are told we are not members of the crew, but we must work all the time and receive only $170 a month.*

At the Barcelona "Centro de los Derechos del Marino" there is also a file containing cases of crew members from underdeveloped countries who sign aboard for a pittance, since anything is better than going hungry.

Other crew members have told how they had to pay manning agencies over three months' pay to get a one-year job aboard, and how nobody was willing to report the fact since if they did they might lose their jobs.

Another abuse is delaying payment of the wages, sometimes by several months; and when the crew members have had enough and say that they are leaving if they do not get paid, they are told that they will have to pay for their passage home, and that anyway they will not be paid because the shipowner has no money or because he argues that he has already paid them in kind (clothes, food etc.). When faced with such a situation, the crew members sometimes seek legal protection.

The "Centro de los Derechos del Marino" in Barcelona filed for a ship to be held on attachment by the court on behalf of a group of Turkish sailors on the grounds of salaries due and unpaid. The judge asked for a deposit of 500,000 pesetas (i.e. well over 3,000 dollars), and the crew members, who had to turn to the Apostleship of the Sea even for their food, could not proceed with the case since they did not have that kind of money, and even if they had scraped it together they might have lost it, since the shipowner would probably have claimed that he had made payments abroad, and would then have gone on to demand damages from the sailors.

Another form of abuse we could mention stems from the fact that when a shipowner registers in one of these countries of convenience, in practice he acquires the sort of rights associated with the corsair's "Letters of Marque". The "Centro de los Derechos del Marino" in Barcelona has also witnessed two cases of shipwreck in which the crew made it to safety but, once ashore, did not receive any compensation. When legal action against the owners was attempted (both having offices in Barcelona), it turned out that the person who seemed in fact to be the owner of the ship was recorded only as a mere agent, and he alleged that he had lost more money than the crew members, since the supposed foreign shipowner had left him in the lurch. And any attempt to take legal action against a company - often just a post box address - in one of those countries is futile.

We could go on and on through an interminable list of the consequences of this thoroughgoing corruption of the shipping business, against which international agreements, trade unions such as the International Transport Federation, and organisations such as the Seafarers' Rights centres and the Apostleship of the Sea, are all powerless to do anything other than raising their voices in protest over and over again, and trying to help the individuals caught up in it, though mostly with no positive results to show for their efforts.

# the crew member

## 3.1 The crew member's world

*It is a characteristic feature that inmates arrive at the establishment with a 'presentation culture' they bring with them from a 'normal world', a lifestyle and a routine of activities taken for granted, up until the moment they enter the institution ... However stable the personal organisation of the recent entrant might be, it formed part of a wider sphere of reference, situated in a civil setting: a cycle of experience which confirmed a tolerable conception of the ego and permitted him a set of defensive mechanisms exercised at his discretion to face up to conflicts, discredit and failures.*[86] A person embarking for the first time as crew member on a vessel undoubtedly arrives with what Goffman calls a "presentation culture". To a certain extent, each crew member arrives with a "culture of his own".

On a Spanish ship there will be crew members from the Basque Country, from Galicia, from Andalusia, from Castile, from Catalonia and so forth. There will be men from coastal towns and from inland towns. Some will come from seafaring families (especially the Basques and Galicians) and will find on board people from their own towns or cities and will be able to cultivate their own eating habits and regional peculiarities. Others will come from families which have no idea what a ship is like, and these will encounter ways of speaking and customs which are strange to them.

The problem will be more serious in the case of ships with international crews with mixtures of races, cultures, religions, languages, etc. In these cases, and especially when the crew member in question is the only one from his country on board, there will be a major contrast between his former world and the one he now finds. The distance between the two worlds may arise in various ways:
- Language: the sense of isolation and of a being a stranger in a place largely depends on language. Being surrounded by people who speak a different language, all the more so if it is unfamiliar, gives rise to a clear feeling of marginalisation.
- Eating habits: although the food at sea is never the same as on land, on German ships one eats in the "German style" and on Spanish ships in the "Spanish style". And this relates not only to the type of food as such, but to the atmosphere in the dining room, the drinks which accompany the meal, and so forth.
- Religion: amongst a Christian crew, religion will not be of great importance, although a non-believer majority will make it more

difficult for a believer who wishes to practise his faith, due to lack of a congregation to back him up. More serious, however, would be the case of a Muslim amidst a crew of another religion, or simply atheist. During Ramadan, for example, Muslims have very strict rules regarding food, and at no time during the year may they eat pork. If no consideration is shown towards a Muslim crew member he will experience serious problems of conscience or will just have to go hungry. Rules about prayer, too, call for understanding to be shown.
- Attitudes: the attitudes, behavioural norms and rules for co-existence can, on ships with international crews, create barriers and differences and foster the formation of subgroups, and these would be points to be highlighted when a crew member encounters people from different worlds.

However, there are other problems of "change of world".

A citizen alternating between work and family and friends, who engages in each activity in a different place, who in his free time puts his professional role aside and is not disturbed as he sleeps (except for some professionals, such as doctors and others on call), who may be a member of a sports club, member of a group of friends, husband, father and son, etc., would were he to embark find that aboard ship he is sailor, cook, oiler, officer or captain twenty-four hours a day.

Day after day he will be dealing with the same people. If there is a heavy sea when he finishes work, the boat will continue to pitch and heave; if his services are needed, he will be woken in the middle of his sleep; his Sundays will be the same as his Fridays, and so forth.

Goffman[87] asserts that "deculturalisation" can occur in the case of long-stay inmates. Men who have spent many years at sea quite frequently become to a certain extent maladjusted in the family environment. Indeed, a seaman who while at sea dreams of his family sometimes feels disappointment[88] upon homecoming, especially after long periods at sea (six months or a year). This is the feeling of being a stranger in what a person considers to be his real world. A sailor returning home after months away is sometimes unintentionally received like a stranger; one example of this is the sad experience of reunion with the young child who hardly recognises the father and looks at him with misgiving.

It is this phenomenon which leads many sailors, after fifteen or twenty years at sea, to try to remain on land and yet to fail through inability to adapt to life on land in general.

Life at sea is tough due to the isolation, uprootedness and so forth, but it is convenient in terms of having a peaceful routine, development of habits disrupted only by emergencies, lack of the day-to-day problems encountered in city life; a sailor can even, up to a point, forget about the education of his own children, not out of lack of interest but because, being far away, there is little he can do about it. That being the situation, sailors end up living life with a different mind-set. Finally, even if a sailor does not earn much money, on board he lacks for nothing, and when he arrives in port he always has sufficient money for anything he wants.

With reference to Sommer[89], and applying his studies to the nautical sphere, we might state that the "totality" of the ship institution leads sailors to experience deculturalisation, takes away a certain amount of ability to handle life on land. Seafarers depend on the ship to meet their daily needs, and little by little they lose certain habits necessary if they are to maintain good social relations on land. The longer sailors spend at sea, the harder they find it to adapt when they return to land.

### 3.1.1 Seamen's awareness of themselves

Seamen are clearly aware of "being different" and of their job being a great service which is nonetheless afforded little recognition by society. Tony Lane[90] says ... *seamen state that they are a race apart, although it is never exactly clear what they mean by it. This is partly because seafarers have inadequate knowledge of other isolated workers to make rich and well packed comparisons.*

We might think of any profession or trade on land, such as bus driver or laboratory chemist, to take two examples. They, too, will surely feel that society's regard for them is not in accordance with the service they provide, though they will not normally feel this as deeply as does the seaman.

One of the main reasons for this is the seaman's feeling of absence, of being forgotten, for he sees that his town and his house operate without him. When he reaches a port he sees a city, some lights if it is night by then, but he knows that he does not belong to that world, that he is a stranger. And when he sets out to sea again he sees a city brimming with life, but over the bows an empty horizon; when he sees that he would like to spend the weekend in dock and the vessels finishes loading up on a Friday so as not to waste time in port; when he sees all that then he thinks that he counts for nothing.

An old German captain said at the beginning of the 'seventies: *All my life I've paid taxes and so helped to finance services for the citizens. But what have I got out of all that, when I'm always away at sea?*

Unless they make an effort to keep informed and take part in events in the outside world, their families and society in general, seamen will live like people absent and will create their own world. Everybody has a tendency to "take the line of least resistance", and indeed, the less one does the less one feels inclined to do. It is thus tempting during long voyages, with day after day at sea, to sink into the limbo of routine, and that attitude, week after week, year after year, leaves its mark on character, on a person's awareness of his own way of existing.

In speaking of roles in section 2.3 we noted that each person endeavours to implement his role in accordance with a schema or model he has learned, and this attempt to take it on will help the seaman, as it will any other professional, to become aware of himself.

## 3.2 Reasons for becoming a seaman

We are undertaking analysis of the vessel as total institution and have in this respect drawn certain parallels with and differences from other total institutions, such as barracks, psychiatric institutions, convents and so forth.

The entry of an inmate (his/her reasons and the circumstances surrounding entry) is undoubtedly a factor of special importance when it comes to undertaking sociological analysis of an institution.

Entering a prison, a psychiatric hospital or a barracks is, for inmates as such, compulsory. Other personnel, though they may live there for a certain number of hours, are there to ensure that inmates comply with the purpose for which they were interned or to take care of other professional and human matters or questions of administration and organisation. Such people cannot be classed here as inmates.

In a barracks there are the professional soldier inmates, there because that is their chosen profession while at the same time subject to the general regime of life in the institution. The others, the bulk of the soldiers, are there out of obligation. This undoubtedly has a special effect on their attitude, and it is therefore in these institutions that secondary adjustments are most fully developed.

In convents, the inmates enter of their own free wills and furthermore take vows (usually of chastity, poverty and obedience) which lead them to accept in advance a certain way of life which they have embraced for itself and not as a means of obtaining an income or meeting other material needs.

On a ship, too, the inmates (the crew) embark of their own will, but that will is not always free and may be conditioned by circumstances or need.

Of all the institutions mentioned here, the ship is the easiest to leave later, though not just whenever a seaman might wish, but once the vessel is, for example, back in a port in his own country and the notice laid down in his employment contract has been given.

Prisoners, army recruits and inmates of psychiatric hospitals, on the other hand, cannot decide of their own free will when they wish to leave. In the case of a convent, it is objectively possible to leave whenever one wants, although subjectively there are other obstacles to so doing (of conscience, of a potential feeling of failure, etc.).

To return to the vessel institution, we will now undertake analysis of the reasons for which a crew member embarks. We will initially take as a basis some surveys, about which we will make some observations.

1. Survey by the Apostolado del Mar in Spain, carried out amongst Spanish seamen in 1984 in the ports of Barcelona, Bilbao, Vigo, Cádiz and Valencia[91]. Within the merchant navy sector, 602 valid questionnaires were completed.
   When asked: What was the main reason why you became a merchant seaman?, the replies were as follows:

| Out of vocation | 28.2% |
|---|---|
| Financial | 21.6% |
| No other work available | 19.3% |
| Family tradition | 10.1% |
| Don't know/no reply | 8.6% |
| Other | 6.9% |
| Problems with studies | 5.3% |

If we look at the total, we will see that the financial motive and that of no other work being available account for 40.9%, while the percentages for reasons of vocation or family tradition account for 38.3%. The survey's tables of cross-referenced variables show that of the 170 interviewees with advanced qualifications (officer ranks), 44.7% declared reasons of vocation and 13.5% family tradition. Of the other 432 interviewees, with lower qualifications, 42.3% pointed to financial reasons and 25% to the unavailability of other work, while vocation was mentioned by only 20.3% and family tradition by 8.6%.
2. Survey carried out by the ICMA (International Christian Maritime Association) in 1988[92] in 59 ports throughout the world and amongst 4,525 seamen. The replies received to the same question as in the first survey were as follows:

| Career choice | 1252 seamen |
| --- | --- |
| Need for a job | 1226 seamen |
| Vocation for the sea | 890 seamen |
| To earn money | 730 seamen |
| Seeking a better trade | 603 seamen |
| Family tradition | 322 seamen |
| To see the world | 52 seamen |
| Desire to travel | 26 seamen |

Note: some seamen gave more than one answer.

We could state that choice of career, vocation for the sea and family tradition, a desire to travel and see the world, account for a total of 2,542 replies, while the factor of needing a job, a desire to earn money or seeking a better trade account for 2,559, showing a balanced result at international level.

This study revealed the financial factor as having greater weight amongst Brazilian, Greek, Hong Kong Chinese, Indonesian, Italian, Korean, Pakistani, Filipino, Sri Lankan and Taiwanese seamen, while vocational or professional reasons carried more weight with Burmese, German, Indian, Japanese, Singaporan, British, American and Yugoslav seamen.

While no firm conclusions can be drawn, we can see that the second group has more representatives from the developed countries than the first, and that this can be explained.

On the one hand, there is a need generally experienced by the inhabitants of underdeveloped countries to seek a living outside of their towns or cities, and on the other the fact that most of the crew members from developed countries hold positions of authority, while the crew members of other countries mostly occupy posts lower down the scale.

- Study carried out in 1979 by the Apostolado de Mar de Argentina[93].
  To the question: Why do you devote yourself to seafaring?, put to 110 merchant seamen, the following replies were received:
    - Necessity: amongst the South Americans, this reason was cited by 40% of the officers and 53% of the ratings.
      Amongst the Europeans, necessity was given as a reason by 16% of officers and 12% of ratings, while amongst Oriental seamen it was given by 91% of ratings and by no officers; amongst North Americans no officers gave this reason, while 50% of ratings did so.
    - Vocation: amongst the Latin Americans, this was a reason for 55% of the officers and 42% of ratings; amongst Europeans it was a

reason for 32% of the officers and 49% of ratings; amongst Orientals, it was a reason for 100% of the officers but for no ratings, a result repeated amongst the North Americans.
- Adventure: amongst Latin Americans, this was cited by 5% of both officers and ratings; amongst Europeans, it was 52% for officers and 19% for ratings; amongst Orientals it was a reason for 9% of ratings, and amongst North Americans it was a reason for 50% of ratings.

These data are doubtless insufficient to draw any broad conclusions, though we could conclude that seamen basically go to sea for three reasons: out of vocation (or professional choice), out of financial need and out of a desire for adventure and to see the world.

This last reason is given especially by young people. In the 1970s, when was a considerable demand for labour on ships, this made it easier for many young people to embark; they did not stay long, however, embarking only for short periods basically out of a desire to have new experiences.
– We might refer also to a large-scale study carried out in France between 1967 and 1969[94], in which vocational reasons (whether directly, as in "the call of the sea", or indirectly, as in "desire for adventure" or "yearning for freedom") predominated amongst French merchant seamen, while the weight of family tradition in the field of trades in general was found most notably in the fishing sector, followed by the merchant navy and, behind them, farmers, small shopkeepers, etc.

The basic interest of the replies to the question about the seamen's reason for embarking lies, within our context, in finding out how voluntary was that embarkation, or perhaps more precisely, whether the voluntary nature, which in the last analysis is always there, was fruit of a quest for personal realisation or simply a way of surviving.

Both reasons have sufficient weight to be taken into consideration.

Generally speaking, officers are more likely to feel that they became seamen out of vocation. That is natural enough, since in principle those who go in for a career usually do so because they feel attracted to it.

Amongst the ratings, however, there is a higher percentage who claim to have embarked for financial reasons. Here, however, a reservation should be made: many crew members and even officers chose the seafaring profession because their towns or cities of residence held out few alternatives, or possibly because it was the most common profession within their family and friendship circles. Many of them will reply that it was because "there were no other jobs" or "I needed a job"; the fact that they may be telling the truth does not mean, however, that they felt no attraction towards the sea.

Another factor to be taken into consideration is that most seafaring folk, even those who enjoy their profession, are convinced that it is one of the toughest and that if they could find a job on land then they would stay on land.

Amongst the officers, where there may be considered to be the highest percentage of vocation, there is also quite possibly the highest percentage of leaving the profession, probably because they are the ones best equipped in terms of qualifications.

It is a feature of the navy that after a few years people try to find a land-based alternative. And this, in combination with the idealist and romantic overtones of the word vocation, undoubtedly influences many when it comes to attributing their choice of work to employment or financial reasons. If we look at the Apostolado del Mar survey of 1984[95], will see that questions numbers 5 and 6 raised the main problems of the merchant navy. The results were:
- In first place: 49.5% unemployment (in the navy) and 21.1% the lack of work on land.
- In second place: 27.9% lack of work on land and 12.6% unemployment.

From this we can see that unemployment in the navy is seen as a bigger problem than lack of work on land.

From the point of view of this study, the important thing is to point out that, whether from fully worked-out choice or because they do not know what else they could do, most merchant seamen go to sea, at least initially, because they feel attracted to the seafaring life.

Having said this, we must also acknowledge that there are those who go to sea because that is the only solution they have managed to find. This cannot be considered to be the case in present-day Spain, however, where unemployment rates in the merchant navy are extremely high. It is the case, on the other hand, in some so-called Third World countries, where the international agencies go in search of crews which make few demands. Here we find men going hungry, who cannot support their families and who have seen in the sea the solution to their woes.

In 1989, for example, there was the case of a crew member from Equatorial Guinea who had gone to sea for a monthly salary of Ptas. 5,000 (approximately £25). The reason was quite simply that he was hungry and without a roof over his head, and aboard ship he found a bed and food and, "on top of all that" a wage.

As time passes the reason which had led a person to go to sea for the first time fades in importance, while his ability to get used to that type of life becomes more important. Thus we find seamen who embarked for the first time full of enthusiasm but who have become disenchanted with time, and others who embarked by coincidence but gradually arrived at an increasing identification with their jobs.

Thus, in considering how closely a merchant seaman relates to his job we might state that vocation generally plays a major part and that the seaman, though he might leave the sea if a good opportunity arises on land, usually feels an attraction for the sea which goes beyond the bounds of the strictly professional.

Another different aspect is the disenchantment he may begin to feel and, above all, the deterioration his quality of life might undergo. This aspect of quality of life is highly important. Lack of communication, isolation, loneliness, powerlessness, routine, monotony, lack of enriching leisure time, are all aspects which will often bring seamen to find life at sea distasteful or even repugnant.

In any case, to return to the subject of the beginning of the chapter, it is important to bear in mind that people going to sea for the first time usually do so because they want to, and often have their hopes placed in the job and a desire to see the world.

By the time seaman are setting out to sea again, not for the first time but after a period of holidays, their reasons will by then be less vocational. Seamen returning to the same ship or to a new one after enjoying a few weeks at home are not usually very cheerful, and even those who like their job will complain and feel that they are returning to a prison from which they emerge from time to time but to which they must always return.

Seamen are people who are just passing through. When at home, they know they are just there for a while and will have to leave before long, and when on board they feel that it is just for that voyage and then they will return home again.

Such impressions will naturally vary from one person to another, depending on whether they are married or single, the links binding them to their families or their life on land, and so on.

One thing is quite clear, though, and that is the considerable number of hours seamen usually spend in bed. It may be that they cannot sleep eight hours continuously and may claim that the vibrations, noises or movement of the ship do not allow them to rest as well as they do at home. But one common factor aboard ship is a quest for how to make the time pass as quickly as possible. Boredom, lack of outside stimuli, and occasionally problems of getting on with shipmates, mean that seamen frequently take to their beds ("to have a bit of a read and grab forty winks") to shorten time. Another way of attempting this is through alcohol, a means of escape into which many fall.

Long faces and the odd glass too many are common as ships set out to sea, when seamen have just left their families.

From the point of view of the total institution, then, how can we classify the inmate (or crew member) in terms of his wish to be shut up in the ship?

Firstly, of course, he is there because he wants to be there, although this must be qualified because, due to circumstances, seamen sometimes do not in fact have any other option.

Secondly, for many seamen there exists, quite apart from the strictly financial aspect, a factor of professional satisfaction or simply of the type of life they hope to achieve.

Thirdly, the highest of hopes can be dashed when a crew member feels lonely and sees himself forgotten as a person. A seamen can come to see himself as just another part of the ship and that all that matters to the shipowner is contracting freight.

That is, crew members may feel that they entered the institution of their own free will, that for many there is a feel for the sea and that they become accustomed to the vibrations of the vessel and the very routine, but that they feel imprisoned because they feel an increasingly strong desire to experience life like a normal person (husband, father, and so forth).

Paul Chapman[96] points out that the reasons for which people go to sea vary from one Third World country to another, and that financial reasons generally predominate given that wages on land are very low. And in many of those countries, being a seaman confers a certain social status. In the Philippines, according to Chapman, the seafaring profession is well respected. Many Filipino seamen are middle class and have a reasonably good education. Others, however, go to sea to escape poverty. And Koreans, according to Chapman, remain on land as soon as they manage to find a similar wage in their own country.

### 3.3 Recently embarked seamen

A person joining ship alone for the first time and encountering a ready-formed crew is an outsider who will have to try and integrate into that new human group. That person will have to approach the new group, with the final intention of becoming part of it.

The greater the differences between the cultural norms of the group from which the new crew member comes and those of the group into which he means to integrate, the greater will be the difficulty of the process, quite apart from personal predisposition and aptitudes.

A person who is a member of an endogroup governed by specific cultural norms does not at first analyse the world in which he moves, but rather *feels it as a field for his present and potential acts, and only secondarily as an object of his thoughts ... That person seeks scaled knowledge of significant elements, and the degree of knowledge desired is in correlation with its signification potential.*[97] That is, the degree of interest a person will show in going more deeply into the various elements of his day-to-day life will depend on his personal interests, his functions within the group, and so forth.

Alfred Schutz is of the opinion that the knowledge of a man who acts and thinks within his daily life is:
- Incoherent: does not form part of a coherent system of knowledge, but varies according to what suits any particular time.
- Partial: a person is only interested in knowing certain things about the world in which he lives.
- Incongruent: a person can accept as valid attitudes which contradict each other, depending on the role he is playing at any given time. He may reproach in a subordinate an attitude which he himself adopts towards a superior.

Despite all this incoherence and incongruity, the system of knowledge acquired thereby becomes for group members a set of rules and habits which permits them to understand each other, which locates them and provides them with the security required to "know the scenario they move in".

Thus, a person acting in a particular way is understood to have a certain intention and, conversely, a person with a certain intention is expected to act in a particular way. And this will remain valid for such time as situations and circumstances arise that are similar to those already known, for such time as confidence in them is retained and the rules and customs handed down by our predecessors is considered to be valid, for such time as this utilitarian knowledge surrounding us is sufficient to get by with and as long as those rules and customs are equally valid for the other members of the endogroup.

Into this reality, this world into which the members of a group (here, the crew) are perfectly situated, there appears a stranger, the newly embarked seaman. That man will look upon all those rules and attitudes in a much more critical spirit, as a spectator. He may know many things about the group, but it has never been part of his life-story. He will be able to accept that he and they will thereafter have a future and even a present in common, but for him the past is missing. When the others discuss what happened on the last voyage, when they pass comment on what happened to this or that person, he will remain silent, being in Alfred Schutz's words "a man without history".

We might consider here the typical case of military service. New recruits are likely to be the object of "pranks". They are easy prey for the veterans, for on arrival they feel disconcerted or even full of fear, and this makes them an easy prey to jokes. At the same time the veterans have a status which nobody challenges. They are owed natural respect. They "have history", the new recruits do not.

The new arrival thus finds himself as an observer of a group unknown to him, yet as an immediate candidate for becoming yet another member of that group. Moreover, he is a candidate who needs to feel as quickly as possible a member of that group. And here we are speaking basically of a person setting foot on board ship for the first time.

For such a person, the concept of "recent arrival" is fully applicable. There are nonetheless other degrees of this same condition. From the greatest to least strangeness we might mention:
- the case of a person already a seaman, who has already been to sea, but is joining a ship of foreign nationality, with a crew of another nationality or other nationalities.
- the case of a person joining a ship flying his own country's flag, but belonging to a company he does not know and, therefore, with companions new to him.
- the case of a person who, after a holiday period, joins another ship of the same company, or event the same ship he was on before. In this last case, especially if the crew has changed little, the new-arrival feeling practically does not arise.

To return to the case of a person going aboard ship for the very first time, or that of a man joining a ship he has never been on before, or maybe a foreign vessel, the attitudes he sees and which may seem to have little to do with him, which he sees from outside, will become transformed into situations which he too has experienced. The ideas the stranger has of this group, and conceived from position of the group he has come from, are of no use for the purposes of comparison since they will be seen by those he is joining as prejudices.

All people have mental frameworks, codes for interpretation, the ones which hold in the human group in which they live. More or less preconceived ideas about other outside groups or activities are framed from this perspective. If we were to carry out a survey into how the average citizen sees the members of an African tribe shown in a television documentary, how he sees the world of cinema actors, or the very life of a sailor, we would see that we find more or less stereotyped or commonplace opinions. It has often been said that many foreigners see Spain as a place full of bulls and flamenco guitars, while we imagine Germans drinking beer, wearing leather trousers or dressed as soldiers, and Americans as cowboys.

Such commonplaces or prejudices clearly become less rigid as people form a wider world view. The narrow views have today been altered through the media and travel. But something usually remains, for in order to overcome many of these prejudices a deeper knowledge of the various human groups is sometimes required.

A person arriving on board a ship encounters a new working realm, one which from land can only be known through cinema or novels. The outsider thus finds that as he gets into the group there is a change of view which leads him to perceive that what he had thought formerly, his previously unquestioned code for interpretation, is not entirely useful in the new social setting. And the outsider will have to make an effort to "translate", not necessarily in terms of language (though this can of course also occur in the case of a foreign vessel), but in terms of suitably interpreting the words, gestures and exclamations inherent to what might be termed the subculture of seamen.

Moreover, a new arrival cannot limit himself to interpreting what is happening around him, but must himself take a leap in order to form part of his surroundings. As Alfred Schutz notes in the work cited, "he who was until then a spectator takes a leap from the stalls onto the stage". He will therefore inevitably have to alter his preconceived ideas and, in interpreting what is happening around him, will begin to interpret himself. And he will realise that things are not how he, from his group of origin, had thought they were.

An outsider will need time to get used to the new group, and the more consolidated that group is the more time this will take. And clearly, if a large number of people join a ship for the first time without having known each other beforehand, the notion of outsider will be more diluted.

All the guidelines which form an element of security for the members of a group (being the rules of play and of meaning on which their language and relations rest) are for the outsider an uncertain terrain through which he moves cautiously and carefully.

Hernández Izal[98] notes that, in sociological terms, there are three channels for the integration process: the biological, the affective and the mental.

Regarding the biological channel, Hernández Izal asserts that certain features mark out the seaman, such as his way of walking, used as he is to the pitching and yawing of ships, sharp long-distance sight (especially in the case of deck crew), a certain way of lighting cigarettes while shielding them from the wind, and on small boats which move a lot, a posture when in bed in order to maintain a stable position and not be thrown out of the bunk.

In terms of sleep, a further feature may be that of not sleeping all in one go, but rather twice in a day. A man on watch from 12 to 4, for example, might get up at 10 or 10.30 in the morning and eat at 11 (a normal meal: soup, pasta, meat, etc.). At 12 he would go on watch until 4 in the afternoon, At 6 he might have his evening meal and then go to bed around 8 o'clock, since at 11.45 he will have to get up to do the midnight to four in the morning watch. Such a man would be obliged to divide his sleep into two sessions and become used to having a meal when he has only just got up, having his "breakfast" at midnight.

What is more, seamen may have this pattern of watches on one voyage and then change to another timetable on the next voyage. And if to this we add timetables altering upon entering port, when practically the entire crew is on duty, the result is that seamen acquire considerable ease of adaptation to changes of sleeping times. This has the compensation that, once on board and whatever the timetable, all follows a tight routine. Newly arrived men will have to adapt to this new way of living, which they will gradually adopt as their own.

As regards the affective aspect, a man joining ship will seek to become friends with the crew members, starting with those whose character and role played on board are closest to his own. Seeking out individual friendship will then serve as a basis for integrating into the larger social group of the crew. The person befriended will to an extent act as an "interpreter" for the new man, helping him to decipher the codes of meaning he comes across. The new crew member will seek acceptance as the answer to his solitude and as an instinctive quest for fellow-feeling.

A person can, as in the case of a single-handed yachtsman, choose to be alone, but if a man who forms part of a crew is not integrated into it and feels marginalised, then he will experience a real hell which may end in personal problems or refuge-seeking in alcohol and drugs.

Finally, Hernández Izal speaks of ways of thinking, referring to the relative value which seafarers confer upon time. A seaman joining a ship knows from the outset that he has a number of months ahead of him, during which he will be at the disposal of the ship. Thus, if the voyage between two ports takes a few days more, or if when the ship arrives at the port it has to ride at anchor, this affects him differently from the way it would affect a land-based man.

When a ship is drawing close to port the crew begin to feel a certain nervousness, and if they had been calculating that on that day after supper they would be going ashore and they are then left riding at anchor, that is a blow to their expectations and puts them in a bad mood. This happens not so much due to a matter of time, but out of a desire to break with routine and make contact with civilisation again.

But once they are used to the idea of lying at anchor, then it is no longer a matter of one day or two days. Seamen are used to being always on call. For them it is normal for their services to be required even in their free time, so that notions of free time are very different from those of land dwellers. This is why for many land jobs seamen are valued for their availability.

Seamen can also turn their hands to many tasks. At sea, everything has to be resolved on board and a dose of imagination has to be brought to some tasks.

Seamen also develop an awareness of being "different". It is said at sea that there are three types of human beings: the living, the dead, and seamen. They refer thereby to the difference there is between seamen and land dwellers. That difference, often cause for complaint and a feeling of marginalisation on the part of seamen, is also felt as a sort of quiet pride.

There are further connotations, such as a tendency towards authoritarianism (in reference to the hierarchical schema discussed above), confidence in the rest of the crew (crew resting place their trust in the professionalism of those on watch), and a mistrust of those who supposedly look after their interests on land (trade unions, professional associations, etc.).

## 3.4 Potential personal consequences of life on board ship

Any activity leaves its mark in one way or another on a person engaging in it. People employed in the same profession usually present some features in common, and these similarities are due not only to the adoption of their own gestures or terminology but, at a deeper level, to the way in which people have recourse to the social means available to them to consolidate the positions corresponding to them by profession.

In analysing this reaction, account must be taken of the pressures to which people will feel subjected and the circumstances in which they will be worked out. From this we will be able to derive keys to explain certain types of behaviour.

### 3.4.1 Mutilation of the self

If we compare here a ship, on the one hand, and other total institutions such as prisons, barracks and psychiatric institutions, on the other, we will see that there are major differences. People entering the second group of institutions suffer depersonalisation: they have their own clothes taken from them, they are assigned a number and, worse still, they lose their freedom to leave of their own free will.

On a merchant vessel that is not really the situation. From the outset, the seaman embarks of his own free will, even though his decision may be conditioned by situations of need or even family tradition, situations which in any case lead the person to take a decision. The crew member enters into a commercial relationship with the shipowner, outside of which the latter has no authority over him.

Merchant seamen can always rescind their contracts whenever they feel that is appropriate, although in this they are subject to the ship being in port and, normally, to the period for which they were contracted having elapsed, except where they are prepared to bear the financial cost of early termination.

Merchant seamen retain their own clothes and, within the ship, are masters of what they do in their free time, all the more so if in port. As, moreover, the crews of merchant vessels are not numerous (the maximum being on passenger vessels, where there can be 200 or more), the crew are not assigned numbers or cards.

Finally, and unlike in a military academy, there is no wish to cut the seamen off from his own world, no interest in "taming" or "depersonalising" people. The shipowner wants the boat to work and therefore requires the crew to guarantee its operational capacity. The shipowner may often try to ensure the wellbeing of the crew with a view to creating a better atmosphere aboard ship, with the attendant better performance of crew members.

It is important to take note of this distinction, as otherwise confusion could be created.

There is a nonetheless a break between the world of the crew member and the outside world, and in this respect the self does undergo mutilation. We could refer here to the famous phrase of the Spanish philosopher and essayist Ortega y Gasset: *I am myself and my circumstances.* Family and social setting, habits, climate, food, and so forth, form part of the self, that is, all that allows a person to recognise himself or herself, as if looking in a mirror. When "transplanted", a person has the feeling of having in some way lost his/her identity.

This would give rise, on the one hand, to a need for that person to find new points of reference upon which to rest his/her identity. But if the place in which people find themselves tends towards group homogenisation and attenuation of individual characteristics, individuals will find themselves seeking out some corner which, in whatever situation, allows them to feel different from the rest.

We will turn now to the aspects which can influence this "mutilation of the self" on a merchant vessel.

With the exception of passenger vessels, uniforms are used little on merchant ships. Uniforms are garments which in some way take away the personality of individuals, making them uniform within a group. In the case of the officers, of course, this will not normally be viewed with displeasure, but rather as a distinction. This is different for the crew, where uniforms will be seen rather as working clothes and their use considered to involve loss of their own personality.

Where private space is lacking, this can as we shall see later lead to mutilation of the self. People need some space, however small, in which they can feel they have privacy, which nobody can interfere in, where they are free to do what they like, where they can be in communion with themselves.

Although increasingly less, there are still ships in which cabins are shared. In the case of passenger ships, until not so very long ago there could be as many as eight crew members to a cabin. What privacy did such persons have, where could they be peacefully alone with themselves? Some space in which people can put their photos, a few ornaments, a music system and so forth is essential for them to feel even minimally masters of their own fate.

Those merchant seamen who had to share cabins suffered mutilation of their selves. And that would be all the more so if they had to share with persons of other races, with other customs, perhaps even a smoker along with a non-smoker or the company of somebody with low standards of hygiene.

Another mutilating factor can be a feeling of being little respected or even mistreated. Situations can arise in all working situations where superiors who feel undervalued then humiliate employees under them. At sea, moreover, that possibility extends into free time, for as we saw in looking at persistence of roles, the relationships deriving from professional rank persist into rest time, twenty-four hours a day.

If, in spite of experiencing a change in his circumstances and therefore to some extent in himself, a crew member finds a place in that new community, he will be faced with a situation which can be experienced positively and negatively at the same time. Negatively, when on arrival in port a person is identified to the outside world as a crew member of the vessel "x", as stated on the pass which crew members receive in many ports for going onto land.

When a crew member finds aboard ship companions he does not get on with, persons with whom for cultural or social reasons, and so forth, he does not feel at ease, that sense of belonging to a crew can lead to his feeling debased.

The positive side of it is that, being far from home, from his world, when the crew member goes around distant ports, or even when simply at sea, he needs even from the affective point of view to feel that he is a member of a community, as a means of overcoming a feeling of solitude.

It has been found that when one is far from family and friends there is a need to find some alternative that resembles a family. That is why on long voyages crew life is more intense, closer-knit, out of the need for mutual and reciprocal support which the crew themselves feel.

### 3.4.2 Breakdown of the usual relationship between the acting individual and his acts

A person carries out a number of acts of which he is master and needs to feel himself master. These acts sometimes amount to a mere minimum expression, as when a person grumbles or looks annoyed when something goes against them but they do not dare to reject it openly. This can occur in a workplace or faced with anybody in authority.

In a total institution this can give rise to the "looping" effect, such that a show of discontent, however small, can give rise to a reaction which leads to a further deterioration of the situation.

Under military discipline, a gesture can be reason for a superior to reproach a subordinate, are there are even situations in which knowledge of a soldier's weak point can be used by superiors to submit him to disciplinary measures.

On merchant vessels, especially nowadays, this cannot be said to be the case. On ships flying European flags or flags of other developed countries, the power of trade unions is of more significance than any remains of military discipline there might be on board.

The situation can be different with crews from the Third World, especially when the captain and several officers are European, for these last will enjoy working conditions very much better than those of the crew, and their word will be accepted without question by the shipowner and sometimes even by port authorities. This situation can also arise with captain/officers and crew of the same country, where the shipowner affords special treatment to the former so that they help him to keep the crew "toeing the line".

We must bear in mind, too, that the captain, above all, has to ensure that the shipowner keeps him in his post, and that he is the shipowner's representative on board ship, so that under maritime law he has certain prerogatives of civil law for dealing with emergency situations.

On a European-based merchant vessel the use of such prerogatives would have to be proved justifiable, or the captain may otherwise be held to account. The captain of a Third World flag ship has considerably more scope for action, and crew members may find themselves subjected to humiliation and abuse; a captain might, for example, order an officer to and able-bodied seaman's work.

In other cases, where a crew has protested about unpaid wages and has threatened strike action, the captain has on arrival in port presented a suit for mutiny and won compulsory repatriation of the individuals causing problems in the crew, who were thus sent back to their countries and placed on a blacklist of men who would not be taken aboard ship again. (In some Eastern countries, repatriation for the crime of mutiny is even punishable with the death penalty).

The credibility which, due to his post, the captain naturally enjoys before any port authority and the difficulties seamen experience in proving any abuse by the captain or shipowner mean that the crew often live in fear and do not dare to voice any demands for fear of reprisals against which they are frequently defenceless. Furthermore, the captain often has men who back him up, often to "get in his good books" or sometimes because men of different nationalities are together on board and subgroups are formed. In any case, the result will often be that the seamen will have to keep silent and conceal what they feel, not claiming what they believe to be just.

The credibility which, due to his post, the captain naturally enjoys before any port authority and the difficulties seamen experience in proving any abuse by the captain or shipowner mean that the crew often live in fear and do not dare to voice any demands for fear of reprisals against which they are frequently defenceless. Furthermore, the captain often has men who back him up, often to "get in his good books" or sometimes because men of different nationalities are together on board and subgroups are formed. In any case, the result will often be that the seamen will have to keep silent and conceal what they feel, not claiming what they believe to be just.

This situation can be suffered by the captain, too. There may be a power subgroup aboard which makes the captain fear for his very life. This can happen, for example, on old, small boats plying routes to certain African countries, with crews receiving little pay yet essential for running the vessel; the disappearance of a crew member, whether captain or seaman, may well be considered an accident of no great importance.

These are, of course, extreme cases. Others of lesser gravity, however, or the cases we have seen where demands may be frustrated by fear or reprisals, are unfortunately very frequent. In any case, on a ship, and especially one out at sea, crew members often have to put up with situations they find unpleasant, trying to pass unnoticed or simply avoiding by all possible means conflicts which will only make their life on board more difficult.

Where violent or stressful situations may be unpleasant in a land-based job, they are more so at sea, for there is no change of setting or role, each member remaining what he is professionally throughout the entire day and coming across any person they do not get on with several times a day.

On board ship the captain has a certain authority, delegated upon the officials, to impose certain penalties, according to the infraction committed by a crew member. Such infringements give rise to different types of penalties, which can even include dismissal or handing over of a crew member to the pertinent authorities where a crime has been committed.

In any case, what is of interest here is the fact that crew members will often feel that there hangs over them an authority against which they have no protection (or at least not at the time), and young inexperienced crew members especially, embarking for the first time as seamen apprentices or oilers, may find, not so much the captain or the officers, but often a boatswain or donkeyman (petty officers), giving out orders which always condemn them to do the most unpleasant jobs.

Finally, crew members disliked for any reason by their companions can be condemned to an isolation which makes their life on board really tough.

And a crew member who for any of these reasons feels that he is marked out by his superiors or even by his fellow crew members, does not have the remedy of going home and trying to regain control over his own person, a feeling of relaxing amongst people he likes, but will rather be subjected in some way 24 hours a day to a working discipline.

Total institutions, and as we have seen we can to some extent include merchant vessels as such, *"... devalue or breach precisely those acts which in civil society fulfil the function of demonstrating to the actor, in the presence of occasional witnesses, that he has a certain mastery over his world, that he is a person equipped with the self-determination, autonomy and freedom of action inherent to an adult."*[99] Being unable to express oneself as one would wish, the possibility of being the butt of jokes, the feeling that there exists 24 hours a day an authority to which respect and obedience are owed, can harm or even take away a crew member's potential to feel that he is his own master.

An important factor, possibly the most important, is the crew member's feeling that he is not free to leave the vessel. This is obvious enough at sea, but can also be felt in foreign ports, for if a crew member leaves the ship before his contract expires he will have to pay the return passage out of his own pocket, and then only as long as the boat is left with sufficient crew and the captain authorises him to disembark and obtains the pertinent permit from the local police.

### 3.4.3 Response of the crew member to his situation aboard ship

Goffman[100] says that in total institutions inmates can show different types of reaction to the situation in which they find themselves. One of these is what he calls "situational regression" about which he continues: *the inmate withdraws his apparent attention from all that is not to do with things immediately relating to his body, which he sees from a perspective different to that of the others present. Drastic abstention from all active participation in relationships arises in its purest form in psychiatric hospitals, where it is known by the name of regression.*

At sea, when a crew member has spent months on board ship, and especially aboard ships such as petrol tankers or container ships which spend only a matter of hours in port and this often at terminals which are far from any city centre, he begins to feel a steadily increasing lack of interest which shuts him up inside himself.

The lack of fresh stimuli on long crossings, with only sea and more sea, and always the same faces and exchanging the same words, compounded by small crews and spending long hours alone, can create in crew members a lack of interest in anything other than their daily activities and their own thoughts.

A second attitude would be what Goffman calls the "intransigent line". The inmate faces up to the institution with a deliberate challenge and refuses to cooperate with the personnel. According to Zurcher[101], the intransigent ones on ships are the ones who vociferously verbalise their discontent with the ship and with everything, though with the paradox that such people often become deeply involved in the total institution.

It is common aboard ship to see an attitude of dislike, of rejection of one's own job. It can at the same time be observed that many of these rejecters manage to find in the situation they detest a reason for self-esteem at the hard life they manage to withstand. With heads held high, they can be loud in condemnation of the shipping company and society as a whole. The permit themselves to despise those who sleep snugly in their own beds each night at home, although they acknowledge that such people are the ones who know how to live and not those who are at sea.

Another tactic according to Goffman is "colonisation", in which the establishment or institution becomes the inmate's entire world. At least while they are on the high seas, the ship becomes for the crew member the entire world and within it he will try to construct as pleasant as possible a life by seeking out as much pleasure as he can achieve.

A crew member who feels really at home aboard will nevertheless sometimes disguise this to an extent, for "normal" behaviour is to talk of being able to leave those four ship sides as soon as possible and go off on holidays or find work on land. A crew member who rarely expresses any desire to leave the sea is considered to be a lost cause.

In any case, and despite complaints about life on board ship, the behaviour of many seamen shows that they feel at ease about life aboard ship, and the routine of life at sea leads them to acquire habits they will not find easy to lose later on.

Joseba Beobide[102] describes the case of a deep-sea fisherman who had no family and when the ship got back to the base port after a voyage of six or eight months, while his companions prepared to enjoy to the hilt the weeks of holiday they were owed, would immediately seek out another vessel to embark upon. While he was at sea he was as alone or in as much company as anybody else aboard, and he then felt just another member of the crew. It was on land, where everybody else had a family they could rejoin, that he feel truly marginalised.

Another way of adapting to the surroundings presented by Goffman is "conversion". As he puts it: *while the colonised inmate constructs for himself, with the limited resources available to him, something akin to a free community, the convert adopts a more disciplined, moralistic and monochromatic orientation, presenting himself as one upon whose institutional enthusiasm the entire crew can always count.* The colonised crew member feels at home aboard ship, despite its shortcomings, since on it he will be developing a vocation, a hobby, living in a world which is his and he has made his.

The convert crew member decides to enter into the shipboard dynamics, for by adapting them and pleasing those in authority and organising the ship he have a better life. He will accept that there are those with authority aboard and will adapt his actions to that situation, avoiding confrontation with anybody.

On a ship, as in most total institutions, the inmate (or crew member in this case) will normally develop pragmatic tactics, which will include a mixture of secondary adjustments, conversion, colonisation and loyalty to the group. This can also give rise to a dual game, in that the inmate of the ship institution speaks one way when he is with his peers and another way when he is with his superiors.

A greater or lesser ease of adaptation to life on board will also depend upon the type of life the crew member had before embarking. Some find the cabins unpleasant due to vibration and noise, sometimes lack of ventilation, and limited space, while for others from a more humble previous life this will be paradise.

Even if the ship can be considered a total institution and many points can be found in common with prisons, hospitals, psychiatric institutions, and so forth, there is always a clear distinguishing feature, which is that in the last analysis the crew member has embarked of his own free will and is bound by an employment contract which in the worst of circumstances will, once the set period aboard ship has passed, leave him free to embark again or remain on land.

### 3.5 Private space aboard ship

A crew member's main place for getting on with his private life is his cabin. The cabins are small, with just enough room for a bed, a table, a chair, a wardrobe and a small washbasin. The cabins become larger as professional category increases, although their is usually a clear distinction of both size and finish between those of the crew and those of the officers. The captain, chief engineer and first mate usually also have an office in which to work, and the captain often has a small room in which to receive visitors, especially when in port.

On modern ships, each crew member has his own cabin, though on older ships, and especially passenger ships, there are shared cabins.

In his cabin a crew member finds his private nook. It is here that he can put up a photo of a loved one, hang a poster he likes or a flag, keep a souvenir of a port, his personal effects, books, clothes, etc. Some might have a plant, artificial flowers, or even a small pet such as a bird, a fish or the like. Sometimes there will be a small larder with the odd tin of food or some biscuits from his native region, a bottle of spirits, cigarettes and so forth. One way or another, then, according to each person, the cabin will be a place of his own, a hideaway in which he can feel truly in communion with himself.

Visiting another crew member in his cabin is rather like entering a neighbour's house. One asks permission and, once invited in, is usually offered a cigarette, a beer, a glass of something. It is in the cabins that private conversations take place, photos of wives, children, one's town or city are shown, or the purchases one made in the last port. The host wants to feel like somebody welcoming another person into his home. Refusing a beer or a cigarette can at times appear impolite.

The communal areas are basically the dining rooms and lounges.

Mealtimes are times for relaxing, chatting, feeling that one is a member of a community. And after meals, in free time, that same dining room or lounge will become a venue for playing cards, watching a video or just chatting.

The stern is another place crew members can meet, have a beer and pass the time. In good weather, the deck is a good place to sit chatting, stretch the legs or even play games, as long as the ship has no deck covering. Some large, modern vessels such as supertankers even have a swimming pool, gymnasium and games room, while nowadays there are also video games. A crew member undoubtedly needs leisure areas and it is important that, given that he is shut in, these be as spacious as possible.

The private space will thus not merely be a hideout in which a crew member can be alone, but also a space in which, together with his companions, he can enjoy the feeling of being at home. When sailing the high seas, with cold and sometimes rain, going into a warm room and sitting with a couple of mates to have a cup of tea or coffee will provide a crew member with a feeling of wellbeing and intimacy.

As we have seen, modern ships with good physical facilities but small crews sometimes lack this welcoming environment which only people can create.

## 3.6 The leisure time of the crew member

If we look at the distribution of work at sea we find that, at sea, on a sufficiently crewed ship, the standard division of eight hours' work, eight hours' leisure and eight hours' sleep is fulfilled. At sea, going from one's cabin to workplace does not require any bus journey; one can go from one part of the ship to another in a couple of minutes. What can nevertheless happen is that apart from the watches (four-hour shifts) or the jobs entrusted to them, crew members find themselves obliged to do overtime. In any case, on a merchant ship right out at sea there is usually time for leisure. So how is this leisure time spent? Seamen, apart from the hours they really devote to sleep, spend a lot of time lying on their bunks reading novels or magazines. This is connected with the fact that seamen cannot always sleep enough hours at a stretch and so spend a few more lying on their beds, though without actually sleeping. The bed is at times also sought out as a way of "killing time".

Those not on watch or working usually choose to devote the midday hours to taking a nap. The most lively time for conversation and communal games is after dinner (dinner usually being at 6 p.m.). This is the time for games (mostly cards, ludo or dominoes) or watching a film. On a ship with a good atmosphere, this can be a truly friendly time.

In 1982 Francesc Larrauri and Jesús Carbajosa[103], psychologists and merchant navy pilots, carried out a study of leisure on 42 Spanish vessels. In analysing the importance of leisure, they stated: *Leisure is free activity in which men look at the value of reality, and without any utilitarian quest, without having to submit themselves to the rules of useful effort, let things be as they will, savour and enrich themselves disinterestedly with them ... Leisure is not just more rest, for resting is stopping work in order to regain strength and be able to work again. Leisure is not having fun, because having fun is forgetting oneself. Leisure is not rest or escape from anything, but enjoyment and opening out to everything. Leisure is the opposite of 'necotium' (utilitarian dealing with things). In short, leisure is contemplative and enriching possession of reality.*

The authors undoubtedly offer a very lofty idea of leisure, almost akin to a form of mystic contemplation. There is no doubt about the importance of that "contemplative and enriching possession of reality", and it is also clear that on a merchant vessel, in the course of a long and peaceful crossing there is the time and opportunity for it. Another matter is whether anybody has the innate and/or educational disposition to live out that concept of leisure.

It is nevertheless important to stress the distinction that Larrauri and Carbajosa draw between leisure and business, and between leisure and rest. I feel that we can assert simply that one form of leisure is disposing freely of time to do what we like.

Leisure, expressed in one way or the other, is doubtless of fundamental importance in people's lives, and especially so in a sphere in which as we have seen above there arises persistence of professional roles over the course of days, weeks and months.

When the weather is very bad, when outside of their working hours crew members have no idea what to do with themselves other than stretch out on their beds, or when excess of work deprives them of that bit of free time, not just for sleeping but for feeling master of their own time, then a feeling of tiredness, disgust and demotivation grows quickly.

It is on large passenger liners, where the passengers are seeking out that very leisure, that peaceful living of the hour and the minute, that waiters especially often have to work 14 or 15 hours a day. Sometimes for ridiculously low wages and, moreover, with a need to appear pleasant as otherwise there will be no tips and they might lose their jobs. This is what happens on large cruising ships with crews from the farthest-flung reaches of the planet.

As Larrauri and Cabajosa also say: *Man is animal of leisure because he needs it to live, in order to be biologically viable ... Leisure is at the same time an essential note of human conduct as properly human ... Leisure can confer sense upon work, but cannot itself be personally assumed without work ....*

It is obvious that there is a need for leisure for the psychological equilibrium of a person, just as there is for work. That equilibrium is lacking in a person who has all his hours empty and with nothing to do all day, and is also lacking for those who have no time available to feel even minimally masters of themselves.

So how do seamen fill their free time, what do they do for leisure? There are people of all sorts on ships, varying greatly in cultural level, character, interests and tastes. We will nevertheless refer to a survey carried out in 1982 by Larrauri and Carbajosa. The three questions below were passed around aboard 42 vessels, with the following results being obtained.
- Question: What do you do in your free time?
  Reply:
  At sea, 86% devoted their free time to getting together with their friends and drinking, 12% to reading and 2% to studying.
  In port, 86.7% spent their free time going out for entertainment, while 13.3% went on cultural trips.
- Question: What would you like to be able to do?
  Reply:

At sea, 72% would like to be able to engage in cultural activities, 14.7% in sports and recreational games, while 13.3% did not reply.
In port, 53.3% would have liked to undertake cultural activities, 26.7% amusements, while 20% did not reply.
– Question: Why don't you do that?
Reply:
At sea, 70.6% alleged lack of resources (material and human), 16.1% lack of willpower and 13.3% did not reply.
In port, 63.3% alleged lack of resources (material and human), 13.3% lack of willpower and 23.3% did not reply.

Although it would have been instructive to know the type of vessels, routes and distribution of those surveyed by professional grade, if we undertake a little analysis of these results we can draw a few conclusions.

The vast majority spent their free time in the way that came easiest to them: chatting and drinking at sea and having fun with no great mental effort in port. A large majority, though not so great this time, stated that they would have liked to do something with rather more content, more along cultural lines, while the reason they gave for this mismatch between what they did and what they would have liked to do was lack of resources.

When a vessel is to spend two or three days in port, some are keen to find out what there is of interest there, and they spend their free time rather as tourists might. If the crew member in question has already visited that port many times he might devote the time to strolling about and experiencing the atmosphere of the city for a few hours. Others under the same circumstances confine their interest to the first group of bars they find near the port.

Deep down, everybody likes to convey an image of having a certain amount of culture. For that reason I feel that the replies stating that they would like to spend their free time on more cultural activities may reveal a desire to make a good impression, which is corroborated by alleging a lack of human or financial resources as the reason for not doing so. Clearly enough, a lower-rank crew member who may speak no language other than his own will have more difficulties making himself understand than will an officer who can get by in English and has had an education which makes access to many of the cultural activities referred to easier. Many officers nonetheless also take the line of least resistance. But this tendency not to make suitable use of free time has another important explanation: lack of stimuli.

Culture has to be cultivated, in a process in which one develops an appetite for assimilating new knowledge, while at the same time one appraises things in a new way. Life at sea is poor in stimulus. Day after day one speaks with a small group of people, and the news that reaches the crew comes over the radio and normally in only brief form. Free time has to be organised with what there is on board.

A person leaving work on land can find concert halls, sports centres, cultural centres, theatres, cinemas, or can simply go round to a friend's house. Society on land is broadly diversified so that a person who works at a keyboard all day in an office can on leaving the office find a more or less wide range of possibilities for filling the free time. At sea all this has to be organised oneself. Crew members can, of course, organise domino, draughts or chess championships, or several music enthusiasts can get together and form a small band. But this has be organised oneself and therefore calls for special initiative. But when one is tired of sea and more sea, and may be in a low mood and with thoughts set on how long is left to get back home, it is not so very easy to create those situations in which the leisure activities we would like to enjoy are indeed those we engage in.

Ships these days normally have video, so it is possible to watch films. But watching films on a television in a room in which there may be four or five people who chat as well as watching the film is very different to the situation twenty years ago, when some ships had a projector for showing films. Several films were taken aboard for each voyage, and the sessions would bring the entire crew together in an atmosphere much more attractive than that created by a television. The setting up, the large sheet on the wall, the lights turned out and the festive feel of cinema day gave it a very special flavour: cinema day was a holiday. I have seen strong, gnarled sailors with tears rolling down their cheeks watching a drama film amidst a tomb-like silence, or laughing their heads off, each laugh louder than the last, at a comic scene.

One important aspect of leisure is hope. Larrauri and Carbajosa assert that the value of free time increasingly lies not in possessing it but in it being attractive. This suggests to me the importance of hope. Any leisure activity, when prepared with hope and expectation, brings comfort and compensates the effort or pressure of work.

Games of cards, often mentioned in this work, can become truly festive occasions. If people come together with enthusiasm, have their spirits lifted by an atmosphere of enjoyment and friendship, then the occasion can be really marvellous. Teams are sometimes formed to compete against each other, so that the games session is anticipated with delight throughout the entire day.

Activities of a more cultural type will be important for the overall development of a person. On cargo ships on long voyages there are hours to devote to study, to cultivating some intellectual interest; the problem lies in there being fewer support resources, fewer people with whom to share the activity, which can thus become an isolating factor.

For pleasant co-existence on board ship, it is important that crew members take part in shared leisure activities. If during free time each one shuts himself away in his cabin, the weight of solitude and lack of communication gradually become greater and crew members lose any feeling of belonging to a common family.

Something similar happens in port. It is important to go on cultural visits, but also that they be shared. If a seamen devotes his time to walking around a city's streets alone he will see things which may be new, but he will remain as alone or more alone than at sea. That is why seamen's welfare centres like "Stella Maris", "Flying Angel",a.s.o. are important, offering sports, games and excursions, but as a group.

In speaking of leisure, an interesting article by Ronald Hope[104] shows the importance of the captain's attitude on the atmosphere at sea. He tells how in 1952 he embarked as a consultant on a 28,000 ton BP tanker with a crew of 40 men. There was no cinema or video on board, no swimming pool and no air conditioning, and the crew could drink only up to two beers a day if the captain gave his authorisation. Seeing that the atmosphere on board was very boring, he suggested that the captain organise something. It seems the captain was rather sceptical, but did agree to do so. Darts and cards championships were organised, along with games of cricket on deck.

The captain himself took part and was eliminated in the first round of darts by an oiler. The captain's participation as player or referee was one of the reasons behind the success achieved, for a genuine team spirit was achieved thereby. Hope later joined another tanker of the same type and proposed a similar idea to the captain, only to be told "They want nothing to do with me, and I want nothing to do with them". The captain did authorise Hope to organise contests and competitions, but they met with little success. Hope attributed this to the fact that the captain took no part in them.

Hope explains in his paper the important role of the captain in life aboard ship. He does not think that the captain has to be the organiser of things, but he does have to lend encouragement. The assistance of the radio operator can be enlisted to write a daily ship's newsletter to liven up day-to-day life. It is also important that the captain knows the name of each crew member. And he mentions the case of a captain who on his birthday invited the entire crew to take a drink with him.[105] Hope is critical of the mentality of many captains, concerned only about the working efficiency of their crew and not the quality of their leisure. This, in Hope's view, is a serious mistake, for seamen who do not have an enriching, amusing and pleasant leisure time are more likely to succumb to drink, drugs and dozing away time, and such persons will not then be in the best condition for efficient work.

This problem of leisure time at sea is aggravated when crews are small. One has only to imagine the case of a crew of twelve, of whom four are on watch, four are sleeping prior to taking over the watch themselves and, of the remaining four, two have no desire to do anything and the other two will thus not be very highly motivated to organise anything.

Physical exercise is important. Some ships have a gymnasium, though even here a certain amount of willpower is required, or they have organised games to encourage people to participate. Easier to take up are ping pong or swimming, especially on large supertankers with routes through warm zones.

### 3.7 Communication with other crew members : the importance of language

Human expressiveness can be objectivised, that is, can arise in such a way that the person producing it and the person receiving it can interpret it in the same way.

There are expressions, such as facial gesture or tone of voice, which denote a state of mind or an attitude, such as irritation or anger. In principle, such gestures simply have a value at the time they arise. However, if in addition to gestures and raised voices somebody, say, throws a knife at another person and that knife sticks in the wall, that knife stuck in the wall acquires of itself, and beyond that mere moment, an objective symbolism of anger, of violence.

Human beings produce objectifiable signs which taken out of the context and the time in which they occur retain an objective meaning, for which they were in fact created. Berger and Luckmann state in this regard: *Language is human society's most important system of signs ... We cannot speak of language when a person grunts, howls or boos, even though these vocal expressions can become linguistic when integrated into an objectively accessible system of signs. The common objectivations of daily life rest primarily on linguistic significance ... An understanding of language is therefore essential for any understanding of the reality of daily life.*[106] Language has rules to which I must adhere when I speak and which I bear in mind when interpreting others. Through language I can communicate my subjectivity to an interlocutor, while at the same time language allows me to appraise my own subjectivity more fully. That is, when I express a feeling, in addition to communicating it to another person the very act of expression makes that feeling more intelligible. When I speak to somebody, the language I use must be common to both of us if there is to be any real understanding.

Shannon[107] establishes the following system of communication, following the schema of telephone systems:

That is, there is a source or brain from which there emanates a message, which in order to be transmitted needs a coding system (language), which will need a medium or channel of communication (the voice, for example) which will in turn permit the receiver to pick up that expression which it will decode in order to convert it into a message which may finally be understood by the addressee.

Without looking into the matter any further for now, we can see the importance of the coding and decoding action, requiring for emitter and receiver a common knowledge of a coded symbolism.

Within a family there can be more or less invented expressions which have an immediate meaning for the members of that family but none for an outsider. Thus, when shared, language is a point of union, and when not shared becomes a marginalising element.

When I speak with my family using expressions which do not belong to the common language, but are full of meaning within that family, and I do so in front of an outsider, that outsider will feel excluded unless I accompany what I say with an explanation.

It is a common enough experience to be with people who allude to expressions or words which mean nothing to us in that context but which, amongst them, cause delight and amusement. In such a situation, we feel that we are being made fun of, or at the very least excluded.

To return to the factor of the common link, language allows expressions to be coined to typify situations or human relations. If I say "the tax man is drowning me in taxes", I am referring to something that does not happen only to me but to people in general, and my own experience is therefore recognisable within a common experience.

Language permits me to see myself situated in the world into which I am integrated. Through language I recognise myself. Language further permits making abstractions of specific situations and expressing a whole conception of the world by means of a system of symbology.

In fact, behind language lies a whole cosmovision. For this reason, two different languages are not just sets of words written and pronounced differently. They are ways of seeing and interpreting a world, with philosophical, religious, social and cultural connotations. Any differences between the cosmovision of two peoples will go into the real differences between their languages.

What is understood to be a just man in an authoritarian society, in which the head of family or tribal chief can ordain the lives of the others, is very different from what would be so understood in a democratic society. The concept of a good father in an Oriental society will contain implicitly within it a duty to choose a good husband for his daughter, while in Western society he would be expected to respect his daughter's own wishes in the matter.

Language, then, is a fundamental vehicle of understanding between people, of recognition of the person as such and of objective construction of a world, recognised by the words one has learned from childhood.

On ships, as in others spheres of life and work, we can distinguish two levels of language: the common language, the language of the nation of its crew members, and the language inherent to the seafaring profession.

At the level of language, although there will be peculiarities according to the region or zone of origin of each crew member, there will be a significant common link, and this will permit perfect understanding between the members of the crew. Even if we take the case of Spain, where there may be Basques, Galicians, Catalans and Castilians together on the same vessel, and although each group may speak its own language between its members, Spanish will serve as a vehicle of understanding between all of them.

However, when a ship contains crew members who speak different languages, then the panorama is very different. And here we have to make the further distinction of whether these are European languages only or European languages alongside Asian languages. In the case of European languages there will be difficulties of comprehension, for a Spaniard will speak of "barco", an Englishman of "ship" and a Frenchman "bateau". Behind these words, however, the sense of what a ship is will be more or less similar.

The concept lying behind the word equivalent to ship in a Polynesian language, however, may be very different, conjuring up a rudimentary craft made from tree trunks.

What we have in the first case is a language barrier, which may isolate a person when he does not understand the language of the others and thus prevent him communicating properly. This can be solved as he learns the different words which in one language are equivalent to those of another language. The process will be more complicated, however, when not only are there different words but also different conceptions of the world. Here there will be a real barrier which will be a considerable obstacle to mutual comprehension, even when the initial barrier of words has been overcome by all the crew members learning, for example, a practical level of English. The different underlying cosmovision will nevertheless remain.

This is an aspect which must always be borne in mind, so that we do not think it is all just a matter of the meaning of a few words. Indeed, between nearby cultures we sometimes find differentiating aspects, words which have very different meanings. Insults, for example, vary widely from one language to another. This means that feelings can be hurt and misunderstandings occur simply by reciprocal lack of understanding of the value of certain expressions.

Nowadays, when crew members from the most far-flung reaches of the world enlist aboard ships, many of them from truly primitive cultures, it is important, and especially for those such as the captain and officers who have to direct life on board, to take an interest in these situations and try to find out about the peculiarities of each human group, aiming to ensure the best possible integration of all crew members.

A person who due to speaking a language different from the others is deprived of sharing conversation, laughing at jokes or celebrating something, will suffer profound isolation and will be unable to feel reaffirmed as a person amongst the others.

Leo Kreiss, national director of the Apostleship of the Sea in Germany and chaplain of the port of Hamburg, said in his address to the I.M.L.A. conference in Rijeka in 1986, *it is difficult to speak of comradeship aboard ship when a ship with a crew of 26 has 11 different nationalities, as in one case I knew ...*

Work can be accomplished using signs and rudimentary English, but rest periods will see the creation of small groups which split the crew. And this same lack of communication can arise between officers and crew. Clear orders cannot be given, and if somebody wishes to explain why he does something in a certain way he will find himself unable to do so. Even explaining the need for medical assistance at the next port becomes a major difficulty. There is a great difference between meeting people of different cultures on a holiday or business trip and living day after day together in a small space.

### 3.8 The solitude of the seaman

The solitude of the seamen is practically a cliché. In speaking of a seaman's hard life, the first problem that usually arises is that of solitude, a factor closely bound up with the seafaring profession. We will now go on to look at some aspects of seamen's solitude and to try to find ways of reducing it.

#### 3.8.1 General factors relating to solitude amongst seamen

Sometimes we speak of solitude, other times of isolation. Spending days and weeks with the same people, without being able to travel freely, without change of surroundings or company is and remains one of the great problems of life at sea.

Nick Perry[108] refers to "tankeritis" [109], the reaction of individuals who impose self-isolation upon themselves as a result of a loss of outside stimuli, which makes them indifferent on the one hand and leads them to set up their own world, on the other. The typical reactions in such cases include talking to oneself, laughing to oneself, gesticulating and, in general, living in isolation from others. Perry gives it this name because it occurs particularly on oil tankers, which undertake long voyages and, when they do arrive in port, very often remain moored alongside a jetty, far from built-up areas.

Another aspect stressed by Nick Perry is that solitude leads people to idealise what they yearn for. Seaman in their solitude usually bring up idealised memories of home and of the family which do not always coincide with the true situation. Similarly, when on land they tend to fantasise somewhat about their life at sea. The result is that this dissociation between fantasy and reality leads them to a feeling of growing discontent.

In speaking of the relations of seamen with their families[110] we will again stress this dissociation, which has the result that seamen, as the years go by, find increasing difficulty in rejoining life on land.

#### 3.8.2 Reduction of crews and increased solitude

Solitude has become a cliché of the seafaring profession, and not without reason. Although seamen are in the company of other crew members , companions, with whom they spend a lot of time, their distance from their homes and families, and being unable to go home at the end of the day, undoubtedly induces a feeling of solitude.

This solitude can be more or less severe, depending upon both the situation of the individuals themselves and the atmosphere on board.

Individuals with no strong affective links on land will not suffer from solitude except in the sense of limitation of their chance of speaking to other people or relating to society in general. Young, single men with a desire to see the world, though they may at times think of their family and friends, will experience solitude in a different way from the married men with children. And sometimes it will, of course, depend on a person's character; some people feel perfectly content alone, while others cannot bear it.

These are factors about which little can be done. Men with strong affective links will not stop having them, and men who cannot stand solitude will continue to suffer its consequences. And there will in any case be a certain element of simply getting used to it, which also plays an important role.

As for the atmosphere aboard, this can depend on diverse factors such as:
- the total number of crew;
- the design of the vessel;
- individualising tendencies;
- personal affinity;
- type of voyages.

### Number of crew members

This is a factor with considerable influence on the other factors.

On a ship with a large crew there will be a larger proportion of similar professional and cultural level and, if there is a diversity of languages, there are more likely to be several crew members who speak the same language. Furthermore, on large ships a large crew will provide a sensation of more company than would the same ship with a small crew.

And a further two cases can arise: a) vessels designed for a crew of thirty, where the crew is reduced to twelve, and b) vessels designed from the outset for a crew of twelve.

Even if the size of the vessel is the same, and the feeling of solitude depends partly on the space-crew ratio, solitude will be more noticeable in case a).

### Design of the vessel

If the ship has been designed for a crew of twelve, the cabins will be in line with this, as will the dining room and communal areas. There will be twelve or thirteen cabins, all will eat in one dining room or maybe two, and the lounge will be of the right proportions for the number of people it has to accommodate.

If a vessel has been designed for a crew of thirty and that crew is then reduced to twelve, we will find from the outset that the cabins will be distributed by zones or decks, according to the professional category of the crew members, but in such as way as to always have a number of cabins together. Where the crew is reduced, without undertaking any refurbishment work, there would in this example be eighteen cabins left empty and, added to that, the twelve crew members would probably be divided into groups of four per cabin zone. Seeing empty cabins of itself tends to increase a feeling of solitude. And if the vessel had three dining rooms and only two or even one are now used, the unused spaces, unless converted to other uses, will also create a greater feeling of solitude.

If, on the other hand, the vessel was actually built for a crew of twelve, spaces will be well used, with none left empty, and the sensation of solitude will not be so acute.

### Individualising tendencies

Anthony Stringfellow[111] of the Apostleship of the Sea in Liverpool, asserted in relation to solitude: *I think perhaps the problem has got worse than it used to be. Nowadays, of course, everyone has his own cabin, and more and more of them carry their own stereos and now videos too. Then he has his own duty-free drinks and increasingly, I'm sorry to say, his own drugs. But I think with all this personal technology there is a tendency for people to isolate themselves more than they used to do. On top of that, ships today have much smaller crews, and that means the men have fewer chances of being together, of even meeting each other just in passing in different parts of the ship. This aspect of the problem has even been officially recognised - naval architects and shipowners are now thinking of ways of designing the accommodation so that in the normal course of moving about they can ensure that people have a chance of meeting each other.*

Similarly, Rodney Wilson[112], an English ex-cook, commented: *Sometimes you're sitting there in your cabin when a companion comes down off his watch and all you hear is the gurgling of a tap being turned on and then a little music.*

It should not be deduced from this that if cabins are shared the crew members feel less alone. Indeed, as we saw in section 3.5, crew members need a space to themselves in which they can commune with themselves in privacy. The problem arises when a person shuts himself away inside himself, as if trying to flee from the ship, as if trying to forget he was in the middle of the ocean.

### Personal affinity

In order to be able to overcome isolation within the crew itself, there must exist certain affinities which cannot in principle be assessed but can be facilitated. People of common customs and languages will always find it easier to get on, and that affinity can be facilitated in broad terms by controlling the composition of crews.

There are, of course, other factors, such as the character of each individual and his personal circumstances, which are truly difficult to foresee. The entire personnel department of a shipping company should nevertheless bear in mind, in addition to the professional aspect of each crew member, his personality in terms of enhancing a good atmosphere on board. This is of course totally impossible when shipping companies do not have their own crews, but rather have them supplied by manning agencies, an increasingly common situation especially on ships flying flags of convenience.

### Type of voyage

The longer the voyage the more time the crew spends far from home and the more influence the atmosphere on board will have on the sensation of solitude. On a ferry covering, for example, the Barcelona to Palma de Mallorca route, the crew will hardly have any chance to decide whether they get on well together, for they will often spend their free time off the ship and during the eight-hour journey each one will be getting on with his/her own job. Crew members will of course feel more or less content depending on what their workmates or immediate bosses are like, but that will be only the same as in any job, both on land and at sea.

On long voyages, on the other hand, a lack of affective ties and progressive isolation of a person can have harmful effects.

Barny Mousa, a Zanzibari seaman, told how a waiter on board a merchant ship which undertook long voyages from Australia to South America, after spending a while gazing in reverie at the sea leaning on the rail, jumped overboard: "Maybe he was thinking 'Why didn't I get a letter last port?'", remarked Mousa.[113]

### 3.8.3 Boredom

Martin Dyer-Smith has taken a close look[114] at this subject. There is a conundrum implicated in smooth running systems and high levels of training. The expectation that something untoward will happen reduces with system reliability. Confidence increases with training and experience. These two factors can coincide with lethal effect. The bored are a danger to themselves, and others, since their behaviour may become increasingly erratic. Mean performance may improve, but fluctuations become more and more pronounced.

Dyer-Smith feels that boredom is the problem most difficult to confront in modern industrial society. It has consequences at individual level (depression, alienation, suicide, etc.) and on a general level (accidents due to inattention, drowsiness, slow reflexes, etc.). Experience of boredom varies from one person to another, and the boredom of listening to a monotonous speaker is not the same as the boredom of the unemployed person or a man on lookout at sea.

Dyer-Smith quotes the remark of a captain: *On the bridge you are on half-brain. Most of the time it's like being in a dream ... I don't need a brain anymore.*

Dyer-Smith carried out a three-month study into the behaviour of the watch aboard a small cargo vessel, observing that:
- watchkeepers find day watches more boring than night watches;
- bored watchkeepers avoided rather than sought compensating stimulation.

From this Dyer-Smith drew the following conclusions:
- *boredom is a form of adaptation to low levels of stimulation;*
- *stimulation does not alleviate boredom but rather makes it worse;*
- *in the absence of other resources, a bored person cannot be held by stimulation;*
- *boredom is really a protection against depression.*

Boredom is revealed as a factor of increasing importance, resulting in a steady loss of interest.

Tony Lane[115] explains how a seaman on lookout perched perhaps 60 ft or 70 ft above the water might feel alone in the universe. *At that height and on a clear night the eye can take in 170 square miles of ocean in a circular sweep. And it is empty.* Lane adds that this *seeing nothing in the middle of the ocean, not even any lights, makes the task indescribably tedious.*

The same author tells of the tendency of bridge officers to establish contact by Morse code or by VHF with other ships in the vicinity, as a means of amusement during the long lookout hours on the high seas. I myself remember one trip from Spain to South Africa during which we met two tankers, one Greek and the other Italian, bound for the Persian Gulf. We spent several nights on the same VHF channel and we set up a chat programme. We even had each person choosing a piece of music to play to the others. Our three ships were travelling at distances of 15 to 20 miles from each other, so we never actually saw one another, but the good wave propagation meant that we could break the monotony of the night watches.

When Dyer-Smith asks who is suited to being a seaman[116], he does bear in mind that a seaman needs technical and intellectual ability suitable for his job. A low level will not allow him to be a competent professional, while too high a level will make him especially prone to boredom.

Life at sea, despite the risks it can involve due to being a profession exercised "at the mercy of the elements", and despite the possibility it offers of getting to know other countries, is a life marked by routine. A ship travels slowly. The speed of a cargo vessel can be reckoned at some 15 knots (about 28 kph), while there are ships that do not exceed 10 knots (about 19 kph) and some passenger liners which achieve speeds of 26 or 27 knots (some 48 to 50 kph). In general, we can state that the average speed of a merchant vessel is around 25 to 30 kph. If we then bear in mind that these vessels cover large distances such as 5,000 miles, between two ports, then we will see that 30 kph must be like a never-ending journey when compared with, say, the speed of a car going along a road. But if we then bear in mind that the ship keeps travelling 24 hours a day, without any rest, we will see that it covers 720 kilometres a day, which does not seem so very little.

If we mention this matter it is because there is a close relationship between this slow but constant progress of the ship and life and work aboard it. If human beings have an innate tendency towards routine, out of a primitive instinct for economy of effort, then the sea is an ideal sphere for it. Faced with a 20-day trip there is no hurry, and work and rest times can be organised. Today, and in six days' time, when we look over the railing it will look as if the ship were in the same place, with the same water and sky. And when coastline does appear on the horizon, it will draw closer only very slowly.

The work itself, except in situations of emergency, is the same day after day. This involves monotony and relaxation of a crew member, especially if the weather is good. That is why crew members setting off on a long voyage often say they're off to the health farm. But, as we will see in chapter five, this monotony naturally has a curved-line development graph. Men setting out to sea for a long crossing are usually bad-tempered. But as the days pass the atmosphere improves, and people fall into a more or less comfortable life. Then again, once a certain number of days at sea have been exceeded people begin to feel that they need other stimuli and the atmosphere deteriorates again. Naturally enough, this cannot be shown mathematically, for it will depend upon many personal and group factors.

In any case, that tedium, that line of days stretching ahead all the same, is fertile ground for the "half-brain" notion referred to by Dyer-Smith. On a merchant vessel on a long voyage there is usually free time in which a lot could get done. But due to being isolated from everything, the content of free time is no long offered from the outside, as can happen on land, but has to be organised personally and thus requires some effort. Faced with such a situation and the lack of outside stimuli, seamen will probably adopt the line of least resistance, living semi-asleep, falling back on simple amusements such as games of cards or ludo.

We should bear in mind that routine is a way of make the time pass quicker, which at heart is what seamen want. Boredom is thus a two-edged sword. One the one hand it induces a gradual loss of reflexes and a lack of motivation. But on the other hand, within certain limits, monotony will help to make daily life more bearable.

Finding a balance between economy of effort and sufficient stimuli to allow a person to feel at ease with what he is doing is an open issue within the broad field of subjects suggested by life and work aboard ship.

## 3.9 Stress and fatigue among seamen

### 3.9.1 Stress

The problems of different languages and of small crews form part of the causes of stress. Paul Chapman[117] notes: *"I once met a lonely Punjabi Sikh who for a year had shared no language in common with anyone on board his ship. He was devastated by the experience. It is not difficult to do one's job in this situation, but the lack of social contact is very stressful."*

The problems of difficulty of communication and of integration, of a sensation of solitude in general, are as we have seen clearly causes of stress. But there are other causes which come from life at sea itself and the very design of ships. Although modern vessels are more comfortable than the old ships (quite a few of which still ply the seas), vibrations and noises, especially in the engine room, can have marked effects on the health of those working in that department.

Changes of temperature are also hard to withstand. Within a single vessel, there can be temperature variation in winter ranging from -10°C on deck to +40°C in the engine room, added to which, during a voyage from north to south one can pass from a harsh winter to a tropical climate in 7 to 10 days.

In coastal shipping and general cargo traffic, trips are usually short and stays in port frequent, though brief. Stopover at a port calls for an entry manoeuvre and another exit manoeuvre, when the whole crew must be on their feet. The hours in port will not usually be relaxed, but normally subject to the pressure of being in a hurry, to problems relating to the load or some document to do with it, and so forth. Moreover, in port letters are received and the crew goes up and down busying themselves at their various tasks, while in their pockets they have letters which they snatch a few moments to read section by section with delight.

If the ship spends the night in the port, there will be a chance to go down on land and that, while it is a relief in that it breaks the routine, is at the same time a source of stress. On arrival in port, everybody goes around tense.

One person highly exposed to stress is the captain, especially when the ship is drawing into port or while coming alongside and moving off. A ship in a zone with a powerful current, or with strong winds, or with an engine fault in a critical situation, is an uncontrollable hulk. And the captain, or the officer on duty in his absence, must give the order which all await to get out of a tricky situation.

The author spent one New Year's Eve in the port of Valencia, with a violent storm which lashed right onto the mooring jetty. Due to the storm the ship, with over 30,000 tons of cargo, began to shift from bow to stern, breaking mooring cables. The risk of lurching into a tanker at the bows and the danger to the seamen each time a cable gave way created a highly stressful situation, one which lasted for all of seven hours.

### 3.9.2 Fatigue

In the world of aviation, fatigue of the flight crew is taken very seriously due to its being considered fundamental to the safety of the aircraft. In the merchant navy and in fishing fleets this would not appear to be at all the case, for it is a factor hardly taken into account.

For the time the voyage lasts, a seaman may be liable to work for days and days without a rest, as might happen when on board amidst a storm which could last a week. Here seamen would have to work with an extremely uncomfortable movement, and even during rest times will find that the ship heaves and almost prevents him from sleeping. And underlying all this discomfort is a backdrop of a certain amount of fear as to whether the ship will withstand the battering. We will refer to a talk given by captain Efraim Marcovitz[118], who analyses fatigue and concludes that it is prevalent on merchant vessels, where long periods of overtime are the norm. And to this are added, in some cases, long periods at sea.

According to Marcovitz, automation on newer vessels means that they can travel with small crews. But the worst of it is that this trend towards reduction has been extended to older vessels, designed for larger crews than shipowners are willing to permit them. And this reduction has led to practices like the single lookout during periods of darkness, which means in the middle of the ocean spending four long hours in pitch darkness without anybody to talk to.

The resolution of the IMO (International Maritime Organisation) number A.722 (18) states as follows: *Fatigue results in the degradation of human performance, the slowing down of physical and mental reflexes and/or the impairment of the ability to make rational judgements.*[119]

The factors causing fatigue vary from one person to the next, but are progressive in their effect.

Marcovitz notes the following causes of fatigue:
- Brief stays in port which, if a seaman is to go down on land, often call for long trips.
- Denser traffic in many of the world's ports.
- Automation. While it may seem contradictory, this has contributed to increasing fatigue on board. Fewer crew members enrol, and when automatic systems fail the crew has to work harder than it would on a conventional ship.
- Flags of convenience which, due to the recruitment of men with little training, lead to quite a high risk of fires and accidents.

The subject of flags of convenience has given rise to much discussion. Some years back, the ITF (International Transport Federation) began a strong challenge to these flags in that the ships flying them often had poor health and safety standards and their crews were paid denigrating wages.

The Center for Seafarers' Rights in New York started a struggle to increase the awareness of North American shipowners and direct defence of rights as evidenced in specific cases. And Apostleship of the Sea centres throughout the world have also taken action in this respect, as has the Centro de los Derechos del Marino in Barcelona, which organised an international seminar on the subject in 1990.

The ILO, through its conventions on maritime working themes and the Memorandum of Understanding on Port State Control, has achieved a commitment from many countries to inspect and monitor the ships of any flag entering their ports. In practice, however, a large number of ships flying under flags of convenience are a clear danger to their crews and to the environment.

There are modern and well-crewed vessels, it is true, but it is also true that there are very many small, old vessels operated by not very solvent shipowners, crewed by men with very low qualifications and working in a parlous state of seaworthiness.

Such conditions lead to crew members living in a state of tension, afraid that some vital organ of the vessel will break, suffering from lack of rest because their cabins are not in a fit state for habitation, from overwork because they are working in an environment where all is falling apart, where instruments fail, in which human work has to make up for what works automatically on other vessels, and all this, with small and scantly qualified crews, is a continual source of fatigue.

We need simply imagine a machine constantly breaking down, calling for repairs night and day in order to carry on, or rusty derricks which threaten to break and cause some disaster if the ship lurches, or holds with hatches which do not shut down properly and have to be secured in great haste at the least sweeping of water; all of this, coming on top of the heaving of a small ship, gives rise to considerable fatigue.

Another cause of fatigue is being unable to sleep peacefully at one stretch. Seamen on vessels with small crews rarely have more than five hours at a stretch to sleep, and if to this is added bad weather then sleep quality is poor, while old and poorly maintained boats will creak and, in general, make noises that will disturb rest periods.

If the ship enters a zone of storms the crew can spend several days unable to cook, eating only sandwiches or cold dishes. The continuous movement alone leads to a feeling of tiredness. And if a crew member falls ill, then the others will have to cover his work.

In aviation, after a certain number of flight hours a pilot takes a rest at home or in a comfortable hotel room. On a ship it can occur that, after eight hours loading in port, arguing with stevedors to get them to stow the load as best suits the ship, there will always be somebody who on setting out again to sea will have to go straight into a watch of several hours. If it is nighttime his eyelids will droop from sleepiness and then perhaps, when the time for sleep finally comes, the lurching or pitching of the ship, together with the noises caused by such movements, will prevent him getting a good rest.

Then the ship may have to be ready only twelve hours later to enter another port for another busy day loading and unloading.

But this factor of fatigue does not seem to matter to shipowners or governments. The sea and oceans are big and there are not so very many accidents; and if they do occur, and if the ship sinks, there will be an insurance policy to cover the material damage. And when it comes to liability it is always possible to blame the captain or the crew in general for lack of skill or for negligence.

## 3.10 Women as professionals of the sea

### 3.10.1 Introduction

This is a subject which remains quite new. Women officers have been aboard some ships in the Spanish merchant navy for over ten years now, while in the merchant navies of other countries they have been present for more than thirty years. They remain a small minority, however, on which little has been written, but a minority which may become more sizable in the not-too-distant future.

On passenger vessels there have in fact always been female crew members working as hostesses, waitresses, hairdressers, and so forth, but their situation does not coincide at all with that of the seafarer we are looking at in this book. Many of those hostesses and waitresses, etc., were and are young girls, doing the work temporarily, or else middle-aged single or widowed women, so we are looking not so much at a profession with the future life outlook of a young person as at work undertaken circumstantially. Any of such women, should she have plans to marry, will automatically abandon the seagoing life.

But when a young woman twenty years of age spends some ten years between studying and time at sea and manages to become captain or chief engineer, this implies an outlook which cannot be dismissed as "doing something out of a spirit of adventure or to get a job". Sooner or later she may leave it, but from the outset a person who chooses a career does so thinking of the future, and a young woman who decides to study navigation is in principle thinking of the seafaring life.

Another factor to be taken into account is that a woman holding a post of authority in a world as traditional as that of ships may find herself in difficult situations.

The seawoman on board must be clearly distinguished from the wife of a crew member, embarked as "accompanying family". These last may not take kindly to the presence on board of a woman officer. On the one had it may give rise to some mistrust, and on the other hand certain reactions on board may lead the female crew member to make it quite clear that she is there to do a job and is not on a pleasure cruise like the other woman. This is clearly due largely to the identification which has existed until recently between the sea and the masculine sex.

Women aboard ship run a special risk of suffering solitude. On a ship crewed only by men there are some mealtime conversations which could not take place with a woman on board. Though she may be treated very well indeed, it will not be easy for her to integrate. At least in the early days, people will lose something of their spontaneity in her presence.

And she herself will have to be cautious. A male crew member, though he may be a mate to many men, usually has a closer relationship with only one or two others, and will go off into port with them; but female crew member will have to be extremely prudent if misunderstandings and gossip are to be avoided. She will not be able to show openly a special friendship with any crew member, for even that crew member himself may misinterpret it.

Here we are clearly faced with a problem of mentality, which with time and habit may be corrected. But planning life as a married woman, for example, is to look at considerable restrictions. There are couples in which husband and wife go to sea aboard different ships and, when one is on holidays, goes aboard as accompanying family of the other, with the holidays of both only occasionally coinciding. There are cases, too, where the husband is on land and the woman goes to sea, but I think such a situation can arise for a period while the couple is young, but cannot work out in the longer term.

As regards motherhood, a woman seafarer practically has to choose between having children and remaining at sea, for if family life is difficult in the absence of the father, then all the more so will it be in the absence of the mother.

### 3.10.2 Integration into the crew

If we think of a cargo vessel, in which all crew members have traditionally been male, the entry of a woman, and not as accompanying family but as a member of the crew, raises a number of question marks.

As against the usual question as to whether women are ready to take up the seafaring profession, Begoña Sagarduy turns the question round to ask whether the merchant navy is ready to receive women[120]. In answer to this, Sagarduy[121] analyses these subjects through a survey carried out amongst Spanish women embarked as cadets or officers on board merchant vessels. According to this study, the ability to accept women as crew members is most widespread among young people, is found amongst a minority of middle-aged people and is non-existent amongst older people.

In terms of education, those with higher qualifications are also the ones most likely to accept women. This may be explicable by the additional fact that an officer may well have no difficulty accepting a woman as cadet, and a woman officer of similar rank may also be acceptable. But accepting a woman as the one who is giving out the orders will, under the traditional male chauvinistic attitude, be more difficult. Most of those surveyed came under the category of cadet or officer. We would therefore have to see whether the crew, men with plenty of sea experience under their belts, found it harder to accept women.

At department level, the deck department was the one where women found easiest acceptance, this being doubtless related to the fact that most of those surveyed were from that department.

Idoia Ibáñez[122], merchant navy captain with the Compañía Logística de Hidrocarburos, in speaking of her early years at sea, tells us: *there were two attitudes ... the attitude of those who would put all my work under a magnifying glass ... and those who would treat me in a delicate, fraternal way, with the kind of consideration shown on board to the wife or daughter of an officer travelling on board ship. So I wasn't really just one of the crew, of the group into which I was trying to integrate ... Moreover, there had arisen within me a responsibility to show the men that a woman could be a good officer in the merchant navy and live alongside them like just another colleague ...*

Ibáñez here raises some very important points. On the one hand, we have the need to feel integrated. The entire problem of uprootedness, communication and solitude is intimately bound up with integration of the person. If crew members get to feel truly integrated within the context of the human group in which they must live and work, then they will have managed to overcome successfully the traumas involved in all total institutions.

Such integration cannot be achieved just with good treatment; one has to feel that one has a part in the jigsaw puzzle. For that reason, the deferential and at times paternalistic and protectionist treatment meted out by some captains or officers towards a female cadet or officer on a ship is something she will take a negative view of, for what she wants is simply to be just another member of the crew, and nothing more.

The other aspect is the need to demonstrate constantly ones worth. When people start a new job, or simply start work in a new place, they need to feel that they are being afforded a certain margin of confidence. If they feel monitored, if they know that everything they do will be subjected to close examination, this can, especially for young or inexperienced people, lead to situations of stress which can even lead them to give up. If on the other hand workmates show confidence in them and accept them, they can go along developing know-how with the necessary peace of mind.

María Cardona[123], engineer officer, discerned three attitudes:
- Those who accepted you as a professional, with only the reservations natural when faced with any person joining a workplace.
- Those who tend to overprotect you simply because you are a woman.
- Those who reject you because they feel that ships are for men.

In this outline, Cardona presents two extreme stances: normal acceptance and out-and-out rejection, without any options. In between these would the attitude Ibáñez describes as being examined under a magnifying glass. Normal acceptance is what anybody would aspire to, while the other attitudes are deformations of a normal reception in a workplace.

Another interesting reaction is that of the wives of other crew members. According to the survey, most of those questioned (38.5%) stated that they had received support from crew wives, though 17.3% felt they had detected signs of jealousy. This is perhaps normal enough. In the atmosphere of land-based jobs relations going beyond friendship can be formed between men and women; at sea, when people are going to be far from home for weeks or months, sharing days and days on end at sea and perhaps going into ports together, it is normal for wives of crew members to feel a certain suspicion if their husbands are going to have a female colleague. It should also be noted that, given the small space in which the crew of a ship moves and the weight of roles in its organisation, greater caution is also to be expected.

### 3.10.3 Access to the labour market

A certain reluctance to accept woman on board can be detected amongst shipowners. In a labour market such as that which prevailed at the end of the 'sixties, with shortages of seamen, there may have been less reluctance. At present, however, when shipowners can have their pick of crews because the supply of seamen is much greater than the demand, it is easier simply to follow the traditional guidelines and not expose oneself to a risk of conflicts on board ship, which could hypothetically occur through taking women on board.

The reasons for rejecting women's access to work at sea would in any case appear to be more a problem of attitude to what is new rather than a deeper underlying problem. Furthermore, in labour markets in general discrimination against women persists even today. And if for any employer an employee's pregnancy creates problems of replacement, this becomes much more serious in the case of a ship, as time off for maternity will have to be much longer.

In this respect, Idoia Ibáñez notes that when she planned to start her apprenticeship as a cadet she was told by one Spanish shipping company that women could go to sea as accompanying family, but not as officers. She later managed to embark with another company and so could continue her career without problems.

Fernando Sánchez[124], head of Fleet Human Resources of C.L.H. states: *The future of women in the maritime world is the same as that experienced by the entire sector ... The ease with which women can integrate into or form part of working teams is in line with the reforms pending in the running of ships.*

This point of view not only does not discriminate against women, but actually sees them as especially suited for taking part in reform of the merchant navy, necessary at times of evolution of computing and automation.

### 3.10.4 The potential influence of women on life aboard ship

We have stated that crew members need to feel integrated and well accepted. The presence of a woman as just another crew member will undoubtedly have an influence on life on board. According to the study by Sagarduy, the presence of a woman leads to more courteous speech and even better personal care of companions.

But the work of women can itself give rise to negative aspects of life in common, relating specifically to the possible harassment to which women can be subjected. In the survey, 57% of the women who replied stated that they had been harassed at some time, while 7% stated that they had been subjected to frequent harassment. As regards the nature of the harassment, offensive expressions and persecution accounted for 44.4%, looks accounted for 38.9% and brushing against and touching 5.6%.

According to Sagarduy, persecution aboard ship is significant when compared with other jobs. Ibáñez speaks of a need for prudence in friendships; going off into port several times with the same male colleague can lead to gossip. All will depend, too, on the personality and general attitude of the female crew member.

Despite all this, most of the women surveyed took a positive view, as did many captains and officers. I believe that the presence of women on board, as old prejudices are overcome, can open up new perspectives and amount to an enriching contribution towards life aboard ships.

### 3.10.5 Women and the exercise of authority

The exercise of authority is always a problem. All in authority have to impose themselves, not by force but rather through their knowledge and aptitudes. Any sphere of social organisation, however democratic, has to have someone holding the reins and using them properly.

We saw in section 3.10.2 that women on ships could encounter attitudes of rejection or find that every step they took was dissected to find flaws. A woman taking up a post as captain, a job which will in any case always be under the gaze of all, will find that that feeling of being on test will certainly increase. This may amount more to a fear that may betray the person who feels observed rather than a real conditioning factor, given that where a person is professionally competent nobody is likely to question their authority.

Idoia Ibañez[125], the first woman to captain a ship in Spain, is quite trenchant in this regard: *Where a captain gives the orders, the crew do not; and for the good of the common maritime adventure, on ships the post comes first and gender afterwards … Human beings in general, whether well-educated or not, are sufficiently intelligent to recognise when the person in authority has sufficient skill for the job*, adding that she never experienced any problems in that respect, with both crew and officers accepting her authority. But she adds that it was not for nothing that she was very demanding with herself and always endeavoured to show greater than normal competence for a seaman. On land it has been found and made perfectly clear that the fact of being a woman should be no obstacle to holding a position of authority; the same should apply in the merchant navy.

### 3.10.6 Family life and professional life

If there is broad agreement on anything it is that for a woman the choice of the seafaring profession means giving up family life and motherhood. If the life of a seaman and husband is incompatible enough already, this is all the more the case for the seawoman and wife.

On the one hand, we have our cultural tradition, which will scarcely accept the man being at home while the woman is off at sea. This, however, is a problem of mentality. More serious is the question of motherhood. Although there may also be some question of cultural charge here, psychology would appear to show clearly the importance for new-born babies and young children in general of having physical contact with their mothers, and of suckling at the breast.

When in chapter four we look at the relationship of seafarers with their families, we will be doing so from the traditional perspective of it being the man who goes to sea. In the case of a woman, these notions would have to be qualified considerably. As things stand today, however, there is too little experience and documentation on the subject to go into it in any depth. Another aspect might be the rate of separation between couples in which the woman or both woman and man are seafarers. In fact, amongst the few women seafarers there are, several are indeed already separated, though detailed data are also lacking here.

# the relations of crew members with the outside world

## 4.1 The relationship of the crew member with society in general

One of the characteristics defining the concept of total institution is the isolation[126] suffered by their members over significant periods of time. This is not so much a matter of the time the isolation lasts as the very fact of belonging to a total institution, which limits the freedom of its members in the sense that they cannot leave it when they wish but are obliged to remain in it without any distinction between working hours and rest hours.

Indeed, when people enter they know that they are giving up a major portion of their freedom for such time as their stay there lasts. This factor involves compulsory separation from the outside world. At the same time, as this separation is a necessary but undesired consequence, inmates will seek out ways of maintaining the greatest possible contact with that outside world.

In the merchant ship institution, when seamen embark they renounce seeing their families for a certain period of time; not only that, they know that they will have to remain more or less distant from the daily life of their cities or towns, from their countries and, in a way, from the world in general.

Being far away not only means difficulty in receiving information but also in some way a gradual decline of interest in the day-to-day events of the far-away place. The isolation thus increases as seamen, over their years at sea, have their own experiences of a world which is by no means akin to that of land-based people. This is alleviated quite considerably in the case of seamen who enjoy frequent holidays, although due to the type of life they still undergo a certain loss of interest in those things which they experience differently.

### 4.1.1 Social identity of seafarers

Seafarers have a truly peculiar social view of themselves. This is demonstrated, as already mentioned, by the old adage among Spanish seafarers: There are three classes of people in the world: the living, the dead and seamen.

Bankston[127] suggests that seamen can be grouped into two types. Firstly, we find those who live with an absent attitude. They retain an orientation towards the outside world, towards land. This type of seamen come over as enclosed in themselves: they speak little, read a lot, elude difficulties, volunteer for nothing, rarely get drunk, dress better than the others and keep tighter control over their money. As Irwin[128] says, this type of seaman makes the most of the situation, adapts himself to privation and retains stronger links with the outside world.

Such seamen are favoured by the anonymous nature of life at sea. The situation of common isolation and the need for mutual support nevertheless give rise to a second type of seamen, who try to organise a new world within the confines of the ship. This will affect the identity of the seamen, who will find their connections with land being eroded. As Hanna[129] says, as seamen build their own structure on board, they also develop rejection of it, for not doing so would mean recognising that they no longer form part of the conventional world. They then seek to criticise even things they may like. Thus, they like to point out they are providing a great service to society, yet society turns its back on them, that if they found a good job on land they wouldn't think twice about leaving the sea, that they do not want their sons to follow in their footsteps at sea.

Socially they display a mixture of attitudes ranging between professional pride and contempt for landlubbers who live peacefully and don't know how hard the sea is, and a certain inferiority complex when they realise that they are living in another world and that on land they feel they are nobody.

Moreover, as Forsyth and Bankston[130] say: *The ephemeral quality of interpersonal relations generates a problematic identity for the seaman. The seaman continually expresses a dislike for ships ... Even so, life on ship becomes more desirable than life on the outside. On the ship at least he is comfortable, sure of his position ...*

The reference here is to that frequent contradiction between what seamen proclaim and what they often really feel. This does not arise out of a wish to deceive, but rather a clash between the cliché (not without foundation) that life at sea is not fit for people and the realisation that they have become so used to that life that, deep down, they identify with it.

Interpersonal relations are initially marked by a working situation and a hierarchical structure which at the very least, as we saw when discussing the crew of a ship, from the outset very much condition those relations.

And even with those with whom there is a closer relationship there will arise the problem that they are sharing not only work time but also part of their leisure time.

If on board there are people who generally get along with each other, then it will not be difficult to extend the professional relationship into one of friendship. However, when there is no such understanding, or there is even animosity, a seaman will have to choose between shutting himself up inside himself and spending his free time alone, or involving himself in a tacit pact to overcome solitude, even if relationships are superficial.

### 4.1.2 Information

Seamen on the high seas are very much isolated from what goes on around them. The radiotelegraph will bring them the most important international news, but the other more minor day-to-day news does not reach them. That is why seamen are often fond of radio (television station signals can no longer be picked up once the ship is more than a few miles from the coast). It is common to see electrical wires emerging out of cabin portholes, attached as aerials to any item on deck. Sailors seek radios with short wave bands, not commonly found in cities but certainly to be found near docks and in ports such as the Canary Island ports, in which any stopover can be used to buy, amongst other things, radios, cassettes and the like.

Spanish *Radio Nacional de España*, for example, can be heard in the middle of the Atlantic using short wave radio, especially news and sports programmes, so that seamen can listen to the Sunday football match results or special broadcasts such as *Españoles en la Mar* (Spaniards at Sea).

Seamen on vessels making coastal trips around their own country can buy a newspaper each time they stop in port, and there are no problems picking up local radio stations and even television. Spanish newspapers, however, are hardly to be found in many foreign ports. The major news, as we have seen, reaches seafarers by radio, while other news will be of more local interest, quite apart from language barriers. Thus, when a seaman returns home after several months away from his country, the fact of not having kept up with day-to-day events only increases the feeling of strangeness we note in section 4.5.

The news of greatest interest, in fact, is that which comes from home and from the shipping company, since the shipping company news refers to trips to be made, relief crews, repair dates and so forth.

The postal service also comes under the heading of information. For seamen, arrival in port is synonymous with the hope of receiving letters.

Quite apart from their importance in relation with seamen's families, letters are also a major source of information, not for the major news of the radio, but the smaller, private news about family life or life in the local neighbourhood. This news, which would be meaningless for anybody else, signifies for the person receiving it a chance to continue to follow what is happening in what he considers to be his world and the place to which he directs his thoughts in order to continue feeling that he forms part of it.

### 4.1.3 Social and political participation: associations and trade unions

One of the main problems seamen face in their attempt to avoid a sensation of marginalisation is their difficulty in taking part in the social and political life of their town, their country. Any potential participation is frustrated from the outset by long voyages, especially to foreign countries. The lack of information referred to in the previous section and difficulty in interpreting news items when one is far from the place and situation in which they arose often prevent any such participation.

Nowadays, when news becomes old from one day to the next, it is very difficult to assimilate it once it has passed.

At political level, there are ways of taking part in elections from a distance, by sending in a postal vote. A person who spends weeks far away from his country has to be put considerable effort into making arrangements to have his vote sent in in the legally established manner and by the due date.

At political level, there are ways of taking part in elections from a distance, by sending in a postal vote. A person who spends weeks far away from his country has to be put considerable effort into making arrangements to have his vote sent in in the legally established manner and by the due date.

But there is another type of association, the type which pursues professional objectives. In this group we find, on one hand, the trade associations such as the *Colegio de Oficiales de la Marina Mercante Española (COMME)*, Spanish Merchant Navy Officers' Association, which in order to expand had to achieve compulsory affiliation of Spanish seamen going to sea with Spanish shipping companies, and, on the other hand, the trade unions.

The leading one at international level is the International Transport Federation (ITF). In Spain there are also the merchant navy sections of the chief trade unions, *UGT* and *Comisiones Obreras*, the latter (the SLMM) being founded clandestinely in the last years of the Franco period under the auspices of Spain's Apostleship of the Sea.

Trade union initiatives were also taken by seamen who joined their efforts from land. Their prominent role when it came to negotiating with the shipping companies and calling a number of strikes were what gave the boost needed to break down the initial mistrust and scepticism of the seafaring seamen.

There are trade union representatives in the larger shipping companies, but in the smaller ones, and especially for sailors on voyages abroad, the fact of spending weeks and months at sea remains an obstacle to any union initiatives.

## 4.2 The ship in port

When people arrive in a country, if only for reasons of work or merely passing through, they go to a hotel, home or private residence. Although such persons still form part of a group they have left behind them, they have entered the new society; they might have first had to pass through customs and immigration checks, but once inside they can move around just like any other citizen of that country.

Even the crew of an aeroplane, when resting in a city, is taken to a hotel, and until such time as they have to fly again can go where they like or receive who they like in their hotel rooms.

When a ship arrives in port, this does not mean the start of a rest period for the crew; they have to remain fully active, attending to their various tasks aboard during loading or unloading.

Moreover, a port is always a frontier zone for them and, therefore, one subject to controls. If it is a foreign country, seamen can only go ashore with a pass issued to them. The physical connection between the ship and the city is the gangway, ladder or just a plank, at one end of which there is often a security guard or policeman monitoring people entering and leaving the ship.

The expression "going ashore", so common among seafaring folk, shows how seamen, even when the ship is in port are not, while they are on board, actually on land, so that each time they wish to gain access to the world surrounding the docks they have to leave their own world, their own haunt, the ship. It should be remembered, too, that the docks are often far from the city, and that there is therefore some distance to walk and a route not entirely free from danger, for walking along docks with containers, train wagons and piled cargo always inspires a fear of attack.

In the words of Roland Doriol:[131]*The first stop in Japan is the Nagoya timber dock ... after we've passed the port fence, we hitch-hike along the main road. But the universal sign of putting your thumb out is no use here, and we have to walk eight kilometres to find a hostel.*

Apart from making you tired, walking eight kilometres along a road running between a dock and a city makes you feel like an outcast. Moreover, quite apart from whether the hitch-hiking sign is understood or not, many people are afraid of stopping and picking up strangers who look as if they've come from distant parts, for fear of being mugged. And once in the city, looking fairly lost, seamen usually just go walking about all over, seeking to enjoy a few hours far from the ship.

When the outing time has elapsed they will have to return to ship, and, once again, the gangway, a narrow passage, will mean leaving the city behind and rejoining the ship's routine. But returning aboard, especially when in a foreign country and the seamen are more or less well-adapted to life aboard ship, is like returning home. It is the point of reference, the place where they feel safe, where they know who they are and what their role is.

On a ship, it is not easy to receive guests. Normally, unless seamen have a special permit from the competent authority they cannot go into the docks, and the coming aboard of non-authorised outside persons is impossible. Although a merchant ship does not have extra-territorial status but is subject to the laws of the country whose port it is in, respect is shown for its internal organisation and, except in the case of a crime or police matter in general, nobody can come aboard without the prior permission of the captain.

During their working hours on board, seamen usually gaze from time to time at the city around them. At night, the lights of the city give a special feeling of life and movement. They see it as a world apart from their own, and one in which they will try to submerge themselves for a few hours, though without at any time losing the identity accorded them through being members of a crew.

Furthermore, the fact noted earlier that the port is a frontier zone means that the seamen are subjected to very tight customs control. Each time they go onto land they will have to pass a check point where they may have to show the things they have with them, or even allow themselves to be frisked. And as ports have been and remain zones through which contraband and nowadays drugs habitually pass, all seamen are in principle suspects.

When ships enter port they do so with the mission of carrying out cargo loading and unloading operations, or passenger embarkation and disembarkation operations, as quickly as possible, with no consideration even paid to the wishes of the crew. A ship might come alongside dock at six in the morning, far from the city, start work, and eight hours later set out to sea again. In such a case, bearing in mind the work the crew has to do in the port and how far they are from the city, it is quite possible that nobody or hardly anybody goes ashore.

Nowadays many ships spend only hours in port, and crew members hardly have any chance to set foot on land. In the case of large tankers, they normally come alongside jetties or tie up at buoys, far from any city and with no chance of going ashore. Tankers on routes to the Persian Gulf, Syria or the Lebanon, to mention a few places, only see land through binoculars, and the only pleasure they will get will be that of receiving or sending a letter through the freight agent.

### 4.2.1 The relationship of the seaman with people who come aboard

It is usually said on ships what when land folk come on board it is only to give you work or make a profit out of something.

This is firstly because the ship or freight agents and the authorities come aboard at any time, without regard to ship mealtimes, and then give out any instructions they deem appropriate. And secondly, because many who come aboard expect to carry away in their briefcases or under their coats a bottle of whisky, a carton of cigarettes, or both.

The relationship of the seamen with the land people who come aboard is not an open one, leading to a person-to-person encounter, but more of a working, commercial or bureaucratic relationship. In some ports, especially where there are language barriers, there will scarcely be any relationship. In the article mentioned above, Doriol[132] tells us: *"In Yokohoma and in Kobe... the ship was loaded up without any unnecessary conversation between the Japanese and the Indian deck officers, whom they ignored entirely. The Japanese have nothing to request, expect nothing... There are brief exchanges between the seamen and the sellers of bits and bobs and electrical appliances ..."*

The stevedores and other personnel usually speak only to their foremen, and the latter will be the ones who say anything that has to be said to the officers of the ship.

The coming aboard of street sellers is a big event. They usually set up their display stands in a dining room on the ship, and offer all sorts of souvenirs and other attractive articles. The crew find this a pleasure, even if only because they enjoy themselves looking at what is on offer. Most of these sellers expect some haggling over prices, which becomes yet another attraction in the purchase transaction. Seamen who purchase something after lengthy haggling go off highly content to their cabins, thinking that not only have they made a good buy but feeling proud of how they demonstrated the art of haggling to their shipmates.

In some African countries a whole avalanche of people come aboard. As Doriol points out, *"real skill is required to distinguish the real security guards and port workers in the midst of the press of visitors selling fruit and souvenirs"*.

The changing attitude of the crew members themselves, depending on the country, is an explicit manifestation of instinctively racist or, at least, comparative attitudes. Spanish sailors have markedly different attitudes when in African ports and northern European ports. In the African ports they will speak familiarly to port employees and people around the docks, with an air of instinctive superiority, while in the northern European ports they will display a respectful attitude, even an inferiority complex. An exception amongst the so-called "ship visitors" are people from Apostleship of the Sea centres and the like, who go aboard ships to provide information about the activities they engage in and to invite crew members to take part in them, to offer cultural and religious products, to offer seamen transport from the ship to their assistance centres, or simply to chat and find out if those aboard have any problems. These visits take place in many ports the world over and are usually well received by the seamen, amongst other reasons because what is offered them is free and disinterested.

The visit of the ship's agent, or agent representing the shipowner, is greeted with expectation, for he will be bringing letters, money, news of how long loading and unloading are expected to take, and details of the next voyage.

If the ship is in its base port or in another not too distant port, then a visit from the shipowner's management staff might be expected, and in their presence everybody will feel to a certain extent the psychological pressure generated by a visit from the boss.

### 4.2.2 The relationship of seamen with the port population: communication and fun

Arrival in port, as long as there is to be sufficient time to go ashore, is a festive occasion for seamen. It means breaking the monotony, getting to know something new, getting in touch with home, having fun.

Just as for land dwellers, within the gamut of amusements seamen are attracted by the frivolous because it provides easy and immediate satisfaction, while any other more humanly rewarding activity such as cultural visits or attempts to get to know the people there a little more seriously is always more difficult and calls for more effort.

The fact that seamen spend no money at sea and they receive their pay on arrival in port means that they think about what they will do before they actually arrive, and when they do arrive they try to put to best advantage the status of being rich for a few days.

Seamen often like to take taxis and eat out away from the ship. In ports and the surrounding streets seamen will find brightly lit premises in which they will be able to have a few drinks with friends and, if they wish, enjoy the female company which awaits them there.

As J.C. Healey says[133]: "Seamen in far-away ports are covered by the veil of anonymity. This situation, together with a desire for sexual satisfaction, is bound to affect a seaman's physical and psychological reaction to his home."

This standpoint nevertheless does not imply ignoring the sociological importance of prostitution in ports. Healey is right to refer to two important aspects: instinctive desire and anonymity. And to these we might add the easy availability factor. For seamen, and for anybody arriving in a strange place with no personal link with its inhabitants, is it very difficult to strike up a relationship or friendship of simple human communication with the people in a port so that the seamen can for a few hours broaden the human circle in which they usually move on board.

For a seaman, going to a night spot, even if all he does is have a few drinks and chat for a while with a woman, is an easy type of communication without any deeper involvement. Naturally enough, circumstances and instinctive impulse may, under the cover of anonymity, lead him to something more.

Another characteristic of this situation is the attraction of alcoholic beverages as a quick means of achieving a feeling of fun and lack of inhibitions. Many seamen drink too much when ashore, as a means of more easily and quickly getting into a good-time situation.

Here there comes to the surface the important role of the intrinsically human need for communication, shared by all seamen as human beings. There are many psychological and sociological studies of the role of alcohol and prostitution as substitutes for human relationships to help men overcome the sensation of solitude.

And we should not forget here the importance of the meaning of roles. [134] There exist attitudes which are typically inherent to a certain situation. On ships, going out to have a few drinks can be seen as behaviour expected of the seaman role. Indeed, a seaman with cultural interests who devotes his time to visiting monuments and refuses to go and have a few drinks will probably be regarded as strange. Even amongst those of more serious outlook, it is entirely usual to take a stroll and have a drink.

As we have seen, seamen who need to feel integrated into the human group of the crew will also seek to have some part in the outings of their companions so as to avoid damaging that integration.

But these attitudes will vary according to the port. When it is a port in one's own country, the outing may be to have a meal or go to the cinema and this, added to the greater ease of speaking on the phone with his family, means that the seaman will feel closer to those who await him.

Where seamen are in foreign countries and communication with their homes is more remote, their families will seem like something dissociated from day-to-day reality and seamen will more easily fall into a round of living a make-believe world for a few hours.

An important role is paid in this respect by seamen's centres such as the Apostleship of the Sea and the like, which offer resources for communicating with seamen's homes or spending a pleasant time and entering into human relationships with new people in a simple way and at the same time without any need to indulge in frivolous behaviour. These centres cater for seamen's desire for company and for leisure activities through excursions or other leisure activities.

In any case, seamen returning aboard will have a feeling of wellbeing. As Hahman[135] tells us, seamen go ashore with a desire to have a good time, while upon return they have the feeling of security offered by the total institution.

A curious example cited by Roland Doriol[136] arises among Filipino seamen, who when two or more Filipino ships are in a port at the same time, get together on one of the ships instead of going someplace on land. And in these get-togethers *they exchange not only words but also songs, fish, papers and magazines.*

## 4.3 Passenger ships and relations with the passengers

The passengers here represent a chance of contact with the outside world. In evaluating the relationship of the passengers with the crew, we have to look at two aspects:
1. the role of the passenger in the ship institution.
2. the different type of contact crew members can have with the passengers, according to their department and professional category.

1) In the case of a ferry, with crossings lasting a day or a night, we may consider that the passengers play no role within the ship institution. They are merely passing through and will not bring the crew into any greater contact with the outside world than would the time they spend in port each day. The possibility of contact will be minimal, even for the waiters.

In the case of cruiser liners, and years ago the transatlantic liners which were filled with emigrants, the situation was completely different, for on them the passengers came in a way to form part of the total institution.

The situation of crew members and passengers is , of course, totally different. Both embark of their own free will, but while one group is going to work, the other is going for pleasure (cruiser ships) and to change country; while some are going in order to earn money, the others are going to spend it. Crew members will be spending a number of months aboard, depending on their contracts, and will over that time go where sent. Passengers will be embarking for one or several weeks and will choose the voyage they feel they will enjoy most or the one which suits them best. The crew members have a daily job to do, while the passengers have all their time at their own disposal.

For the passengers there is a role to be played, that of passenger, and they will at all times retain their various identities, as bank clerk, shopkeeper, architect and so forth, will retain them throughout the entire crossing, and everyone they meet will soon know who they are and what they are doing aboard. The crew members, however, are as we have seen identified by their job or profession, during both working and leisure time.

Out on the high seas, neither passengers nor crew members can disembark physically, so that passengers will also suffer the effects of being confined. Passengers will nonetheless not experience seamen's personal and family problems and will indeed come aboard in a rather superficial manner.

As regards the hierarchical schema, the passengers do in some way lie within it, in the sense that they too have to respect rules concerning order, peaceful co-existence and safety on board. When compulsory exercises for abandoning ship are carried out on passenger vessels, a certain authority is exercised over the passengers, as all are required to go up on deck with their lifejackets on. And in the event of an emergency the passengers will have to obey down to the last detail the instructions given by the captain and officers.

The captain is the highest authority on board, for both crew and passengers, having the authority during the voyage to detain any person who threatens to disturb life on board seriously. What is more, some weapons are usually carried on board passenger liners to deal with particularly grave situations.[137]

2) If we turn our attention now to the relations which can arise between crew members and passengers, we might state that, in terms of departments, the one with most contact with passengers is the catering department, and especially the waiters who serve in the dining rooms or bars or clean out cabins and are thus in regular contact with the passengers. Within that department, pursers and chief stewards will also come into contact with passengers, since they will be supervising the work of the catering staff and will pass through all the public areas of the vessel.

The department with least contact will be the engine department, with the exception of the chief engineer, who along with the captain and chief officer, usually takes meals with the passengers. Other engine department crew, on the other hand, have virtually no possible contact with passengers, while deck hands will have contact to a certain extent as they go about maintenance tasks on deck, keep an eye on gangways in port and the like.

Of the deck department, therefore, the captain and the first officer (called in some countries the deputy captain) are the ones having most relations with passengers, so that in this case public relations can be said to come after nautical requirements.

Some consideration should be given, too, to the younger officers, who will make use of the time the cruise or crossing lasts to form the occasional friendship with certain passengers.

Indeed, from the sociological point of view there is a major difference between a cargo ship and a passenger ship. In the former the life of the crew is very much to the fore. The reasons for this are very simple. Outside of the crew's life there is no other possibility for relations on the high seas. Moreover, on freight ships living conditions are much the same for captain and apprentice alike. The captain will have a better cabin that the apprentice and will enjoy certain prerogatives not enjoyed by others, but there is a certain homogeneity, especially where all crew members are of the same nationality.

On passenger vessels, the fact that there are crews numbering two or three hundred or more, and that crew members live so separated from each other, means that many do not even know each other. The professional categories here are much more clearly demarcated. Officers wear uniforms, live on the upper decks of the ship and have a certain, although limited, relationship with the passengers.

Ratings often have to put up with considerable discomfort and deprivation. It is well-known that on large and luxurious passenger liners there frequently arise situations of exploitation and marginalisation of Third-World country crew members, who are called upon to work hard for little pay and are, on top of all that, subjected to threats.

To return to the sociological differences which exist between the various types of vessels, we could conclude that there is more crew social life within the internal atmosphere of the cargo vessel institution than on a passenger liner.

## 4.4 The relationship of crew members with their families

Within the theme of relations of seamen with the outside world, the relationship with the family is of crucial importance. Indeed, many seamen leave the profession due to being tired of living always far away from their families. As a primary and basic social group, the family requires its members to live alongside one another. Not only are the most intimate links forged within the family, but it is also the setting for transmission of all the knowledge, ideas, values and attitudes which will form the sociocultural backbone of those born into it.

It is for this reason that the seafaring profession has always been seen as incompatible with a traditional family life, and for that same reason relations maintained with their families are for all seamen and in spite of circumstances a priority objective outside of their strictly professional objectives.

Living apart from the family has negative consequences for both the seaman and his family. "He becomes a visitor in his family.[138] As we will see in the sections which follow, the seaman's situation of always passing through, gives rise to serious problems when it comes to organising family life, both at the level of relations with his partner and with his children.

### 4.4.1 Seamen's family problems

To say that the seafarer's life and family life are incompatible is practically a commonplace. Images of seamen who see a son or daughter for the first time when they are already a year old, or seamen who arrive back home and find that their young children burst out crying because they don't know them, have been and are still used in novels and films.

In the 'seventies, with the gradual improvement in the system of holidays, leading to four months aboard ship and two months at home, the panorama improved substantially, though this did not entirely put an end to all the problems which life at sea raised for families.

At a forum in Lübeck (Germany),[139] one seaman's wife noted the improvement made in the merchant navy by the possibility of wives maintaining more continuous contact with their husbands through more frequent holidays, accompanying their seamen husbands on some voyages and the availability of facilities for telephone contact from the sea.

This opinion most likely came from the wife of an officer or captain, as they find it easiest to embark as accompanying family, and officers are the ones with most access to the ship's telephone or radio system. These improvements are nevertheless real, as are all those relating to comfort on board ships; we cannot make generalisations, however, but must rather acknowledge that there are considerable differences between different types of ships.

It was in the 'seventies, in fact, when ships flying flags of convenience began to become frequent, and with them crew members from the Third World who could be taken aboard for voyages of one year or so.

The process of dismantling of the fleets of the so-called industrialised countries in favour of the free-flag countries led to a massive rise in the number of cheap-labour crew members willing to accept long periods aboard ship and conditions of comfort and safety on board very far below the levels reached on modern ships operated by conscientious fleet operators.

In any case, with more or less frequent holidays, the seafaring profession creates serious difficulties for family life.

Craig J. Forsyth and Robert Gramling[140] have made a study of the strategies used by seamen's families to adapt to the situation of absent husbands and fathers.

And in recent decades many studies have been made of the effect of working hours on family life, from which it has emerged clearly that non-traditional working hours or schedules are problematical for families.[141]

Merchant seamen represent an extreme form of abnormal work schedules, although their problems differ only in degree from those of other workers with unusual timetables. Families with non-conventional working schedules cannot expect to be able to put in place conventional systems of organisation and roles. Indeed, if they try to do so they will be making a mistake.[142]

In their study of the strategies used by various families when faced with the periodic absences of the father, Forsyth and Gramling found five systems:

- Family authority alternating between husband and wife.
- Conflict type of authority: The wife exercises authority when the husband is away at sea, but they disagree on who has authority when he returns.
- Replacement authority: The authority of the husband/father is exercised by another male relation while the husband is away at sea.
- Contingent authority: There is no transfer of authority, but authority is exercised by the wife for urgent matters, while the husband retains authority at all times.
- Transferred authority: The husband is a periodic guest and the wife assumes the traditional roles of father and mother, except in respect of being the major source of income.

In order to carry out this study, the authors took a sample of 141 families of merchant seamen over a period of 7 years (1981-1987). Of the people interviewed, 111 were merchant seamen, 29 were wives and 23 adult sons or daughters, 89 were officers or family members of officers and 52 lower-ranking seamen or family members of same. The 44% opted for solution c) (substitution of the father by another male family member), 23.4% came into conflict when the husband returned (case b).

**Substitution of the father/husband:** In this type of solution the father or brother of the seaman take on this role in his absence, although it is even more common for this to be done by a male member of the wife's family. When it comes to choosing a place of residence, many families of seamen choose a place close to the wife's family. This gives the seaman considerable peace of mind, given that powerlessness when he is at sea in the face of certain difficulties is a cause of worry.

**Conflict:** The situation of conflict arises when the wife takes decisions and takes over typically masculine tasks in the absence of the husband. When both are together, they share responsibilities. When the husband goes away he realises that she starts taking initiatives on matters he used to decide. The wife, for her part, is annoyed when the husband returns and wishes to exercise the authority to which she has become accustomed.

This phenomenon arises, for example, with the children's upbringing. A woman who has acted as father and mother feels put out when her husband tries to correct certain aspects of the children's behaviour or criticises the way she is bringing them up. And if the wife stands firm, claiming what she feels is her right, then the husband will feel that he is a nobody in his own house and in front of his own children. And a wife who finds herself criticised for what she does when she is alone will at times see her own husband as a stranger who comes and disturbs her life.

In one of the interviews carried out by Forsyth and Gramling, one wife declared:

*I have problems each time he comes home ... his way my way they don't seem to match ... my schedule gets screwed up ... the children don't listen ... he just comes in and takes over like he has been here for two months ... after he leaves I take about a week to straighten it back out.*

While another wife remarked:

*He would come home and cause problems with everybody. He would tell the children they could do things that broke the rules I had made —then argue with me about it. It was good to have him home, but after a few days of arguing he just got in the way. His leaving had sort of a double edge. I missed him ... At some point ... the fighting stopped.*

**Contingent authority:** The most controversial aspect in this case is the upbringing of the children. The mother clearly acts in the name of the father, who is the one who then gives the finishing touches when he comes home. Here, the father has the role of the severe one, which is not easy.

A captain aged fifty or so stated:

*A seaman whose children are well-behaved is lucky. If they're not he has his work cut out for him. If when he comes home he tries to sort them out, then they'll think "that bugger may just as well go back to his ship", but if he does not want a bad time at home and just ignores it they'll think "he's a pushover" and won't get any better.*

**Periodic guest:** The long periods of absence mean that the seaman becomes a periodic guest, on a visit. It is difficult to maintain a stable family relationship on the basis of four months' contact a year (and all the more so if it is only a month).

Due to not having lived home life on a day-to-day basis, seamen arriving home after a period of absence feel like strangers. For the seaman himself the house and the people he left when went away are not exactly the same. It is very common for both the seaman and his family to have the impression that he is there on something like a visit. Apart from the feeling of strangeness which can be caused by the period of separation, another factor of importance is that when the seaman returns home he is on holiday, while the other members of the family may have to continue going about their daily business.

In a family in which the children go to school, or in the case of an older son or daughter to work, and the wife bears the entire brunt of running the home and may even go out to work too, a person who gets up late long after the others, who goes out for strolls because he doesn't know what else to do, who has a clear notion that after so many months at sea it's his turn to have a good time, becomes a guest on a visit. This status marginalises him, for he is different from the rest of his family.

A seaman interviewed by Forsyth and Gramling said:

*My wife does a great job with the kids. I don't want to mess up her system. Sometimes I feel left out... I only put in my two cents when someone asks me to.*

For Forsyth and Gramling, the periodic-guest strategy is the only viable one, in the absence of a close relative. This is because most merchant seamen's families are from a traditional working class background and have certain values and concepts of family roles. When one of these families faces the absence of the father, the initial response is to retain the traditional family structure when it comes to replacing the husband and father figure. If a close relative is not available, then the family begins what seems to be an inevitable transition to the non-traditional family, in which situation the authority of the father gradually decreases while that of the mother increases.

The conclusion of the study carried out by these authors is that families are affected not so much by the absence of the father as by the strategy used. The father accepts being a periodic guest rather than falling into what MacIver (1950) calls a state of "anomie" (lack of social meaning). The state of conflictive authority and that of contingent authority both involve states of anomie for the merchant seaman.

As a periodic guest, the seaman will not have to wage battle with his wife, nor will he have to play a role in which he is uncomfortable before the children. This is the least ambiguous arrangement. The mother assumes a role of laying down the disciplinary rules and takes the necessary measures to enforce them. The father nevertheless retains a highly important function, that of being the breadwinner.

In a study commissioned by the Ministry of Transport and Communications[143] and carried out in Flensburg, Germany, on board fifteen ships on different voyages, 43.9% of the crew members interviewed felt that life at sea was a heavy burden on family relationships, while 23% felt that it only affected them to a certain extent. Family breakup was feared by 36.3%, while 61.5% thought that the absence of the husband was very hard for wives. According to 86.8% of those surveyed, wives were not self-sufficient and when faced with difficult situations had recourse to relatives or friends.

Furthermore, 38.5% had the impression that due to their lengthy periods apart their wives had become more independent and that when the husband, back home on holiday, wished to take certain decisions then tensions arose. This problem occurred basically with crew of a certain age, probably due to their already having formed preconceived notions about decision-making authority in the sphere of the family.

In 1984, a survey carried out by the Apostleship of the Sea in Spain[144] also looked at the subject of seamen's families and, quite apart from specific replies, in the port of Vigo the following words of seamen's wives and children were recorded:

*The husband's presence in the house, during his short stays, makes for an agitated life, as he wishes to live intensely the little time we have together ...*

*Your husband sometimes ends up becoming just a current account at a bank.*

*Living together in peace is difficult when his stays are long.*

*I discuss the important things with my father, but day-to-day things with my mother ... that's our usual way.*

*When my father tells me off, the thing is forgotten the next moment; but when my mum punishes you with chores you have to make sure you do them.*

Both the study in Germany and the survey by the Apostleship of the Sea in Spain confirm the view of Forsyth and Gramling. In relations with wives and children, the avoidance of conflicts of authority by delegating authority broadly on the mother makes for peaceful relations, though it can give rise to distancing.

Seamen wrap themselves up in routine, get used to calm; many aspects of life at sea are tough, but others are comfortable: you have work, but your time off on a merchant ship is yours. Families get used to doing without the husband and father and, even where there are warm bonds of affection, the lack of daily life together creates an enormous gap.[145] Having accepted that life at sea is a serious obstacle for family life, and having seen that the occasional-guest approach seemed to be the best of the possible solutions to division of authority, we should perhaps add some further observations.

It is undoubtedly extremely important for seamen and their families that holiday periods, the time they spend together, are satisfactory for all. If this is not the case, the initial looking forward to meeting up again will be converted into frustration, and this will in the longer term undermine the family relationship.

Seamen must of course delegate day-to-day family authority on their wives, but that should not mean setting the matter entirely to one side, as that does not normally please wives either. Today's communications systems permit more or less frequent contact with the family and thus the possibility of taking part in decision-making or simply sharing problems with the family. Husbands at sea who have participated in this manner will find when they get back home that, although day-to-day life is organised by the mother, they do not have the feeling of counting for nothing. Their children will also feel closer to them. From their position of enforced solitude, seamen can fall into the temptation of creating their own fortresses and shuffling out family problems and, by extension, social problems in general. From saying "I can't do anything from here" it is possible to sink to "I don't care about anything".

Another aspect to be taken into account is the tendency seamen have to fantasise about life on land and about their own families, which often leads to feelings of frustration when reality does not coincide with fantasy.

Having reflected on the problems of the seaman's family, we will now look at what family reunion means to a seaman.

### 4.4.2 Family integration

*One obvious characteristic of the seaman's family is that the seaman goes to sea and, as a result, it is clear that a professional seafarer's family will have to operate within a context of present or potential separation throughout his professional life.*[146] This situation is clearly intrinsic to the seagoing profession. It can be alleviated by frequent holidays, made easier to put up with by better and more regular communications, and so forth, but a seaman's family knows that one way or another it has to live with this situation. This is why, in speaking of women as professionals of the sea[147] it became clear that the greatest problem was not whether women were better or worse accepted as professionals on ships, nor the degree of aptitude they might have for the job, but the repercussions on family life and how in the case of a woman being a seafarer practically meant giving up motherhood and founding a home, at least in the sense traditionally accorded the term.

This separation is the reason why a seaman remains outside the day-to-day events in his family, and as a result outside the taking of many decisions.

Forsyth[148] carried out a study of the occupational traits and relationship with land of the merchant seaman which pre-shape his awareness of family integration.

The occupational factor was measured by five variables:
- factors used to measure the occupational factor:
  - number of years at sea;
  - annual time spent at sea;
  - length of trips.
- factors affecting the isolation experienced by merchant seamen:
  - sailing always in the same ship;
  - always having the same job aboard ship.

According to Forsyth, the seaman who has worked for the better part of his career in permanent positions is more likely to develop interpersonal ties with other seamen, thereby reducing the isolation experienced. Because the seaman spends so much of his time aboard ship, his job status aboard should have a relationship to family integration.

In fact, there is usually more continuity on ships amongst the officers than amongst the ratings, as they are changed from ship to ship more readily. This factor, linked to officers' greater ease of taking part in shoreside associations, for Forsyth makes it easier for officers than for ratings to achieve a higher degree of family integration.

In assessing the influence of occupational traits on the level of family integration, Forsyth considers the following factors:
- The nature of the community of residence should affect the degree of family integration. The size of the community, for example, may be expected to contribute to the degree of social integration the seaman maintains. The size of a community and its level of complexity are considered to be determinants of individual and group integration. [149] Forming part of a community with a complex degree of interaction lends individuals the capacity to maintain links over a distance.
- Geographical mobility is a negative factor for integration. An individual who lives in a fixed place, with more or less stable associates, will find social integration easier than an individual who lives now here, now there, without any fixed core of people with whom he feels he has ties. The seafaring world throws up many examples of men with considerable underlying uprootedness. Such persons may show themselves to be indifferent while others miss their families deeply, and then gradually as they grow older this uprootedness leaves an ever deepening imprint upon them, to the point where they become people who could only adapt with difficulty to a traditional social and family life.

- Participation in religious or other associations is also necessary, for those who endeavour to keep up such institutional affiliations find the effects of their isolation less onerous.
- Education, too, is a factor which helps to maintain a greater degree of integration with the home.[150] A person who has received instruction undoubtedly has available greater resources for distance cultivation of integration into a social group.
- Finally, having children must be considered to be a social binder which helps individuals to overcome the negative social consequences of solitude on board.[151]

Forsyth carried out a study among 132 married seamen to analyse the influence of the above-mentioned factors in family integration of the seaman. Although the duration of trips and the years a seaman has been in the profession are good indicators of family integration, he found that the degree of separation counted in months at sea appears to be particularly influential. What matters is not so much the number of years at sea, or if there are many short trips or fewer longer ones, but rather the total time of separation from the family.

The relationship between status on board and family integration suggests that prestige on board and the degree of social privation associated with status on board is carried over into seamen's associations on land.

A pattern of stable trips, with the same workmates, promotes a relationship between those men both on land and at sea. The effects on family integration of size of community, religious participation, education, having children and being a member of some organisation are in line with general social integration.

Forsyth's study showed that the more time a seaman has spent at sea the less integrated he will be in his family. His family integration is influenced by certain social characteristics. The level of a merchant seaman's family integration depends also on his participation in associations and organisations.

### 4.4.3 Communication with the family

Communication is a basic factor in maintaining integration with the family. Despite distance, there are seamen who continue to take part in all the major decisions taken in their families, while there are others who prefer to delegate all authority in their wives and so remain outside of events which they might have taken part in at a distance. In any case seafarers, and especially married ones, think of their families a lot.

Letters are sacred for seamen. Joseba Beobide, national director of Spain's Apostleship of the Sea and chaplain to the port of Pasajes[152] declared: *"The postal service in Newfoundland is such a sensitive issue that the crew have refused to work because the captain would not go 20 or 30 miles off their course in order to collect the mail. (On fishing vessels the mail is thrown overboard with a buoy by vessels coming from land out to sea and then picked up by the other fishing vessels.)... On one occasion we had been nearly a month at sea when the mail arrived, given us by another vessel, and there was one seaman, the only one, who had not received a single letter. I remember the man being as affected by this as if he had been struck a blow in the face. In an attempt to cheer him up I said, "Come on, man, there may have been some letter they accidentally kept on the other vessel"; his reply was, "When I get home I'll have a thing or two to say to my wife". Fortunately, his letter had been given in error to a companion, who brought it over to him right away. I can still see that man's face now, when he saw that he was after all the same as the rest ... When the mail is received crew members retire to their cabins, disappearing like rabbits down burrows."*

Letters play a very important role in the lives of seamen. Writing letters means communicating with those one loves and involving them in what one is experiencing. A postcard is often just a greeting, without any further content. A letter is different, and most seamen write letters during the trip, this being a time when they converse with their wives and children. As they write, seamen usually look at the photos they keep on their bedside tables or walls. Such times, with thoughts on their homes, are times when they experience intimacy and in a way have their families there in the cabin.

And letters are to be savoured. They are given a quick first reading, to see if there is any news, and then they are read slowly, with relish. In the life of a couple, long letters are a very valid means of keeping in contact.

When a ship arrives in port, two things are of particular concern. One is whether the mail has arrived; all eyes are on the shipping agent's briefcase, from which the bundle of letters will emerge. The other thing is where they can post the letters they have written. On ships which tie up near a city where they will be staying a couple of days, this is not a matter of such great concern, as there will be opportunities to post them. But on short stopovers, sometimes only of hours, everybody makes sure he gets his letters into the hands of the agent.

At the beginning of the year 2000, however, the telephone began to take on an unusually important role, basically due to the proliferation of telephone cards that make it possible to call anywhere in the world at economic rates. Talking represents immediacy, as well as the opportunity of listening to the voice of a loved one. For this reason, obtaining these telephone cards has turned into a sailor's main objective upon arriving at a port.

At seafarer's welfare centres, such as Stella Maris and other similar centres, this is the most requested service, as is the internet, which, little by little, is taking on greater importance, because not only does it allow for receiving and sending emails, but also the possibility of attaching photos, as well as chatting or looking for newspaper articles from any country.

One method which does not find a warm welcome is that of sending recorded cassette tapes. In Joseba Beobide's words: *I was surprised at the reaction of the crew, not one of happiness but quite the contrary; they asked me not to have them sent, because they made too strong an impression.*

Hearing voices as if shut inside a cassette box leaves one sad, accentuates the feeling of distance. The telephone, which also has its negative side because it leaves one a little sad due to increasing considerably the desire to return home, has the positive side of being a live conversation and the communication being reciprocal. Upon hearing a tape, you would like to reply but you can't, and each time you play it this gets worse.

### 4.4.4 The family on board

The presence on board of a seaman's wife or even a son or daughter, is an aspect deserving special attention, presenting as it does a facet that does not arise in other total institutions.

**Presence of families in port**

The presence of family members on board while a ship is tied up in port is properly speaking simply a visit, which can also take place in other total institutions. There is one important difference, however, since visits to the inmates of a prison, a convent, a barracks or a psychiatric hospital are external visits which do not include unrestricted entry to the premises, or overnight stays, or unrestricted living alongside all members of the institution.

When a ship enters port, the wives who come aboard, sometimes accompanied by a son or daughter, will stay in the cabin with their husbands and over the days of the stay in port will share with him the cabin, dining room and, in general, all the usual areas of the ship.

An atmosphere different from the usual day-to-day atmosphere is created. At meal times, the presence of family members can cause the drift of conversations to change completely. If there are several wives together, they may talk about the more common themes of life on land, such as their children or the film they saw the night before. Those who have such company will have a feeling of re-integration into that life on land, which seemed to have forgotten about them.

The single men, on the other hand, or those who had been unable to receive anybody, will quite possibly feel a little ill at ease, as if displaced from their own world by people who do not belong to it. An untypical atmosphere may thus be created on board ship in such circumstances.

**The presence of family members at sea**

Particularly amongst the crew members of developed countries, it is quite common for some crew members' wives to travel aboard. This is not so common amongst Third World crews. Without going into great detail, some points can be made about the reasons behind this.

From the shipowner's point of view, a wife can embark for a more or less limited period of, say, a month or two months. Only seamen with individual cabins can have their wives aboard. And family circumstances naturally have their influence: if the wife has children or if she works, she will find that she has only a very limited time for embarking.

Furthermore, except if the home is in a port at which the ship calls quite regularly, embarking will mean travelling to some other city or even some other country, and that will involve expense which cannot always be afforded. If a plane has to be taken, and especially if travel overseas is involved, the cultural level and worldly know-how of the wife will also be a factor of influence.

From all these points it will be clear that the wives of officers, and particularly those from industrialised countries, will normally accompany their husbands more often that those of crew members from the Third World. In this last case the low wages of the crew members, the long trips usually undertaken by ships from their countries, domestic obligations and the scant level of attention often received by such crew members aboard will often be insurmountable obstacles.

The presence of one or more wives on board also has an influence on daily life, especially at meal times. Their presence makes the atmosphere more normal, and gives a fresh cast to the routine of life on board. Conversations will be different and the crew will be more careful and more polite in their speech.

From the point of view of the total institution, if visits in port had no equivalent in other institutions, then the case of a wife travelling with her crew member husband is totally alien to any other type of total institution, given that during the trip she will become part of the crew, even if in the capacity of accompanying family. To that end, she will have to have a seamen's book and be enrolled on board.

She will differ from the other crew members in that she has no contractual relationship with the shipowner and therefore no professional duties or pay; she will have no responsibilities and will not belong to any department. She is simply the wife of a crew member. However, the fact of being on board and of taking part in the overall day-to-day life lends her certain characteristics which make her part of the total institution. She is one more person in a group which remains isolated for such time as the trip lasts. In this situation, she is no more free that any crew member to leave the ship. She will also be subject in a way to authority, not in strictly professional terms but rather as a member of a community. During her stay on board her world will be delimited by the sides of the ship.

She will not become fully integrated on board, however, for apart from being "so and so's wife" she will have no other role and the fact of knowing herself to be a visitor will be an obstacle preventing her really forming part of the total institution. Thus, she will take part in the life of the institution but will not be a member of it as such.

### 4.5 Rejoining family life: returning home

The situation of the seaman on board ship, putting up with pitching and yawing of the vessel, noises and vibration, going here and there wherever he is sent, to places not of his own choosing, in the company of people with whom for the most part his ties are purely professional, is a situation experienced with a feeling of uprootedness from what he considers to be his world, that is, his town, his family, his friends.

Except for the younger men going to sea in search of adventure, seamen do their job, as we have seen, in order to support their families. Although they might initially have gone to sea out of vocation, the toughness of the life they have to live means that they do not take long to come to see it as a sacrifice.

Seamen live, then, thinking of land, of their houses, of their relations. And there comes a day when they go home.

The reaction a seamen, and his family, will feel will be directly influenced by the length of time the separation has lasted. It is not the same to go back home after a fortnight as after three months or a year. The longer the period of separation and the less the communication over that time the greater may be the surprise of the return home.

During his stay on board, a seaman will have spent much time thinking of his family and his return home, often idealising them. When he finds himself back home with his family, even if he is overflowing with happiness he will find once the first few days have passed that he easily feels out of place. Fina Santos,[153] wife of a deep-sea fisherman, who used to spend periods of five or six months away from home, observed: *Many seamen, when on holidays, spend a long time outside of the house, in the bar, with friends, as if they can't stand much time inside the house.*

And a distinction should be drawn between disembarking for holidays and returning home for good to rejoin family life in a stable way. Later we will look at the finer nuances of the situation, but for now we will look in generic terms at what returning home means.

*The man returning home foresees return to a setting of which he always had and believes he still has an intimate knowledge and which he only has to presuppose to orient himself within it. An outsider approaching the group has to anticipate more or less blindly what he will find in it: the man returning home only has to have recourse to his memory. That is what he believes, and due to that belief he will suffer the typical upset Homer describes in the Odyssey, when Ulysses returns to his country after twenty years and does not recognise it.*[154] Over the time he has been away, the seaman will have been thinking about his home just as he left it. As he approaches his home he imagines what he will find, the reaction of the people in it, the smell of the house, the noise of the familiar streets, all that has accompanied him in his memories.

He will nevertheless find that many things and many people are not exactly the same as they were; what is more, in attempting to recognise himself in what was his own setting, he will notice that he too has changed.[155]

Home means one thing for the person who has never left it, another for the person who lives far from it, and yet another for the person returning to it.[156] Home life stands for a number of people, things, experiences, sensations, etc. In the work cited, Alfred Schutz notes that according to a publication of the Marine Engineering Corps, Chevron, a survey carried out amongst US soldiers during the war in the Pacific pointed out that what most surprised them, apart from their families, wives or girlfriends, were everyday things like *"a lettuce sandwich with tomato, fresh milk, the morning paper, the whistle of a locomotive ..."*

People who live regularly in their homes become used to a number of sensations which they are scarcely even aware of. It is normal to see their wives every day, it is normal to talk to their children, it is normal to have coffee and toast for breakfast each day, it is normal to see a certain bus passing the house, and so forth.

Home life is a template for living, a set of customs, habits, traditions, timetables, and so on. All this is reflected in ways of doing things, ways of relating to others, ways of looking at life, of facing problems and of planning the future. The way of life in the home marks the acts of its members.

*The system of significations adopted by the members of the endogroup shows a high degree of conformity. I have a good chance of predicting how others will act towards me, and how others will react to my own social acts.*[157]

As we saw in speaking of the internal life of the ship institution, these connotations also arise in some way in the human group known as crew, the life of which is marked by customs and habits and by interrelation between persons who, from seeing each other continuously, can practically guess at any given time what the other person is going to say.

Within the relationship in the home, there is an awareness not only of "me" and "you" but of "us", showing belonging to the same group. People who usually live together, even where that living together is interrupted on a daily basis by the various tasks each has to do, do not find their living together interrupted and so, when they are together again, can resume their relations entirely normally.

A person who leaves home leaves that microcosmos and no longer takes part in all those details and moments which form daily life and mean that members of the family feel themselves to be such. On departure from home, a person carries away an "us", a relationship, which is as it was on the day he set out on his travels.

From that time, however, he will no longer share his family's experiences, the place they live in, what a neighbour said, what happened in the next town, a joy or disappointment experienced by somebody in the family or by friends. The experience lived day to day is replaced by memories. The people back home are no longer co-participants in a dialogue, in a friendly relationship. The picture he has of them is no longer accompanied by a thousand gestures or expressions. The immediate nature of their relations, in which a word from one gives rise to a word from another, has come to an end.

A person leaving home places a full stop on their lives together and from that time will replace those people with memories, memories which are as if anchored in one instant of time. It is like a photo in which we see a person at a certain time and in ten years time just the same, while if we were to see them in flesh and blood we would see how much they have changed.

At the same time, a person who has left home lives through a number of experiences which his folk have played no part in. He comes into contact with new people, in different situations, and new habits are learned. After a certain time, certain habits of the new group into which he has integrated are even acquired.

We thus find a sort of branching off. The longer the separation lasts the greater the distancing will become, the greater mismatch there will be between the person remembered and the present-day person. There are means of communication, such as the telephone and correspondence. Letters, between people who enjoy facility of expression by that channel and devote time to writing lots of pages, will doubtless help considerably in keeping up to date on the day-to-day events, in taking part in the mutual daily growth as a person. There is nonetheless a big difference between this letter-based dialogue and a face-to-face relationship, for the world in which a person lives from day to day is made up not only of what he thinks or of outside, objective events, but rather a whole wealth of details and a way of living.

Another means is the telephone. Apart from being able to hear the voice and to talk, getting an instant reply, this method is hindered by high cost, so that one cannot describe as much as in a letter.

*From the viewpoint of the absent person, the desire to re-establish the former intimacy, with things as well as with people, is a special characteristic known as "yearning". However, the change we have described in the system of meanings and in the degree of intimacy is experienced by the absent person in a different way than by the household group.*

*The latter continues its daily life within its usual pattern.*[158]

This feeling of yearning can be reciprocal, but there are differences. The absent person finds it easier to evoke the home, the loved ones, for he knows where they live, what they do each day, and so forth. It is more difficult for those waiting back at home to situate the absent one in their minds. A seaman can situate his family with a thought, and can even, by looking at his watch, think that at a certain time they'll be having their dinner or that the children will be in school, or they'll be sleeping.

The seaman's family will imagine him on ship, one that they may not know, surrounded by people about whom they quite possibly know little or nothing, and they do not know if the ship is tossed in heavy seas or sailing calmly, if it will arrive in port on a certain date or will be delayed.

During the time he is away, the seaman has been a member of a crew containing people of different characters, with all together adopting the same timetables, forming relationships, having good times and bad times, giving each other nicknames, doing a job and adopting some kind of internal rules.

A member of a crew acquires a sense of belonging to that human group, and it is in that group that his professional tasks take on meaning through habits inherent to seafaring folk.

Within the framework of total institutions, rejoining external life generally poses problems. In the case of penal institutions, it is worrying to find high rates of recidivism during temporary absence (as in the case of leave permits) or when the sentence ends. What is of interest here is how studies done on the matter reveal the effect of the closed institution on the subsequent development of the person in the outside world.[159] When a seaman returns home, he realises that when he wishes to explain what he has experienced there is a kind of short circuit, and he has the feeling that many of the things he is describing or trying to describe are not being understood. A similar feeling is in fact experienced by anybody who has been on a trip with a group of friends and has experienced a number of events and then finds that all that cannot be conveyed in any meaningful way to those who remained at home.

And Alfred Schutz notes another problem, which he puts as follows: *This discrepancy between the singularity and decisive importance which the absent one attributes to his experiences and the fact that the people at home pseudotypify them and attribute them a pseudo-meaning is one of the greatest obstacles to the mutual re-establishment of interrupted "we" relationships.*[160]

That is, the people who have stayed at home, who have not shared in the experiences of the absent one, will have imagined a world in which the absent one moves which will always be different from his real world. Land-based people see seamen as they have been seen in so many films, and will always situated them in their minds according to frameworks which can quite easily diverge from the truth of the situation.

The seaman returning home thus finds that he has returned to a home which is not the same as the one he left and that the people —including himself— are not the same as they were.

We have a picture from films and novels of the soldier returning from the war and suffering a real shock. It is obvious that in time of war people can experience considerable changes over a short period of time, and that it is therefore only natural that those returning home cannot identify what they find, those they left behind. But, to remain with Alfred Schutz, an important part of the problem is also that the soldier returning home after living for months under a military lifestyle with its discipline and viewpoints suddenly feels deprived of meaning, as a whole range of rules, criteria and even ways of looking at the world lose their significance.

A seaman feels rather disorientated when he returns home. On the one hand, there are the timetables. At sea, lunch is at eleven in the morning and dinner at six in the evening. If he was on lookout from four to eight, then he'd go to bed at ten or eleven and get up at a quarter to four in the morning. Some seamen, when they return home, find that they wake up early in the morning for the first few days, as their bodies have become used to a certain time pattern.

Over the months he has been alone he will have lived in a small cabin, but in it he will have been able to do as he pleases. Now he finds that he has to fit in with a different lifestyle in which he has to participate a lot more. On the ship he simply did his job and in his free time he did not have to talk to anybody if he didn't want to. Such an attitude is not acceptable at home.

If he is a seaman with a position of authority, such as a captain, then on board ship he is the one who gives the orders and who, in a way, everybody serves. An Italian captain told me that one of the things that struck him most when he was on holidays was going to a public office and having to wait in a queue. On the ship, of course, he was used to simply calling and having anything he might need brought to his cabin, or, if on land, having the agent place a taxi at his disposal for getting about in the city. A person who has a post of authority and who is obeyed in the professional sphere cannot usually accept cheerfully having barriers placed on his authority when he returns home, thus becoming just another member of the family.

We thus reach the conclusion that returning home is not easy. Its difficulty will depend, amongst many other factors, on the length of the period of separation, the frequency of such periods and the amount of contact kept with the family. In any case, reunion with the family calls for a certain amount of psychological preparation, patience and mutual understanding. In fact, and except in the odd cases which can be found, as time passes, and especially if the periods of separation are long and the periods together short, distancing occurs between the family members and the seaman. Some people when away from home dream of reunion, but after a few days together again start to argue and do not feel as they thought they would while waiting.

This is one of the reasons why it is said that a person wishing to leave the sea should do so while still young. After twenty years at sea a seaman will find it difficult to adapt again to life on land. Amongst other factors he will have hardly any friends, and the type of work and life on land may not appeal to him. When a seaman retires, too, he will have difficulty getting used to normal land life. Many seamen, once a certain number of years at sea have passed, fear the day when they will be unable to return to their familiar world of the sea.[161] Rejoining home life, then, is not easy either for the person returning home or the one awaiting him. On many foreign vessels, especially ones flying flags of convenience, seamen have only two months' holiday a year. Moreover, if we bear in mind that over that period they hardly ever see their families, then we will see that there really is an imbalance.

On Spanish vessels, with frequent holidays of, say, two months for every four at sea, the problem will lie in that the seamen on holiday will at first be there at home without knowing what to do, given that during that time the rest of the family will have their daily tasks to get on with.

Apart from the specific and particular disconnection between the seaman and his family, there are two factors which stand as obstacles to the seaman's smooth return home: isolation on board, especially in the case of small crews, and social isolation in general. Both factors affect seamen by reducing their capacity for making a successful return to their families[162].

That is, apart from the factors considered so far, such as lack of day-to-day living together and the fact of having lived different situations and lives over lengthy periods, which could explain the difficulty seamen often find in rejoining their own families, there are other factors which simply lead to a loss of sociability, due to the isolation experienced by a person over lengthy periods of time.

## 4.6 Seamen rejoining society on land

Goffman describes a number of mental processes which arise in an intern prior to going out into the free world and upon going out into it. He speaks of anxiety at the idea of liberalisation and stigmatisation. A seaman, after several months aboard ship, more or less separated from a society with which he has maintained irregular contact, highly dependent on the type of route his ship plies, and having received news of events he has not personally lived, has adopted a routine of life, with professional or personal problems which he has gone along solving as best he could, but always as an individual or as a member of a crew.

And in terms of his town or city, when he reaches it after a spell at sea he looks at it all somewhat as if he had to rediscover places. The clubs, recreational associations, and cultural and political associations have all followed their own course and he is a visitor.

Thus a sailor who on board ship had a place, despite all the defects of life aboard and all the isolation and so forth, knew that he was part of a crew and had his particular job in it, feels as the time to leave the ship draws near a certain disquiet, perhaps nervousness or anxiety. This will of course depend on each person, on his family and the relations he has maintained with it, the length of time he has been away, the atmosphere which existed on board, and so on, but he will quite likely feel such disquiet upon disembarking.

On his arrival home, there will be a cluster of sensations. The joy of reunion, the happiness of having a certain amount of time to be with his family again, will be very strong feelings marking the reunion. Simultaneously, however, over the first few days he may feel a certain unease at feeling a little out of place, at wishing to assimilate in a matter of hours what others experienced over months.

And meeting up with friends can be disappointing, when the seaman realises that he in indeed outside the group.

Another experience can be that of a bachelor who may have nobody on land, but who is set down ashore to enjoy holidays though at heart has no clear idea of what he will do.

It is said that seamen do not usually feel they are the same as land-based men. In part they feel superior, and in part inferior. Their hard life, their crossing of seas and putting up with hardships, getting to know far-off countries and always going from here to there lends them something of the air of adventurers in the eyes of "landlubbers" and can often be a source of admiration. They will then feel proud of their job and might feel superior to those around them. On the other hand, in ordinary everyday life on land, when faced with people with other jobs, or when it comes to giving an opinion on sundry matters with which land people have day-to-day familiarity, they may often feel inferior.

As the years go by, a seaman may find it increasingly difficult to take up a job on land. He feels that he doesn't know how to do anything other than sail the seas, and the longer he has spent at sea the more difficult he will find it to get used to the ways of life and work on land.

Furthermore, where the seaman also had a post of authority on board, he may regret going from being someone important in a small community to being nobody in a large community.

This will arise particularly in the case of captains, who aboard ship really are the highest authorities and are not accustoming to having anybody dispute their orders. When they set foot on land they lose that status, and if they take up another job then they are unlikely, at least at first, to enjoy such authority.

## 4.7 Seamen's welfare centres

We have already referred several times to these centres, whose mission is to provide the seaman with a pleasant and welcoming atmosphere which he knows has been created for him and where nobody will try to exploit him but will, rather, try to make a seaman feel that even in a distant port there is someone who takes an interest in him as a person.

Most of these centres belong to the Catholic Church and other religious denominations. The Catholic Apostleship of the Sea centres are usually called Stella Maris, while the Anglican Mission to Seamen centres are usually called Flying Angel. And there are many others of various denominations, such as the Evangelical Deutsche Seemanns Mission, the British Sailor's Society and so forth.

Their importance lies in the fact that nearly all seamen when they arrive in an unknown port usually ask after these centres, which become points of reference and confidence for them.

In order to combine their efforts, the various Christian organisations for seamen have since 1972 formed part of an ecumenical society called the International Christian Maritime Association (ICMA).

What does it mean to a seaman to receive a visit on board ship or be invited to attend a club which is his club, since it was thought up for him? It means knowing that there is a place he can go to seek advice, friendly attention, religious attention, and so forth. It means knowing that someone is thinking of him.

Many ports throughout the world have an Apostleship of the Sea or other similar centres, and seamen very often go to them, even if only as points of reference. Seamen often go to them as a resting stage, for they know that an attempt to help them will always be made there. The existence of such centres means that seamen feel more integrated.

There are at present some 2,400 centres worldwide. International meetings are held from time to time to discuss the most burning issues of the human situation at sea. Nineteen World Congresses of the Apostolatus Maris and seven Plenary Conferences of the ICMA have been held to date. Represented at meetings of ILO work committees, they often intervene before shipowners or shipowners associations to call attention to all the human aspects affecting life at sea.

In Spain, the Apostleship of the Sea was founded in Barcelona in 1929 by Fr. Brugada, and was extended later to other parts of the country. Right from its outset, it has not only turned its attention to the seamen themselves, but has also engaged in important work with seamen's families. At the beginning of the 'seventies it took in the pioneers of the then clandestine Sindicato Libre de la Marina Mercante (Free Merchant Navy Trade Union), by then in the last years of the Franco dictatorship, and in whose work many chaplains of the Apostleship of the Sea were involved. It also coordinated the campaign of seamen's wives for the famous "2 x 5" (two months at home for every five at sea), when in countries such at France terms were by then two months for every four.

In the fishing sector Spain's Apostleship of the Sea, along with that of France, is waging a stern struggle in Brussels to defend fishermen against the Community authorities. In Vigo, the "Rosa Dos Ventos" fishermen's wives association is a major front in the face of fishing fleet owners and before the Ministry of Agriculture and Fisheries, in support of fishermen's rights.

# 5

# crew recruitment and organisation criteria

In approaching this last chapter, we will have to run though the more significant points we have noted in order to seek responses, and to explore what the future may hold in store for the crews of merchant ships and what fields of research are opening up before us.

With this in mind, after setting out the human problems of the maritime profession, we will turn to a number of papers and studies produced in various countries that attempt to find criteria for defining what merchant ships should be like in human terms in the immediate future and what the characteristics of their crews should be.

## 5.1 Merchant ships as total institutions: the implications

We began this work by looking at the characteristic traits of total institutions, and we have indeed found all the inherent features of such institutions in merchant ships.

Can we draw any valid conclusions for the ships and their crews?

The total institution inherently has such a powerful impact on the activity for which it was created that it is difficult to draw the line between the group of human beings as a social nucleus of people living together and that group as the performers of the activity concerned.

Naturally, how well the people involved get on together has an influence on any work, but when this shared life goes beyond the strict limits of the joint activity they are intended to perform, and when the person cannot get away from a given role, then the conditions of life for that person have a decisive influence on his private life, and thus on his capacity to perform that activity.

Let us take concentration camps as an example. Their purpose is to keep people confined while making it as easy as possible for their keepers to stay in control. So what do they do? On the one hand they look for threats they can use, and sometimes make an example of an inmate to instil fear in the others, and on the other they set up a busy schedule of activities so that the inmates get tired and have little time for thinking about other things.

If the institution is a monastery, we can see that the purpose is the contemplative life, study, prayer... All the rules governing the community are aimed at creating life habits through which the monk can attain a degree of personal balance that makes him really capable of leading the life he has chosen.

On a ship, the purpose of the crew, as we have seen, is to make it possible for the ship to undertake certain shipping work. However, if this is to be done, the people who do it must be fed, be allowed to rest properly, and also be able to engage in some level of human relation in order live in a psychically balanced way.

And this is something that the authorities and the shipping companies find very hard to appreciate. They take account of certain requirements in terms of primary necessities, such as food to eat and a bed to sleep in, but when seamen ask for something to enable them to pursue their free time in a rewarding way, the request is regarded as a whim.

The importance of physical exercise, in the form of swimming (in a swimming pool) or table tennis for example, is not recognised. Neither is the importance of not having marginalised individuals aboard. In fact even the need for having a launch to take crew members ashore when the ship is at anchor by a port roadstead is often ignored. And such examples could easily be multiplied...

The problem is that if such elemental factors are frequently disregarded, how can we expect any account to be taken of the importance of creating an atmosphere of togetherness aboard, in which the seafarer can feel that he is a human being first, and then a seaman?

Everything we have said does, I believe, highlight the decisive influence of the man as a person on the man as a crew member.

Some people and bodies have already adopted this view, and so we will devote this last chapter to considering the ships and crews of the future from the sociological standpoint.

## 5.2 The personal and professional significance of good relations aboard ship

While good relations in the workplace are important anywhere and under any circumstances, they are much more important still when the workplace is also the setting for one's leisure time. When this is the case, work-related problems will influence personal problems, and vice versa.

Most problems arising on board stem from people-related problems rather than work-related ones. Cases of psychosomatic complaints and fully-fledged psychological disorders, leading at times to suicide, are unfortunately fairly common in the merchant marine.

And while such problems can easily arise from the isolation and humdrum routine of life on board any ship, we find that on ships in a deplorable state, with crew members who perhaps sleep with a knife under their pillows, the seafarer might well end up feeling that there is no misery like his.

Before officers or captains can take up their posts on board, certain studies on navigational techniques are required. For the levels just below them, some experience and practical knowledge of shipboard work is needed, and for the lowest ranks, some general idea of what a ship is all about is expected. However, no attention is paid to the fact that these people, if they are to do their jobs at all, will have to be able to live together, to be properly fed, to have adequate resting time for recharging their batteries, and to have leisure opportunities to help them remain balanced as people.

A tired, demotivated, anxious, isolated person goes downhill, and his work suffers. Many accidents at sea occur against a backdrop of human failing.

Feeling alone in the middle of the ocean, seeing the people around one as anonymous beings and not trusting them - these things can make life at sea a torture. In the past, even though scant attention was paid to these sociological and psychological aspects, the shortage of seamen induced some shipping companies to go to some trouble over the welfare of their crews. Today, with large numbers of sailors from the Third World ready to man ships at any price whatever the quality of life aboard, the world of the sea has lost ground across the board in the progress towards humanisation that had begun to be made after the Second World War.

Since it is difficult to ensure international compliance with minimum standards, even if they are agreed in theory, then at least those countries which pride themselves on defending the human rights of all workers should be very much aware of the importance of human training for seafarers.

## 5.3 Crew organisation, taking account of sociological and psychological aspects

The number of crew members needed for a given ship is legally stipulated in accordance with the tonnage of the ship and the power of its engine - i.e. the number depends on technical considerations. It is true that when those in charge of factories have to calculate the number of people to be hired to achieve a given output level, they take primarily technical factors into account. When a machine or an industrial installation is designed, attention is given not only to what it can produce but also to how many people will be needed to operate it.

On ships, it is perfectly possible to reduce the number of crew members by bringing in technical improvements and by eliminating certain services. Nowadays the post of the cook can be scrapped thanks to a catering system of the kind used on airliners. The engine can be controlled from the bridge, and so long as a chief engineer and an assistant are kept in that department, nobody else is needed, since watches in the engine room can be dispensed with. If the maintenance work is done by shore teams during loading and unloading, the deck crew can be cut back to the bare essentials too. And then for manoeuvres, a couple of people fore and a couple aft will suffice.

But how well will these people perform? What motivation can they have if they spend days on end with practically nobody to talk to?

The number of crew members stipulated should take account of human communication needs and the need for company as well. Everybody should have somebody else to talk to. Here the number of people is not the only factor: having a language in common, and some cultural points of contact too, are also necessary. The food should not be too alien, and it should be possible to share customs and practices. People need to live in a social nucleus. Sociocultural habits lose their meaning at the individual level.

Furthermore, just as seamen are obliged to undergo medical check-ups from time to time, covering matters such as blood and urine analyses, lung X-rays etc., there should also be tests to check their psychic condition. Such checks would bring down the accident rate, and indeed the suicide rate too.

Other important factors needing monitoring are alcoholism and drugs. The solitary life of seamen, their easy access to cheap drinks and the availability of drugs in certain ports, all make them particularly vulnerable to these. The starting point, of course, is solitude, lack of communication, and personal frustration.

## 5.4 Recruitment schemes for future crews

### 5.4.1 Prior considerations

As techniques are refined, more stringent personnel recruitment procedures are employed in all spheres of human activity.

Let us recall a few points we made previously.

If we turn to astronauts, we see that finding people with suitable technical skills is not enough: other absolutely critical factors are their psychological characteristics and their capacity to face up to tough human-relations circumstances involving a small number of people living in close quarters over a long period of time, and so on.

Of course there is much at stake in that context, such as the very high cost of such expeditions, the risk involved, the close attention to results paid by people and by governments, the deep impression made worldwide by accidents in space ventures, and the general scientific interest in the missions.

If we turn to aviation, we cannot say that greater economic interests are involved than in sea voyages, since in ships the value of the cargo, or the number passengers, may be much higher than in an aircraft.

Nonetheless, in the early days of aviation, flying was seen as dangerous, and aviation companies wanted to earn the confidence of the general public by stressing just how carefully selected the crews were, and the meticulous care taken over everything to do with fatigue and stress in flying crews.

Even today, despite the density of air traffic all over the world and the fact that flying is regarded as the safest means of transport, safer even than travelling by road or even by sea, air crashes are always spectacular, and the causes of them are always thoroughly investigated, partly because the famous black boxes are usually found unless the plane crashes in the middle of the ocean.

With the marine, even though legislation exists in each state and even though there are international agreements, the legislation and the agreements concern themselves more with technical safety provisions (which are often not fully complied with) than with the physical and psychological fitness of the crew members.

Why is this so? Many causes can be adduced, but I would venture the following:

- Navigation dates back to the origins of humanity. It has always been seen as an activity entailing danger, though more on account of the natural elements than on account of any psychological or physical factors affecting the crew members. For centuries, crews were recruited from among the men roaming around ports. The strong would survive, and the weak would end up at the bottom of the sea.
- Navigation has been viewed as a routine matter in technical terms, and as being a suitable activity for the adventurous.
- Sailors have never been seen as needing training, apart from just the basics (e.g. the Seaman Competence Certificate in Spain), which do not really imply any specialist studies.
- Officers have traditionally received adequate technical training, with the subject being taught as a full university degree course in many countries - Spain, for example.

However, providing training on psychological and sociological issues is usually omitted for these officers, even though they will have to organise and control life on board as well as the work done there.

- Although the increasing levels of automation makes the need for high-level technical training for the officers apparent, and even though it is in fact being provided, the idea is still prevalent in the maritime world in general that sailing is just a routine activity.
- Lastly, we could point out that accidents at sea only attract the attention of the press or the general public when a large ocean liner and a large number of victims are involved, or if the accident involves a tanker and the accident causes a large oil slick. Little interest is aroused when a small coaster goes down, and anyway there is no black box to investigate.

These and many other aspects emerge clearly when we see how shipping companies are more concerned with low costs than high skills when recruiting. Still less attention is usually given to the human needs of the crews, which are nevertheless important for greater safety in shipping, quite apart from their essential human importance.

However, increasing importance is being attached to these matters in recent years, particularly among the professional bodies, nautical teaching staff, and psychologists and sociologists who for one reason or another have come into contact with the professional world of the sea.

### 5.4.2 Admission tests for nautical studies

Just as psychological tests are carried out on would-be air pilots, people intending to work in scientific bases in the Antarctic etc., their use is also being considered for people who intend to man ships, particularly the people who will be in charge of them.

Dr. Stanislaw Kozak of the Merchant Marine Academy of Gdynia (Poland) has studied this matter. Having started with initial tests carried out in 1969 at that marine academy in Gdynia[163], Kozak analysed various tests sent to him by various specialists in his country and abroad.

During a voyage to Africa, 42 students on work experience were examined, their social popularity being compared with their academic results. The most popular ones turned out to be the ones classified as melancholic. No relation could be established between their social popularity and types of nervous system or emotional maladjustment. It was noted that a tight-knit group of students quickly fell apart during the sea voyage. It also emerged that there was no relation between social popularity and academic results... [164] Psychologists In the Soviet Union, according to Kozak, when studying "propensity to accidents", showed that many graduates that had been very good students experienced difficulty later in their professional lives in coping with their work both in the engine room and on the bridge.

At the Plymouth School, Kozak goes on, they noted that the traits needed for an engineer officer to concentrate on a task involving technical problems, in a small compartment cut off from the outside, must be different from the traits needed in a deck officer, who has to concentrate on factors that do not depend on him, such as the distance to the coast, the weather, the load and the draught - he is supposed to be able to divide his attention between a number of objects at the same time.

Basing their work on this study, the scientists of the Szczecin Academy concluded that this was at odds with the theory that sought to integrate these two professional spheres, a theory that was very popular in the 1970s and that had some following in Poland too.

The admission procedure for students wishing to study at nautical schools in Germany is different, since before admission they are required to have worked on board ships for 18 or 24 months. Thereafter, they go straight through their theoretical training without further interruption.

In a study from the Szczecin Academy in 1974[165] made during a work-experience trip, it was noted that the personality of the students changed during the course of it. Of a group of 22 students, 9 underwent changes for the better, and the rest changes for the worse.

It was found that they were neurotic and tended to suffer nervous disorders. During the trip, the students gradually fell into a state of interior isolation, their activity level waned, they became apathetic and were prey to some extent to obsessive ideas. In spite of the difficulties experienced, they all continued with their studies, although several months were to pass before they became fully adapted once more... In the view of the authors, the age of the students - all around twenty - had an influence in these changes.

Z. Borucki[166] of that Szczecin Academy set down the following criteria for adaptability to the seafaring profession:
a) assessment of level of achievement in the professional requirements, both technical and organisational;
b) assessment of relations with other members of the crew (social acceptance in the group);
c) assessment and self-assessment of the degree of satisfaction with work and life aboard.

To analyse these criteria, Borucki drew up the following test methods:
a) the "Seaman Appraisal Scale"
b) a sociometric questionnaire
c) a questionnaire on satisfaction derived from the seafaring profession.

The Raven test and others on personality, temperament, intelligence etc. were taken. Personality traits were assessed twice: before going aboard, and again after 6 months aboard. A total of 120 men were surveyed, with a uniform mental capacity. When they were compared with other Polish students, the latter were more extrovert, less prone to neuroses and had much greater capacities for socialising and for aggression.

The features that were deemed most stable were intelligence and temperament. In the fairly-stable group of features were shyness and the need for social acceptance. And lastly, the least stable traits were agitation and aggression.

It was concluded that personality traits were not the only ones giving indications as to the capacity for adaptation: sociological, pedagogical and demographic factors also had some influence.

We believe that it is right to make this distinction between factors that are inherent to the individual and factors that stem from his up-bringing, his environment.

If we take the case of a sailor from Galicia on the Atlantic coast in north-west Spain, a man born into a family of seafarers who has come to regard as normal the abnormal situation of having a father, an uncle and maybe even a brother who are all seafarers, and who then marries a woman who has also been brought up in the same atmosphere, then with the same personal conditions as others, he will certainly adapt much more easily to the sea than someone from inland who has always lived in an atmosphere in which people were only dimly aware of the sea. Indeed, for people with average personal characteristics, factors of environment will have a decisive influence: few things are harder than "changing worlds".

Hence someone from a maritime world, who might in fact meet other people from his region or who will at least have an outlook very similar to his own, will surely have a much easier time adapting to life at sea.

According to a paper by Dragoljub Arnautovic[167] of the Marshal Tito Centre of Naval Universities in Split, experts from all over the world had also voiced the need for candidate selection at the 10th International Symposium of Maritime Medicine held in Riga in September 1986 with the title "Men and Ships in the year 2000".

Arnautovic reported that the Soviet B. Burov based selection on the capacity to adapt to shipboard conditions, while I. Iljin attached greater importance to resistance to physical factors such as sea sickness.

The various types of tests that seemed most important were selected:
- Test on general learning ability - a set which was to contain at least two intelligence tests.
- Test on special abilities, designed to measure technical, motor, visual, eye-motor capacities and eye-hand coordination.
- Test on resistance to sea sickness - necessary since the profession involves constant movement, and it has been shown that from 7 to 10% of the population is incapable of getting used to it.
- Test on professional-motivation capacity - to measure the interest aroused by pursuing this profession.
- Test on the mental health and maturity of the candidates: this measures resistance to stress and frustration, strength of personality, individual psychic energy, sociability, locus control, capacity for adaptation, and freedom from any personality disorder.

In line with what H. Boehm[168] had already said in Opatija in 1982, it seems evident that such selection would help us to avoid making wrong decisions and failing in life - which may have serious consequences individually and collectively, personally and economically.

Staying with the papers from that same IMLA conference in 1988, we may now note the contribution of Onkina T.A. and Vinogradov S.A.[169] of the Institute of Water Transport Hygiene of Moscow in the USSR.

This paper highlighted the incidence of the human factor in the causes of maritime accidents, in the following way:

The notion of the human factor combines three main groups of personality aspects in the integrated framework of personal relations: psycho-physiological, psychological and socio-psychological.

It is known that the task of commanding a ship is characterised by strain and emotional tension, caused partly by the density of information received per unit of time when on watch or by the large number of important objects to be kept under observation, and partly by the need to take decisions against the clock and with personal responsibility for the safety of the ship and the crew. This type of work, particularly the captain's, puts extra pressure on the organism's functional possibilities, primarily in the nervous and emotional sphere, requiring specialised personnel to be selected taking account of both physical parameters and psychological conditions.

Unfortunately, there are no generally accepted ideas on what this selection process should entail.

Be that as it may, the studies of Onkina and Vinogradov on the psycho-emotional status of sailors and data on their psychological adaptation, carried out aboard Russian ships on long voyages, enable us not only to draw up the average psychological profile of the sailor but also to establish certain periodical changes in the nervous and psychic sphere during voyages.

51 to 70% of those surveyed (on various voyages) were seen to be extrovert people, indicating an aspiration to broader social contacts that is probably related to a sharp drop in the usual flow of information from the outside.

The study of how the psychological adaptation process worked, in terms of the duration of the voyage, showed that during the first weeks at see, some degree of internal tension, dissatisfaction with the situation, very low levels of organised activity and unstable moods were detected. These orientative reactions were connected with the need to form a new dynamic stereotype, under a change of environmental conditions. This change led to a stabilisation of psychological state, along with a decrease in internal tension and more positive behaviour. The need to enter interpersonal contacts facilitates to some extent the processes of socio-psychological adaptation both for the individual and for the group collectively.

Later on, as from the third month of the voyage, signs of psychological de-adaptation began to appear, surfacing as an increase in internal tension, and increase in aggressive tendencies and a decrease in behaviour control.

It should be noted that the number of accentuated personalities in the crew doubled after three months, and trebled after six.

An important aspect to take into account here is the long periods of sexual abstinence, particularly in young and middle-aged men. An externally-imposed change in the usual sexual pattern is a cause of some nervous and psychic disorders.

The study showed that 45% of those surveyed had an average sexual constitution, while 25% were sexually strong and 35% sexually weak.

Of the group as a whole, 28% tolerated the long periods of sexual abstinence with some equanimity, while the remaining 72% showed physical disorders in varying degrees. In the sexually strong category, the disorders were apparent even during the first days of the voyage, and were characterised by constant mental fixation on sexual themes. It was in this group that the greatest number of psychotic traits were detected. Abstinence began to affect the sexually average after about two or three months at sea, coinciding with the general psychological de-adaptation experienced then.

It can be concluded from even a superficial analysis that both the likelihood of accidents and the seriousness of their consequences greatly depend on the situation, the time and the conditions in which decisions are taken. Thus one path towards preventing accidents is establishing their relation to psychological personality traits, the psychic state of those involved at the time, and the likelihood of having to take decisions against the clock.

With regard to tensions and bad moods on board, I would like to stress that evolving pattern in which we noted an improvement in the crew's psychic condition over the first few weeks, though falling off again after some three months.

When a ship puts to sea, particularly if a large number of new crew members are aboard, people's thoughts are still land-bound, and if the ship is setting off on a long trip then the prospect of being shut up in it for several months is not exactly conducive to a cheerful mood. But the need for company gradually helps to create an atmosphere of its own in which some good things can be found and need to be found. Yet as time passes, the supply of internal resources diminishes, people get tired of the company thrust upon them, irritability arises, and probably a deterioration of life aboard.

This worsening of the atmosphere will be accelerated as the voyage is due to end if it is going to run over the scheduled time.

Another important factor are stop-offs in ports. A stay of two or three days, with decent chances for going ashore, is appreciated by the crew. If a crew member is in his own country, his wife may be able to visit him, or he may be able to make a lightning visit home.

If it is a foreign port, it offers a chance to break the monotony and to experience whatever the port and its city may have in store.

Just as constantly running in and out of ports with precious little time out at sea between-times prevents community life aboard from developing, so overly long trips with no stop-offs in ports lead to a deterioration in community life aboard.

Large oil tankers, for example, are ships that do long runs (approximately one month), and when they arrive at port they anchor or tie up at mooring buoys or berth alongside a wharf, far from any city.

If they are in the Persian Gulf, all they will see is jetties and oil towers, with the sun beating down fiercely overhead all the while. If they are in port like Rotterdam's Europort, the city is so far away that only a few may get the chance to go there, and even then only on some ship business or with some errand to run and having to come back straight away, with no chance for that leisurely evening stroll around city streets.

On those oil tankers, even though they feature plenty of comforts aboard, people end up unhinged, self-absorbed, and suffering out-and-out claustrophobia, for they spend the four or six months aboard virtually without being able to leave the ship.

This brings an impoverishment in personal relations and a drop in the psychic condition of the crew member. Calling into port, when the visit can be enjoyed, is a source of news and inspires conversations, nourishing that shipboard community during the next voyage. Spending months between the same bulkheads, with nothing new to see or to talk about, drastically impoverishes the potential for dialogue among the crew.

A harbour pilot at the port of Santa Cruz de Tenerife in the Canary Islands in the 1970s remarked that he had gone aboard an oil supertanker for a mooring manoeuvre, and during it, the captain took out a flute and began to play him the latest tunes he had learned.

We will now turn to the paper by F.A. Cavaco[170] of the Escola Náutica Infante D. Henrique at the Rijeka I.M.L.A. Conference.

Cavaco notes that there is a long tradition of people choosing the seafaring career in Portugal, for both economic and cultural reasons. The fragmentation of the crew into groups (fully discussed in this work, particularly in chapter 2) was never seen as a problem in the past, since the crews were large enough to share out the workload reasonably well and thus have enough rest time.

However, at present, with the trend to reduce crew numbers, the smaller the crew the greater the need for the officers to communicate directly with the crew.If this communication fails to arise, the crew members will consider their work to be harder, and they will find that they have no time for resting.

Officers frequently use overtime as a reward for individual cooperation and as a substitute for communication with the crew as a whole.

In fact, on small ships with small crews, there is usually just one mess room, precisely to facilitate internal communication. However, on large ships, particularly, as discussed before[171], if they were originally built with larger crews in mind, then bringing the crew members together is a task for the captain.

Cavaco refers to two studies each made on oil tankers on long voyages, and from these he draws the following conclusions:
– A style that was inadequate for coping with the vast diversity of needs on board the ships was noted.
– A misguided concept of routine was related to the captain and the officers not being suitably prepared to deal with all the human and organisational problems.

We have also frequently noted the weight of routine in the marine profession. This routine, which can be positive in some respects in that the crew members feel well acquainted with what they do, is negative when it implies a passive response to problems - "that's how the sea is" or "what else can you do?".

The approach to exercising command, Cavaco adds[172], cannot be based merely on accumulated experience: a more assertive leadership style is needed.
– As regards stress reactions, these were attributed essentially to very limited social relations on board, to the crew not having adapted to the reduction in crew numbers, and to ship-land communication systems that provided scanty, limited information.
– Lastly, an attitude of resisting any change among crew members was noted, as a result of their inability to solve problems, their inflexibility and their lack of social skills. This attitude is quite normal in such groups.

From this, the study Cavaco outlines makes the following recommendations.

- Leadership should be regarded as one of the most important factors in managing personnel aboard oil tankers. At all levels on board, leadership skills will help to create a better climate and to increase satisfaction and productivity.
- A new type of contract is recommended, designed to take account of social and psychological aspects. The overtime schedule, while maintaining economic stability, should enable a new work climate to be achieved. Moreover, the regional cultures of the seamen ought to be preserved on board ships to avoid alienation, particularly during time off.
- A spirit of critical thought and analysing the facts should be encouraged to overcome complacency and a misguided view of loyalty.

The studies arranged by the Nautical Academy of Portugal are generally applicable to any ship today, particularly when crew numbers have been cut.

Ships spend little time in port, there are few people aboard, and those few are of different nationalities... Some compensatory mechanisms that may have been available in former times are now rare, and social and labour planning for crews adding motivation to their work is more necessary than ever.

Carrying on with our review of the various studies produced on how seafarers might be selected, let us turn now to the one made by Bengt Schager[173] of the Swedish Maritime Academy. Schager tells us how they had pondered in 1992 whether it might be advisable to introduce an admission system for applicants for nautical studies, in view of the great responsibility people on ships had for human life, the environment and economic interests, and he asserts that.

*... there is no reason whatsoever why nervous, stress-prone, easily-exhausted, unbalanced, disorganised or anxious people should receive training for responsible work on a ship's bridge.*

To address this problem, the National Swedish Administration of Shipping and Navigation, the Swedish Shipowners' Association, the Maritime Academy at Gothenburg and the trade unions directly involved in this area agreed to develop a system to check the suitability of applicants for nautical studies. This programme was to be implemented in late 1993 under the direction of the author of the article, Bengt Schager, who writes:

*In the near future ... the role of a maritime officer and especially that of a master is going to change in important respects. Besides being a skilful, judicious and experienced seafarer, the master's other duties are more and more resembling those of an executive. ... Like an executive ashore, the master may have to work with an executive group consisting of his closest subordinates.*

This is an important aspect since traditionally many captains have taken over practically all the functions of command, delegating powers onto the officers on when unavoidable; thus they have come to feel alone with their responsibility, and in the event of the master falling ill, problems have arisen owing to the master having kept information to himself that he should have made available to others. In many cases this attitude is a sign of the captain's underlying insecurity and his lack of confidence in those around him: monopolising certain actions and information in this way can be seen as a means to underpinning his authority.

To return to the article we have been discussing, the aptitude tests proposed for candidates for officer posts in the civil marine concern the following aspects:

- Aptitude for understanding technology. A person who has no feeling for technology and no interest in it is unlikely to be receptive to technology, while other people are able to assimilate it from the outset.
- Intellectual capacity. Candidates should have well developed faculties for reasoning and logic, along with the ability to grasp difficult situations. They should be able to think and react in a reasonable manner, and to make use of complex knowledge. They should also be able to undertake analytical reasoning.
- Perceptiveness. They should be able to register factors in their environment without letting subjective interference come in.
- Sociability. To be able to work harmoniously in such a special atmosphere, it is important to be extrovert, sociable, communicative, tolerant and not to show any leanings towards extreme approaches to life. Candidates must have a firm character.
- Self control. This is important both for the safety of the ship and for various aspects of social life aboard. Naturally, an 18 year old cannot be compared with an adult, but he should display an appropriate degree of self-control for his age.
- Stress tolerance. Working as an officer requires being able to perform simultaneous operations well, without developing psychosomatic disorders, even under very tense circumstances.

Schager[174] ends this section by saying that the idea is not to seek supermen, just people who can pursue their profession in a skilled, responsible manner.

The next problem is of course the nature of the tests to assess the characteristics listed above:

- Capacity for logical thought: this can be detected through certain problem-solving tasks.
- Stress tolerance: here the purpose is to measure to what extent a person's action may be influenced by stress.
- Perceptiveness: this can be measured by the candidate's ability to recall visual details.
- Understanding of technology: this can be measured by how well technical problems are understood, the candidate being expected to adopt a methodical way of thinking.
- The capacity to cope with simultaneous activities: this is measured by getting the candidate to deal with several issues while carrying out one activity.
- Understanding orders: this ability is detected through the candidate understanding written instructions and following them.
- Self-assertiveness: finding out whether the candidate is assertive in his behaviour, whether he is self-sufficient, whether he feels at ease in a group.
- Responsibility: displaying reliability, constancy and resistance when faced with tough tasks.
- Emotional stability, self-control: the aim here is to see whether the candidate is prone to becoming anxious and worried, or whether he remains calm.
- Watchfulness: measuring the capacity to observe changes or signs arising in the candidate's environment.
- Accuracy: finding out whether the candidate can work accurately under normal conditions and under stressful ones.
- Tempo: this involves measuring how long each candidate can withstand, without relief or distraction, a task that is neither enjoyable nor gratifying.

Naturally, test data then needs to be processed, and to be interpreted by specialists. The ideal profile for a seaman is, according to Schager, very demanding.

We can state that a basic characteristic for a seaman is good psychic balance, and of course other aptitudes such as capacity for improvisation, serenity, responsibility etc. However, in intellectual terms, I am not so sure that such a high technical level is necessary.

Evidently, seamen should have a good command of the technical knowledge to be employed, but in the last analysis sailing is not so very complicated, and I believe that the nautical profession can be successfully pursued by the many people who have sufficiently high technical competence, yet who moreover have human characteristics enabling them to adapt to different situations and different people, who can tolerate solitude, and above all, though not so far mentioned here, who have a sense of professional vocation. I have known people who were less than brilliant intellectually, but who were nonetheless good sailors. There will be a good atmosphere aboard if people are in a good mood, and for this, in the teeth of the negative aspects of the profession, one must feel at home with it.

Martyn Dyer-Smith[175] wonders whether there really is an ideal temperament for a sailor, or character traits that should be avoided. According to him, excessive importance should not be attached to the methods currently available for selecting future seamen. He refers to cosmonauts, people who are selected and trained according to the most stringent standards, and remarks that one of them, the astronaut Valery Ryumin, wrote in his diary in 1980 that *everything required for committing murder was present when two men share a cabin measuring 18 feet by 20 feet for two months*. Dyer-Smith takes the view that the most meticulous selecting and the most thorough training can come to naught when the sensation of solitude and the inescapable company of others with whom relations may not be good come into play.

Even so, Dyer-Smith grants that stable extroversion is a favourable trait in a seaman. However, he wonders to what extent we can measure those parameters and also whether those qualities will be necessary in the seamen of tomorrow.

With regard to the first dilemma, he argues that psychology has no universally accepted definition of personality, intelligence, stress tolerance etc., and that furthermore there is no evident relation between them and efficiency in work. Dyer-Smith asks: *If we accept that a quality such as extroversion exists and can be measured, can we be sure that it is a good quality for a seaman? It is true that an extrovert will perform watchkeeping tasks better than an introvert, particularly under stressful conditions, but the same does not appear to be true when night falls.*

Dyer-Smith inclines rather to the view that on ships it is more important to avoid extremes, whether of introversion or extroversion or any other characteristic. He tells us that a mentally retarded person and a genius are both equally out of place on a ship's bridge.

For this author, if alienation and boredom grow, they are no doubt psychosocial factors to be borne in mind when selecting candidates. He says that *a high I.Q. will no doubt help in doing an examination well, but that he does not know how useful it would be in settling the little watchkeeping problems arising after the tedium of four hours of solitude strolling up and down on the fifth day of a three-month voyage.*

While I ventured that Schager's approach was excessively theoretical, I think that Dyer-Smith perhaps goes too far the other way. I agree with him that for seaman it is better to be neither dull-witted nor a genius. However, I believe that there are certain characteristics that in principle, and accepting the risk always entailed in making rules or laws, can be deemed helpful for being a good sailor.

I must insist, as I said before, that it is important for the seaman to feel at home aboard ship. This does not mean that he will never feel tired of it all and yearn for his holidays, but even so he must have some esteem for his work.

Secondly, it is important for him to feel that he is in a habitat in which he can recognise himself.

As has also been pointed out previously, a sailor from Galicia on the northwest coast of Spain, who was brought up in close contact with the marine profession, and who moreover finds himself sailing with other seamen from his own town or some nearby one, has an important head start - he will not feel himself to be an outsider from the outset.

An important condition is no doubt to be a self-reliant person, capable of improvising and taking quick decisions. Such a person will make the most of his spare time, thus avoiding boredom and demotivation. In this sense, we can take the view that selection procedures for future seafarers should be essentially based on psychosocial aspects and not so much on technical-intellectual matters, though staying within the bounds of normal intelligence.

An important aspect for the seaman to find himself in appropriate psychosocial conditions is that the shipping company pay attention to the composition of crews, so that everybody can feel fully integrated aboard. One of the greatest dangers - the isolation of individuals - arises mainly when the individual finds himself out of place, when he has difficulties in communicating with other crew members and being on friendly terms with them. Such isolation comes about when, for example, there are a number of different cultures and nationalities and when one group dominates another. Studying the characteristics of people from each country, and creating an atmosphere of equality (aside from differences of post), are essential if each crew member is to be able to enjoy psychic balance, and if as a result there is to be a good atmosphere on board.

## 5.5 The ship of the future

### 5.5.1 Concerning technical progress

The ship of the future is a ship with high technology, fitted out with electronic devices enabling the navigation and other related operations to be done accurately and simply.

This model of hi-tech ships with small crews is currently seen chiefly in ships from developed countries, with crews from the same nation.

If we turn to ships with crews from the so-called Third World - i.e. with cheap labour - the ships usually has less electronics, but more crew members in exchange.

On such ships, reducing the size of crews is not such an obsession for the shipowner, on account of the low wage costs and in many cases the absence of holiday expenses or welfare benefits.

Captain Jens Froese[176] of the Institute of Ship Operation in Hamburg, says that *controlling and handling all the technical systems is done from the bridge, which is the only place with an operator round-the-clock when out at sea...*

*... A bridge equipped with air conditioning, in which the officer is comfortably seated on a commodious leather chair, presents the risk of making us forget that the ship is still vulnerable to being hit by a large wave. A propulsion failure stemming from technical faults unexpectedly puts the ship in a situation comparable to that of a sailing ship a couple of centuries ago with its masts broken. Although the life-saving resources are much better, in cases of extreme necessity entailing abandoning ship, electronics are of little use in the teeth of the unpredictable strength of natural forces.*

Later in the same article, Froese goes on to warn of the potential risk of increasing electronics as regards ship safety, pointing out that the most dangerous conclusion that can be drawn is to assume that the more electronics (automation) there is, the less need there is for skilled operators. In fact, the opposite is the case, since although through electronics crew sizes can be reduced, the competence of those remaining must be higher.

When complex systems fail, keeping operations safe can only be assured by using first-class personnel. This brings us to one problem with automation: the fact that it can lead to a loss of competence in the manual and mental sphere.

Froese also draws attention to the need for ship operators (as he calls them) to be able to sail under traditional conditions when the automatic systems fail. One of the hallmarks of sailors over history has been their capacity for improvisation, for coping with the unexpected by availing themselves of their deep professional knowledge.

The often hostile environment in which navigation occurs and the possibility of break-downs means that sailors cannot restrict themselves to being mere operators of an instrument that tells him what to do. Computer systems have a wide range of problems - not just technical, but ones relating to human error. People working on land with computers often need technical assistance, and that is not available out at sea.

Froese attaches importance to simulation possibilities, fitted with many of the electronic devices used aboard, to simulate various situations, and even to deal with them in a fully or partially automatic way, or in an entirely manual way.

### 5.5.2 The ideal crew on the ship of the future

Martyn B.A. Dyer-Smith[177] wonders: *Who will be suitable for living aboard the ships of the future? In my opinion, those who can tolerate isolation and are capable of working in a non-stimulating environment... I believe that however valid personnel selection is and however thorough their training, small international crews will not be viable in the long term. It will probably be necessary to redesign a community on board, one in which normal people can live.*

For his part, Juan Ribera Alsina[178] declared: *... We believe that numbers of watchkeeping personnel, the ones that really stay aboard, should not be sized in terms of the tonnage and horsepower of the ship - other kinds of criteria should be used, probably of a sociological kind.... rather than technical ones... In any event, I would like to point out that that we should be going towards smaller crews, though through high technical standards, assistance services for the ship, and very safe ships that really must be more comfortable for those inside, particularly if we accept more feasible, more human shipboard schedules for the crews.*

In the same Round Table, S. Hernández Izal[179] explained: *the individual becomes or can become a chronic ultra-rootless case, and such individuals can scarcely offset their sociological deficiencies with purely material remedies (e.g. more pay, more comfort)...*

If we look at it a different way, there is something in common in all three opinions set down: there is a problem beyond the technical problem on the ship, i.e. the criteria aimed at getting crew members to live in the full sense on board. It its contradictory to invest in improving technical facilities while forgetting about the repercussions on the people.

Taking a short-sighted view, automation and technical advance in general can be seen simply as a way of cutting costs in the means of production or in services.

Taking a slightly broader view, we can see that at the heart of scientific advance, before it gets manipulated by other interests, is progress, and that progress as such always means a step forward for humanity, in other words an improvement in living conditions. Evidently, lowering costs will mean greater access to certain goods or services, yet if this improvement for some consumers leads to a deterioration in the quality of life for the producers, we are contradicting the general principle of progress as it should be. This is particularly valid today, with the great social awareness that exists.

Technical progress on ships up to a few decades ago led to improvements in the life of crews: ships that were more comfortable, cleaner, quieter, safer, with better food, better cabins etc.

Naturally, as ships were modernised, the number of crew members went down - just think of the crew needed to manage the rigging on a sailing vessel, or the people needed to run a steam ship's engines.

However, this reduction, which evidently entailed moving into the growing problem of unemployment, did not have a negative effect on the quality of life on board: despite the cut-backs, there were still enough people to establish basic human relations, and then the reduction also meant relieving the overcrowding in shared cabins and improvements in living conditions in general.

The psychosociological study carried out in Germany in 1974[180] takes as its starting point that loneliness stemming from isolation and separation from one's family is a factor that is inseparable from the marine profession. It can be attenuated, but not eliminated.

As a way towards solving this, it was suggested that sailors should generally have the option of returning to shore life after a certain length of service at sea, so that some link could be preserved between the life spent at sea and the subsequent job ashore, the link concerning not only knowledge but also pay. The sense of "transitional profession" would thus lose its negative overtones.

To achieve this, the professional associations and the trade unions as applicable should bring about a situation where nautical qualifications are a requirement for officers, and experience a requirement for subordinates, for the purpose of gaining access to certain shore jobs linked to the sea.

### 5.5.3 The viability of ships with downsized crews

The subject of cuts in labour is one which is not, as we have said, exclusive to the sea. In every industrial or economic activity, attempts are made to reduce staffing levels to cut costs.

The factors to be considered with respect to cutting down crew sizes[181] are wide-ranging. Crew costs certainly have a significant impact on the total running costs of a ship, which is why efforts are made to reduce the number of crew members.

The question Dyer-Smith[182] asked himself is also being asked by many other researchers dealing with the psychological and sociological problems of seafarers.

Thus T. Munk[183] reflects on the extent to which it is possible to subject crews to an excessive workload while still keeping the ship working safely and efficiently. Munk refers to projects for remote-controlled ships, with only one or two men aboard; these do not seem feasible in the near future, since there have to be people on board to take decisions in the light of changing circumstances. For that purpose, a suitably skilled crew is needed, which moreover leaves us with the question of how many members that crew needs to have.

According to Munk, *experience shows that a crew of six may be enough on a small coaster if the work to be done is suited to a crew of that kind. Such a crew would comprise a captain, two deck officers, a chief engineer and two versatile seamen.*

It is to be assumed that on such a ship the engine would be controlled from the bridge, where three people could reasonably share out the usual watchkeeping work between them. The chief engineer would cover general engine control, and the two seamen would act as hands for all the jobs required, whether on deck, in the engine room or in the kitchen. Ships of this kind usually adopt a pre-prepared catering system for food.

The question Munk asks is whether any ship can be manned by just six people, with human work being replaced by automatic systems.

Munk also says that *One criterion when deciding on crew downsizing should be that the safety, efficiency and reliability of the ship are not adversely affected.*

There are many activities that can be tackled ashore, such as certain maintenance and repair work, and then the work involved in loading and stowing can be carried out by shore-based personnel.

As we mentioned in section 2.10.2, even back in the early sixties, some German merchant ships were taken over upon arrival at base by a crew whose role was to relieve the sea crew for the two or three days that the ship might be spending in the port.

If it proved possible to do that at a time when crewmen were desperately sought after for the merchant marine, with the companies going to considerable lengths to offer ever better conditions as regards pay, work and holidays, it is not beyond the bounds of possibility to think that some similar system, adapted to our own times, might be designed.

Yet the fact is, as we have said before, that the widespread move to register ships under flags of convenience, and the flood of cheap labour being signed on, is putting off a promising project which will have to be implemented sooner or later.

Munk also stresses what he sees as necessary conditions for arranging crew reductions:
- The ship must be designed and fitted out to reduce the workload for the crew and to reduce the risk of accidents and equipment breakdowns.

- The crew must be instructed and trained accordingly.
- The operational procedures must have been established and tested, so that the efficiency of the ship under every imaginable situation is assured.

This can all be analysed using the differing criteria of navigation, manoeuvres, docking and undocking, loading and stowage, fire prevention and fire-fighting, etc.

However, there is another very important factor that Munk also takes in: *social life on board*.

The crew member, as a person, has social needs, and if they are not met his psychic balance will be affected, and consequently his professional performance too may suffer.

Solitude is a terrible burden for a crew member when he has nobody to talk to, either because there really is nobody, or because he does not get on with the people there are around him. Feeling alone is very hard to cope with.

While it is inherently important for any crew that the make-up of the crew and the layout of the space available be conducive to good social relations between crew members, it becomes still more important on a ship with a reduced crew.

Many psychologists and sociologists have studied this matter and agree on the importance of common areas such as mess rooms, day rooms and games rooms being comfortable enough to induce the crew to use them, making them places for meeting and thus avoiding isolation in the cabins.

Mealtimes are important. On ships with traditional crews (20 to 40 people), as we said when talking about the crew in general, there are usually two or three mess rooms, divided along professional-category lines.

This custom is questionable, and present-day social-living patterns may possibly be tending to do away with such distinctions in favour of a better communal spirit among the entire crew.

On ships with crews of six or ten, this problem becomes much more acute, since then we would find that only three to five people would be sharing a mess room, and of them there would probably be one or two who would have to have their meals at a different time on account of the watchkeeping schedule. The result is that they would end up having their meals virtually alone. And if on top of this people of different nationality and language are brought together, the results can be really catastrophic.

To make a reduced crew viable in human terms, it must be ensured that its members can communicate without difficulty, that they are all compatible in terms of habits, that they have adequate common areas to meet in, and that life and work on board are organised in such a way that no crew member is permanently condemned to seeing nobody and talking to nobody for days on end.

Undoubtedly, a change in the social attitude of the crew is needed in this. Up to now, owing to traditional reasons and cultural differences, the hierarchical pattern of ships went way beyond what was prompted by labour considerations, and it permeated every aspect of life on board.

In addition to the social evolution of our own times, which perforce leads to a change in such patterns, change becomes urgent and essential on ships with reduced crews. And in fact on ships with 7 or 8 crew members, all of whom are European, there is indeed a trend towards working and living as a team, without the customary social differences.

Such a cut-down group must necessarily change its outlook, and links as colleagues and members of the same team must weigh more heavily in human terms than differences in post or role on board.

### 5.5.4 The crew member's relation with his own world

In this context, some allusion needs to be made to the problem of communication with the family and with society in general. We have seen how important information in general is, and frequent communication as well, so as not to feel cut off from the world one has left behind. For a member of the crew of a coaster plying between the ports of his own country, this problem will not be very acute, but it will be for a sailor who flies thousands of miles to board a ship and who, for the duration of the voyage, will only get news from home through the odd letter which may anyway take weeks to get to him, or news of some important event that reaches him on board or through the press at some foreign port.

This is the situation of thousands of sailors on long voyages. Henning Puvogel[184] describes in a very simple and true-to-life way how it feels to go aboard a ship scheduled to make the journey between the Pacific and the Gulf of Mexico and find an incomplete crew that is resigned to its fate, with half the navigation instruments not working properly, with the air conditioning and the washing machine not working at all, and the conditions in general being very different from those portrayed to that writer back in Hamburg when he was signing on as first officer. He being thousands of kilometres away, and sailing in a climate and seeing countries so different from his own Northern Europe, any complaint or demand would pass through a long filter made of weeks and silence. In the end, the conviction that one has been forgotten about, and having no choice but to get through the duration of the contract somehow, leads to an attitude that can run from stressful frustration to demotivation and indifference.

The problems of stress, fatigue and lack of motivation are linked to this feeling of being miles away from home. It is often the case that the shipowner hires the ship to a charter company, the latter seeking the cargo and organising the ships. The crew will be at the orders of the charter company, although the crew members are actually in the service of the shipowner with whom their contracts were made. The result of this situation is often that nobody seems to take any interest in the crew - unless it is to seek replacements at the slightest sign of delay.

People need to feel that they have professional links and to know who they must turn to if they have a problem in order to seek some response. Seamen need to feel that they matter to their families, to society in general and to the companies employing them.

## 5.6 The profile of the captain on ships in the immediate future

Having ultimate responsibility, a ship's master has naturally always needed to have adequate technical skill and also the skill to lead a community of people living and working on board, people that are to a greater or lesser extent isolated from their own worlds. What degree of importance was attached in the past to the human aspect is not our concern here, since we are concerned rather with analysing what the master should be like today and in the near future. Nowadays, all large companies have a human resources department, since companies are convinced that having suitable personnel and studying their behaviour and human needs is of vital importance in getting the most out of their work. This is a cold, mercantilist approach, and yet for that very reason it shows just how important the whole human factor is, even from the point of view of mere work performance. If we accept that, we surely ought to realise how important this is from the standpoint of the human dignity of work. A captain should have qualities that not everyone possesses. Y. N. Yegorov and V.V. Kormachev[185] carried out research involving 105 officers who had taken a ten-month course for candidates for posts as captains, the research employing a questionnaire concerning 16 personality factors.

The personality traits analysed were divided into three broad groups: business qualities; communicative qualities; personality qualities. The personality qualities covered practical aspects and communication-activity aspects, as well as the person's own knowledge, own perfection and own achievement.

Those in charge of ships are people who are involved in business terms (instrumentally) in that they have to achieve effective results from the crew, and at the same time they also have a contributory and emotional role (personality).

A low level of individualism reflects an absence of tension in dealings with other people and the capacity to make more objective assessments of reality.

A person in command must be capable of delegating, listening, and giving everyone the feeling that their contribution is of value. For that purpose, the person in charge must have confidence in himself, the confidence born of that natural ascendancy or authority needed to maintain an active relation with the various members of the group.

Values such as tolerance, social responsibility and self control speak for themselves as qualities that people in positions of authority should possess. All these qualities assist in interacting more actively and rationally with other participants in convergent activities. I would like to add here that anyone in authority must feel social concern for the persons under him, such that when people from different countries or continents are brought together on a ship, the person in charge takes an interest in their sociocultural peculiarities in order the better to understand their behaviour and to achieve a positive atmosphere on board.

## 5.7 The human factor at sea: research fields opening up

Throughout this book, we have sought to present the human problems of ships in a systematic manner, following the scheme of total institutions.

Each of the various sections dealt with are themselves fields open to research. Sociology and psychology have much to tell us.

An important task in this respect is to make a compendium of the great variety of articles, tests and studies carried out on these aspects, to analyse them by spheres, and to do thorough work on specific criteria that may help to bring the seafaring profession up to date.

We have twenty-first century sailing techniques with nineteenth century crew schemes.

Topics relating to flags of convenience, dummy shipping companies, crew downsizing and internationalisation require a thorough-going study for the purpose, among other things, of serving as a base for approaching changes in national and international legislation.

The notion of authority reconciling hierarchical and democratic requirements is also a highly important issue for the very efficiency of shipping. The relation between the human factor and accidents has been one the elements that has done most to prompt interest in recent years in the subjects of social relations and life on board ship.

The value of communication within the crew and between the crew and the world outside, the notion of family, and innovations such as the incorporation of women as seafaring professionals, are just some of the other aspects to be studied.

Work which is both systematic and creative is needed for this.

Social evolution follows different paths from technological evolution, even though there is of course some interdependence between them. Technological evolution, once produced in the laboratory and tried out in practice, can spread rather quickly. Social evolution, on the other hand, can only be initially channelled and fostered, since applying it requires a gradual change in mental attitude in the people and bodies responsible for making it a reality.

# postscript

If I have learned anything over my long years as a student, a seafarer, a nautical-studies lecturer and director of the Barcelona Apostleship of the Sea, it is the fundamental importance in all spheres of life of how people get on and how they deal with each other.

The great strides that science has made over the course of our century has led to the younger generations being given ever greater knowledge of physics, mathematics, computing etc. Science has come to be seen as the key to the future, and the area of choice for devoting one's life.

However, hand in hand with these great strides made by science, we are witnessing alarmingly individualistic trends, showing no respect for the planet we live on, threatening the future of humanity and bringing dehumanisation in their wake.

Environmental groups have emerged to counter this, and the terms "solidarity", "common good" and "mutual respect" have pervaded countless documents and papers.

Yet it would seem that we use these terms for the sake of appearances, while underneath we are caught up in a race in which man is increasingly at the service of technology rather than the other way round.

Studies have been made and are being made in various countries on life aboard ships, particularly from the psychological point of view. These have been prompted essentially by business interests choosing to invest in them through a realisation that human factors are involved in pursuing the economic activity - the economy is one of the major driving forces behind research. The human factor began to arouse interest when insurance companies had to foot huge compensation bills as a result of accidents. As the technology has become more sophisticated, the consequences of human error have become more serious.

The loss of human life in shipwrecks, such as the case of the Titanic, prompted a review of lifesaving systems and safety in general, but nobody gave any serious attention to the psychological burden of people feeling isolated, cloistered and so on until giant oil tankers, carrying hundreds of thousands of tons, began to ply the seas with reduced crews, endangering not just the ship itself but also the environment, with the potential for entire strips of coast being devastated by huge oil slicks from shipwrecks (as in the case of the Exxon Valdez and other ships).

When referring here and there to the great importance attached in the aviation world to rest and good psychic aptitudes in flying crews, we hinted that human concern for these people does not appear to be the real motive: the real concern is keep the aircraft in good condition and to safeguard the company's reputation from being dented by air crashes.

As we have already noted, living conditions on board ships improved significantly in the 1960s and 70s. Why? Mainly because shipping companies were falling over themselves to recruit crewmen. When crews from the Third World began to come in on a large scale, the improvement work commenced was quickly dropped. So do Korean sailors not have the same human needs as English or Spanish ones?

The fact is, quite simply, that these people come from places where living conditions are very precarious, and they will "settle for anything".

At the same time, automation cleared the way for reducing the size of crews, and hence getting a higher return from shipping.

But...

Did anyone spare a thought for what it means in human terms to spend several months in the company of just five or six people, perhaps with a different language and nationality?

Did anyone think about what it means when a letter takes weeks to get to the person it is addressed to, or about the difficulties sailors have in attempting to phone home from out-of-the-way places?

Did anyone ashore consider what it feels like when you do not know the shipowner and have the feeling that nobody cares in the least about you?

Even so, over recent years, there has been growing concern over the human problems involved and their influence on accidents.

Behind these studies we encounter business interests once more, along with a question: who could ever withstand life on such ships?

Nevertheless, any effort to improve living conditions on ships and any concern for the physical and psychic well-being of sailors is welcome, since whatever the motives, the result is positive.

Yet if there is any real concern to make life at sea more humane, then international agreements should set down and demand compliance with the pertinent regulations, so that any crew, whatever its nationality, can pursue its profession in the most human and dignified way possible.

Sociology and psychology should move into nautical schools in force, at all levels, in the clear knowledge that proper human education is as important as proper technical education, so that crews on ships can have a life as well as do their work.

# bibliography

# bibliography

## Books, articles and talks/lectures

ANDERSON, N. *The Hobo*. University of Chicago Press. Chicago, 1923. (Article).

ARMSTRONG, R.M. *Joseph Conrad: The Conflict of Command*. Yale University, vol. 26. New Haven, 1971. (Article).

ARNAUTOVIC, D. *Psychological Selection of Aplicants for Nautical Schools*. IMLA. Rijeka, 1988. (Paper).

ARSENAULT, R. *Status; has the traditional mariner been forgotten?*. Trial, vol 28. Louisiana, 1992. (Article).

AUBERT, V. *A total institution: the ship in the hidden society*. Bedminster Press. Totowa, New Jersey, 1965. (Article).

AUBERT, V. *The hidden society*. Transaction Books. New Brunswick, New Jersey, 1982. (Article).

AUBERT, V.; ARNER, O. *On the social structure of the ship*. Acta Sociologica, vol. 3. Oslo, 1958. (Article).

BACKHAUS, A. *Sozialhygienische Erhebungen zur Problematik der Freizeit der Seeleute*. Hamburg, 1968. (Lecture).

BANKSTON, W.B; FLOYD, H.H; FORSYTH, C.J. *Toward a general model of the process of radical conversion: an interactionist perspective on the transformation of self-identity*. Qualitative Sociology, vol. 4 (winter). Lousiana, 1981. (Article).

BARNES, B.L. *Relationship between mental health and job efficiency*. Acta Psychiatrica Scandinavica, vol. 69. Oslo, 1984. (Article).

BEOBIDE, J. *La soledad en la Gente de Mar*. VII Jornadas del Hombre de Mar. Stella Maris. Barcelona, 1993. (Article).

BECKER, G. *Der Mensch an Bord*. Nautischen Verein. Wilhelmshaven, 1981. (Lecture).

BERGER, P. *Invitació a la sociologia*. Editorial Herder. Barcelona, 1992. (Book).

BERGER, P.; LUCKMANN, T. *La construcción social de la realidad*. Amorrortu Editores. Buenos Aires, 1968. (Book).

BOEHM, H. *The social climate on board towards enhanced efficiency*. International Conference on Shipboard personnel. Opatija, 1982. (Lecture).

BOEHM, H.; VIVEROS, A. *Balancing jobs and family life*. Philadelphia Temple University Press. 1981. (Article).

BOSS, P. *A clarification on the concept of psychological father presence in families experiencing ambiguity of boundary*. Journal of Marriage and Family, vol. 29. University of Southwestern Louisiana. 1977. (Article).

BOSS, P. *The relationship of psychological father presence, wife's personal qualities and wife family disfunction in families on missing fathers*. Journal of Marriage and Family, vol. 42. University of Southwestern Louisiana. 1980. (Article).

CARDONA, M. *La mujer como profesional del mar*. VIII Jornadas de la Gente de Mar. Apostolado del Mar. Barcelona, 1994. (Paper).

CAVACO, F.A. *a moderating factor of stress in the crews of Portuguese oil tankers*. IMLA. Rijeka, 1988. (Paper).

CHAPMAN, P.K. *Trouble on Board*. Itaca. New York, 1992. (Book).

DECKER, K.R. *Coping with Sea duty: Problems encountered and resources utilized during periods of family separation*. E.J. Hunter and D.S. Nice Pareger Publishers. New York, 1978. (Article).

DOWN, B. *On Course Together*. British Library. Norfolk, 1988. (Book).

DYER-SMITH, M.B.A. *Boring work*. IMLA. Portugal, 1994. (Paper).

DYER-SMITH, M.B.A. *Enhancing safety and quality through focusing on the human factors in shipping*. IIR Conference. London, 1993. (Lecture).

DYER-SMITH, M.B.A.; STEIN, M. *Human resourcing in the European marine industry*. 5th European Congress on the Psychology of Work and Organization. University of Rouen. 1991. (Lecture).

ENCANDELA, JOHN A. *Danger at Sea: Social Hierarchy and Social Solidarity*. Journal of Contemporary Ethnography, vol. 2. Sage Publications. London, 1991. (Article).

ETZIONI, A. *A comparative analysis of complex organizations*. Free Press. New York, 1961. (Article).

FORSYTH, C.J. *Father Alienation: A Further Analysis of Familial Managment Strategy Among Merchant Marine*. International Journal of Sociology of the Family, vol. 22. University of Southwestern Lousiana. 1992. (Article).

FORSYTH, C.J. *Determinants of Family Integration among merchant seamen*. International Journal of Sociology of the Family, vol. 18. University of Southwestern Louisiana. 1988. (Article).

FORSYTH, C.J; BANKSTON, W.B. *The Merchant seaman as a social type: a marginal life-style*. Free Inquiry in Creative Sociology, vol. 11. University of Southwestern Louisiana. 1983. (Article).

FORSYTH, C.J; BANKSTON, W.B. *The social psychological consequence of life at sea: a cause model*. Maritime Policy and Managment, vol. 11. Hants, 1984. (Article).

FORSYTH, C.J; GRAMLING, R. *Merchant Seamen: Historical Stereotypes and Current Status Dilemmas*. Free Inquiry in Creative Sociology, vol.13. University of Southwestern Louisiana. 1985. (Article).

FORSYTH, C.J; GRAMLING, R. *Adaptative Familial Strategies Among Merchant Seamen*. Family and Economic Issues, vol II. University of Southwestern Louisiana. 1990. (Article).

FRICKE, P.H. *Seafarer and Community*. Rowman Littlefield. New Jersey, 1973. (Article).

FROESE, J. *More electronic improved safety or more risk?*. Safety at Sea International, vol. 306. International Trade Publications Ltd. U.K. Surrey, 1994. (Article).

GOFFMAN, E. *Internados, ensayo sobre la situación social de los enfermos mentales*. 2 ed. Amorrortu Editores. Buenos Aires, 1972. (Book).

GONZALEZ PINO, E. *Las Tripulaciones de la Flota Mercante de la C.E.E.*. Departamento de Ciencia e Ingeniería Náuticas. Barcelona, July 1993. (Doctoral Thesis).

GRAVE, W.; HUGHES, M. *Reexamining the ecological fallacy: a study in which aggregate data are critical in investigating the pathological effects of living alone*. Social Forces, vol. 58. University of North Carolina. 1980. (Article).

HAHMAN, E. *Seamen ashore*. Yale University Press. New Haven, 1952. (Article).

HANNA, C.F. *Complaint as a form of association*. Qualitative Sociology, vol. 4 (Winter). Lousiana, 1981. (Article).

HEALEY, J.C. *Foc'sle and glory hole: a study of merchant marine and his occupation*. Merchant Marine Association. New York, 1936. (Article).

HERBST, P.G. *Interpersonal Distance Regulation and Affect Control on Merchant Ships*. European Journal of Social Psychology, vol.1. Work Research Institute. Oslo, 1971. (Article).

HERBST, P.G. *Socio-technical Design of Ship Organization*. Work Research Institute. Oslo, 1968. (Article).

HERNÁNDEZ IZAL, S. *Aproximación a la sociología marítima*. Librería Bosch. Barcelona, 1988. (Book).

HERNANDEZ IZAL, S. *Buques con tripulación reducida*. IV Jornadas de la Gente de Mar. Apostolado del Mar. Barcelona, 1988. (Paper).

HILL, J.M.M. *The seafaring career*. Headly Brothers, Ltd. United Kingdom. 1972. (Book).

HIRSCHHORN, L. *Beyond mechanization: work and technology in a postindus age*. Cambridge Mit Press. 1984. (Article).

HOHMAN, E. *Seamen ashore*. Yale University Press. New Haven, 1952. (Article).

HOPE, R. *Spare time at sea*. The Nautical Institute on Command. London, (Article).

IBAÑEZ, I. *La mujer como profesional del mar*. VIII Jornadas de la Gente de Mar. Apostolado del Mar. Barcelona, 1994. (Paper).

I.M.L.A. *2nd International Workshop on Human Relations and Conditions on Board Ships*. Rijeka, 1988. (Paper).

I.M.L.A. *8th International Conference on Maritime Education and Training*. Oeiras (Portugal), 1994. (Paper).

IRWIN, J. *The Felon*. Englewood Clifs. Prentice-Hall. New Jersey, 1970. (Book).

JACKSON, B. *In the life: versions of the criminal experience*. New American Library. New York, 1972. (Book).

KAPLAN, I.M. *Women who go to sea: working in the commercial fishing industry*. Journal of Contemporary Ethnography, vol. 16. London, 1988. (Article).

KLEMPERER, E. *Reduction of ships' crews. Factors to be considered*. IMLA. Rijeka, 1988. (Paper).

KOBURGER, CH.W. *Man is the limiting factor*. International workshop on human relationships on board. Bremen, 1982. (Paper).

LANE, T. *Grey dawn breaking-British Merchant Seafarers in the late twentieth century*. Manchester University Press. Manchester, 1986. (Book).

LARRAURI, F. *Psicología penitenciària: observació i predicció de la conducta en els permisos de sortida*. Justiforum, vol. 1. Barcelona, 1994. (Article).

LEMMERT, E.M. *Human deviance, social problems and social control*. Englewood Cliffs. Prentice-Hall. New Jersey, 1967. (Article).

LISCH, R. *Totale Institution Schiff*. Dunker und Humbolt. Berlin, 1976. (Article).

MARI SAGARRA, R. *Aproximación al método de evaluación del riesgo de incendio estructural y global de los buques*. Departamento de Ciencia e Ingeniería Náuticas. Barcelona, 1991. (Doctoral thesis).

MIDDLETON, R. *Alienation, Race and Education*. American Sociological Review, vol. 28. U.S.A., 1963. (Article).

MILLER, M.L; VAN MAANEN, J. *Traditional and non-traditional seamen*. Urban life, vol. 11. London, 1982. (Article).

MOSCOVICI, S. ET ALTRI. *Psicología Social I*. Ediciones Paidós. Barcelona, 1985. Book.

MOSCOVICI, S. ET ALTRI. *Psicología Social II*. Ediciones Paidós. Barcelona, 1986. Book.

MUNK, T. *Safety considerations in the design and operation of a six-men refrigerated vessel*. Managment and safety - The Nautical Institute. London, 1991. (Article).

NOLAN, B. *A possible perspective on deprivations*. P. Frike Editor. Seafarer and Community. New Jersey, 1973. (Article).

NYLEHN, B. *Socio-Technical Analysis of Ship Organization*. Institut of Industrial Social Research, Technical University of Norway. Trondheim.

OLIVER, C. *Seminario de recursos humanos y dirección de personal*. Colegio de Oficiales de la Marina Mercante Española. Barcelona, 1990. Seminar.

ONKINA, T.A; VINOGRADOV, S.A. *Psychological Selection of Ships' specialists as the factor of prevention of sea ship accidents*. IMLA. Rijeka, 1988. (Paper).

OSTERWALD, C. *Die Technik und der Mensch an Bord - aus der Sicht eines Seemannspastors*. Manuskript eines Vortrages anlässlich des Deutschen Seeschiffahrttages. Emden, 1980. (Lecture).

PERRY, N. *Conflict on Board Ship: An Interpretation*. The Sociological Review. University of Strathclyde. United Kingdom, 1974. (Article).

PERRY, N.; WILKIE, R. *Social theory and shipboard structure*. Part I, Journal of Maritime Studies and Management, vol. I. London, 1973. (Article).

PUVOGEL, H. *Die letzte Fahr der Scarabea*. H.M. Hauschild, GmbH. Bremen, 1992. (Book).

RIBERA, J. *Buques con tripulación reducida*. IV Jornadas de la Gente de Mar. Apostolado del Mar. Barcelona, 1988. (Paper).

RODRÍGUEZ-MARTOS, R. *I. Seminario sobre convivencia a bordo*. Facultad de Náutica. Barcelona, 1992. (Apuntes).

RODRÍGUEZ-MARTOS, R. *Trabajo marítimo y familia: dos realidades en tensión*. XVIII Congreso Mundial del Apostolado del Mar. Mombasa, 1987. (Lecture).

ROSENHAHN, D.L. *On being sane in insane places*. Science 179. Washington, 1973. (Article).

SAGARDUY, B. *La mujer como profesional del mar*. VIII Jornadas de la Gente de Mar. Apostolado del Mar. Barcelona, 1994. (Paper).

SAGARDUY, B. *Presencia de la mujer en la marina mercante*. Escuela Técnica Superior de Náutica y Máquinas Navales. Portugalete, 1992. (First - degree dissertation).

SANCHEZ VERDUGO, F. *La mujer como profesional del mar*. VIII Jornadas de la Gente de Mar. Apostolado del Mar. Barcelona, 1994. (Paper).

SCULL, A. *Decarceration, community treatment and the deviant: A radical view*. Englewood Cliffs. New Jersey, 1976. (Article).

SCHAGER, B. *Training. A new assessment for applicants*. Bimco Butlletin 4/93. Copenhagen, 1993. (Article).

SCHILOH, A. *Sanctuary or prison: response to life in a mental hospital*. E. Wallace, 9-24 New Brunswick, NJ. Transaction Books. New Jersey, 1971. (Article).

STARR, P. *The transformation of American medicine*. Basic Books. New York, 1982. (Book).

SYKES, G.M; MESSINGER, S.L. *The inmate social system. Theoretical studies in social organization of the prision*. Social Sciencie Research Council. New York, 1960. (Article).

SOMMER, R. *Patients who grow old in a mental hospital*. Geriatrics 14: 586-587. Cleveland, 1959. (Article).

SCHUTZ, A. *Estudios sobre teoría social*. Amorrortu Editores. Buenos Aires, 1974. (Book).

TONNIES, F. *Community and Society*. East Lansung Michigan State University Press. 1957. (Article).

UNTERWAGNER, J. *A professional sociologist at sea*. Slippery Rock State Coll. Pennsylvania Sociological Society. Pennsylvania, 1977. (Lecture).

VAN DER RYN, S. *College in live. In total institutions*. E. Wallace 69-86. New Brunswick, NJ. Transaction Books. New Jersey, 1971. (Article).

VARONA, L.R. *Entidades Psiquiátricas más frecuentes entre los tripulantes de la marina mercante. Factores predisponentes*. Revista del Hospital Psiquiátrico de la Habana, Vol. 26. La Habana, 1985. (Article).

WEEDFALD, A.A. *Personnel Handling on Merchant Ships*. Vantage Press. New York, 1956. (Article).

WEISAETH, L. *Torture of a Norwegian Ship's Crew: The Torture, Stress Reactions and Psychiatric After-Effects*. Acta Psychiatrica Scandinavica. Oslo, 1989. (Article).

WICKSTROEM, G.; LEIVONNIEMI, A. *Suicides among male Finnish seafarers*. Turku, 1985. (Article).

YEGOROV, Y.N; KORMACHEV, V.V. *On personality traits conducive to successful performance and psychological compatibility of ship commanding personnel.*. Soviet Journal of Psychology. Madison, 1990. (Article).

ZURCHER, L.A. *Social Roles: Conformity, Conflict and Creativity*. Sage Publications, Inc. Austin (USA), 1983. (Abstract from book).

ZURCHER, L.A. *The sailor about ship: a study of role behavior in total institutions*. Social Forces, University of North Carolina. 1965. (Abstract from book).

## Studies and surveys

APOSTOLADO DEL MAR. *Estudio sociológico hombres del mar*. Dep. de estudios migratorios y Dep. de investigación sociológica. Madrid, 1972. (Survey).

APOSTOLADO DEL MAR. *Estudio sociológico*. Dep. Invest. Sociales. Madrid, 1984. (Survey).

CARBAJOSA, J.; JIMENEZ, J. *La utilización del tiempo libre en la mar*. Barcelona, 1980. (Study).

CARBAJOSA, J.; LARRAURI, F. *El ocio en la mar*. Centre de recerques i estudis marrítims (CREM). Barcelona, 1982. (Study).

FACHHOCHSCHULE FLENSBURG. *Sozialpsycholo¬gische Untersuchungen an Bord Deutscher Schiffe*. Forschungsstelle für Schiffsbetriebs-technik. Flensburg, 1974. (Survey).

BENJAMIN, R. ET ALTRI. *L'univers des marins*. Etude sociologique sur les marins de commerce et les pêcheurs francais. Fondation pour la recherche sociale. París, 1969. (Study).

INTERNATIONAL CHRISTIAN MARITIME ASSOCIATION (ICMA). *Surveying*. London, 1987. (Study).

ORGANIZACIÓN MARÍTIMA INTERNACIONAL. *Informe para el Comité de Seguridad Marítima*. London, 1992. (Study).

STELLA MARIS. *Trabajo de Investigación*. Buenos Aires, 1979. (Survey).

STELLA MARIS. *Tripulantes del Tercer Mundo en buques de bandera de conveniencia*. II Jornadas del Hombre de Mar. Apostolado del Mar. Barcelona, 1986. (Round table).

STELLA MARIS. *Buques con tripulación reducida*. IV Jornadas de la Gente de Mar. Apostolado del Mar. Barcelona, 1988. (Round table).

STELLA MARIS. *La mujer como profesional del mar*. VIII Jornadas de la Gente de Mar. Apostolado del Mar. Barcelona, 1994. (Round table).

WARWICK. *Worldwide Demand for and Supply of Seafarers*. Warwick University Institute of Employment Research. 1990. (Study).

# notes

# notes

[1] GOFFMAN, E. *Internados. Ensayos sobre la situación social de los enfermos mentales*. Buenos Aires, 1972, p. 13.

[2] PERRY, N. *Conflict on board ship: an interpretation*. University of Strathclyde, United Kingdom, 1974.

[3] See (1), p.17.

[4] See (1), p.19.

[5] See (1), p.18.

[6] See (1).

[7] AUBERT, V. *A Total Institution: The Ship in the Hidden Society*. Totowa. New Jersey, 1965.

[8] NOLAN, B. *A possible perspective on deprivations*. New Jersey, 1973, pp. 85-96.

[9] AUBERT, V; ARNER, O. *On the social structure of the ship*. Oslo, 1958.

[10] ENCANDELA, J.A. *Danger at sea. Social hierarchy, and social solidarity*. Denver, 1991.

[11] FORSYTH, C.J., BANKSTON, W.B. *The merchant seaman as a social type: a marginal style of life*. Louisiana State University, 1983.

[12] See (10).

[13] JACKSON, B. *In the life: versions of the criminal experience*. New York, 1972.

ROSENHAHN, D.L. *On being sane in insane places*. U.S.A., 1973.

SHILOH, A. *Sanctuary or Prison: Response to life in a mental hospital*. New Jersey, 1971.

SYKES, G.M., MESSINGER, S.L. *The inmate social system. In theoretical studies in social organization of the prison*. New York, 1960.

VAN DER RYN, S. *College live in. In total institutions*. New Jersey, 1971.

[14] See (10).

[15] See (13).

[16] HIRSCHHORN, L. *Beyond mechanization: work and technology in a postindus age*. Cambridge, 1984.

[17] WEEDFALD, A.A. *Personnel handling on merchant ships*. New York, 1956.

[18] SCULL, A. *Decarceration, community treatment and the deviant. A radical view*. New Jersey, 1976. New Jersey, 1976.

STARR, P. *The transformation of American medicine.* New York, 1982.

[19] See (10).

[20] AUBERT, V. *The hidden society.* New Jersey, 1982.

MILLER, M.L., VAN MAANEN, J. *Traditional and non-traditional seamen.* U.S.A., 1982.

ZURCHER, L.A. *The sailor aboard ship: A study of role behavior in a total institution.* N. Carolina, 1965, pp. 389-400.

[21] DYER-SMITH, M.B.A., STEIN, M. *Human resourcing in the European marine industry.* Rouen, 1993.

[22] HELBIG, K. *Seefahrt vor den Feuern.* Hamburg, 1988.

[23] See (21).

[24] PERRY, N., WILKIE, R. *Social theory and shipboard structure.* United Kingdom, 1973.

[25] ETZIONI, A. *A Comparative analysis of complex organizations.* New York, 1961, pp. 160-172.

[26] See section 1.2.

[27] FORSCHUNGSSTELLE FÜR SCHIFFSBETRIEBSTECHNIK. *Socialpsychologische Untersuchungen an bord deutscher Seeschiffe.* Flensburg, 1974.

[28] NYLEHN, B. *Socio-technical analysis of ship organization.* Trondheim.

[29] ZURCHER, L.A. *Social roles: conformity, conflict and creativity.* London, 1983.

[30] See section 2.5.4.

[31] HERNÁNDEZ IZAL, S. *Aproximación a la sociología marítima.* Barcelona, 1988, p. 15 (Introduction to Maritime Sociology).

[32] See (31).

[33] LANE, T. *Grey Dawn Breaking - British Merchant Seafarers in the late twentieth century.* Manchester, 1986.

[34] BERGER, P.L.; LUCKMANN, T. *La Construcción social de la realidad.* Buenos Aires, 1968. (The Social Construction of Reality).

[35] See (34).

[36] op cit. - see (34).

[37] See section 2.5.4.

[38] In legal terms, the various roles making up a crew are fully dealt with in national and international legislation. Book III of the current Spanish Code of Trade covers maritime trading in full, and Part II in particular covers the people taking part in maritime traffic. There is also a great deal of legal bibliography, particularly concerning the figure of the captain.

[39] VIGIER DE TORRES, A. *Derecho Marítimo.* Madrid 1977 (Maritime Law).

[40] WADE, W.C. *Die Titanic. Das Ende eines Traumes.* Munich, 1984.

[41] See section 2.5.4.

[42] See (1), p. 76.

[43] The author experienced this on a German ship which had no fixed time for lunch or dinner, but rather a two-hour period during which people came and went as they pleased. The result was a complete lack of warmth in the atmosphere, and thus what is usually a time for being with others and enjoying their company became a time of icy solitude.

[44] See (1), p. 175.

[45] See (1), p. 177.

[46] See section 3.2.

[47] See (31).

[48] See (1), p. 181.

[49] See section 2.3.1.

[50] ZURCHER, L.A. *Social Roles: conformity, conflict and creativity.* London, 1983

[51] See section 3.2.3.

[52] See section 2.3.3.

[53] See (1), pp. 199-200.

[54] See section 2.3.3.

[55] See (50).

[56] See section 3.5.

[57] See section 2.2.

[58] PERRY, N. *Conflict on board ship: an interpretation.* United Kingdom, 1974

[59] See (58).

[60] See section 2.3.2.

[61] See (58).

[62] See (58).

[63] HERBST, P.G. *Interpersonal distance regulation and affect control on merchant ships.* Oslo, 1971.

[64] See section 2.3.3.

[65] See (63), p. 53.

[66] See (1), p. 319.

[67] See (31).

[68] See (1), p. 51.

[69] See (50).

[70] See section 2.6.

[71] GONZALEZ PINO, E. *Las Tripulaciones de la Flota Mercante de la C.E.E.* (Merchant Marine Crews in the E.E.C.) Barcelona, 1993.

[72] See section 3.6.

[73] See sections 1.2 and 1.3.

[74] CHAPMAN, P.K. *Trouble on Board.* New York, 1992 - p. 5.

[75] HERNÁNDEZ IZAL, S. *Buques con tripulación reducida.* (Ships with small crews) Barcelona.

[76] See section 3.7.

[77] See (63).

[78] See (72).

[79] MARCOVITZ, E. *Fatigue aboard ships.* Portugal, 1994.

[80] See (79).

[81] MARÍ SAGARRA, R. *Aproximación al método de evaluación del riesgo de incendio estructural y global de los buques.* (An approach to the method of assessing structural and global fire riks in ships) Barcelona, 1991.

[82] See (31).

[83] ITF, Marine Bulletin, London, 1994.

[84] See (33).

[85] See (75).

[86] see (1) pp. 25-26.

[87] see (1), p. 26.

[88] see section 4.5

[89] SOMMER. R. *Patients who grow old in a mental hospital.* Cleveland, 1959.

[90] See (33).

[91] APOSTOLADO DEL MAR: *Encuesta Nacional a Marinos.* Madrid, 1984.

[92] INTERNATIONAL CHRISTIAN MARITIME ASSOCIATION: *Seafarers' Survey.* United Kingdom, 1988.

[93] STELLA MARIS: *Trabajo de Investigación. Parte I: Situación socio-cultural y religiosa de los marinos.* Buenos Aires, 1979.

[94] BENJAMIN, R. et al., *L'Univers des Marins.* Paris, 1970.

[95] see (92).

[96] see (75).

[97] SCHUTZ, A. *Estudios sobre teoría social.* Buenos Aires, 1974, pp. 95-107.

[98] see (31), p. 66 et seq.

[99] See (1), p. 53.

[100] See (1) pp. 70-73.

[101] See (50).

[102] BEOBIDE, J. *La soledad del marino.* Barcelona, 1993.

[103] LARRAURI, F; CARBAJOSA, J. *El ocio en la mar.* Barcelona, 1982.

[104] HOPE, R. *Spare Time at Sea.* United Kingdom.

[105] The author has had personal experience of the significance of parties involving the whole crew. On board the bulkcarrier "Lukua", on which he undertook part of his nautical practicals, was a Basque capitain, Mr. Gregorio Arrinda, by then close to retirement, who attached considerable importance to parties. On his birthday there was a special lunch for the entire crew and later (it was a Sunday) singing and revelling until close on dinner time. And with the same captain the author had occasion to celebrate Christmas and New Year's Eve, with festivities well into the early hours. Those on watch were relieved so that they could join in. Thus, even on Christmas Eve, nobody felt lonely; each no doubt remembered his family, but nobody could feel alone or isolated.

[106] See (34), pp. 52-65.

[107] MOSCOVICI, S. et al. *Psicologia Social II.* Barcelona, 1986, p. 535.

[108] see (24).

[109] From the type of vessel known as "tanker" (oil tanker).

[110] see section 4.3.

[111] see (33), p. 44.

[112] see (33), p. 49.

[113] see (33), p. 45.

[114] DYER-SMITH, M. *Boring Work.* Portugal, 1994.

[115] see (33), p. 64.

[116] see section 5.4.2.

[117] see (75).

[118] MARCOVITZ, E. *Fatigue on board ships.* Lisbon, 1994.

[119] INTERNATIONAL MARITIME ORGANIZATION. *Report for the Maritime Safety Committee.* London, 1992.

[120] SAGARDUY, B. *La mujer como profesional de mar.* Barcelona, 1994.

[121] SAGARDUY, B. *Presencia de la mujer in la marina mercante.* Portugalete, 1992.

[122] IBAÑEZ, I. *La mujer como profesional del mar.* Barcelona, 1994.

[123] CARDONA, M. *La mujer como profesional de mar.* Barcelona, 1994.

[124] SANCHEZ, F. *La mujer como profesional del mar.* Barcelona, 1994.

[125] see (123).

[126] see (1).

[127] BANKSTON, W.B., FLOYD, H.H. and FORSYTH, C.J. *Towards a general model of the process of radical conversion: an interactionist perspective on the transformation of self-identity.* Louisiana, 1981.

[128] IRWIN, J. *The Felon.* New Jersey, 1970.

[129] HANNA, C.F. *Complaint as a form of association.* Louisiana, 1981.

[130] Forsyth, C.J., Bankston, W.B. *The socio-psychological consequence of life at sea: a cause model.* Hants, 1984.

[131] DORIOL, R. *Informe de un sacerdote obrero jesuita sobre su vida con los marinos.* Paris, 1991.

[132] See (132).

[133] HEALEY, J.C. *Foc'sle and Glory Hole: a study of merchant marine and his occupation.* New York, 1936.

[134] See section 2.3.1.

[135] HAHMAN, E. *Seamen Ashore.* New Haven, 1952.

[136] See (132).

[137] At the beginning of the 1970s the author experienced a situation of semi-mutiny aboard a passenger liner, arising out of a clamour to free a stowaway. In the face of the danger posed by the threatening attitude of many of the passengers, measures were taken to detain the ringleaders and shut them up in padlocked cabins until the ship arrived in port.

[138] FORSYTH, C.J., BANKSTON, W. *The merchant seaman as a social type: a marginal type of lifestyle.* Louisiana State University, 1983.

[139] *Lass Anker Fallen.* Bremen, 1993.

[140] FORYTH, C.J., GRAMLING, R. *Adaptative Familial Strategies Among Merchant Seamen.* University of Southwestern Louisiana, 1990.

[141] BOHEN, H., VIVEROS, A. *Balancing jobs and family life.* Philadelphia: Temple University Press, 1981.

BOSS, P. *The relationship of psychological father presence, wife's personal qualities and wife family dysfunction in families on missing fathers.* Louisiana, 1980.

[142] See (139).

[143] MAU, G., GASSNEN, V., LANGHANS, K. and JENSEN, H.J. *Sozialpsychologische Untersuchungen an bord deutscher Seeschiffe.* Flensburg, 1974.

[144] See (92).

[145] RODRIGUEZ.MARTOS, R. *Trabajo marítimo y familia: dos realidades en tensión.* Mombasa, 1987.

[146] DECKER, K.R. *Coping with Sea Duty: Problems encountered and resources utilized during periods of family separation.* New York, 1978, pp. 123-129.

[147] See section 3.10.

[148] FORSYTH, C.J. *Determinants of family integration among merchant seamen.* The University of Southwestern Louisiana, 1988.

[149] TONNIES, F. *Community and Society.* Michigan State University, 1957.

[150] MIDDLETON, R. *Alienation, Race and Education.* U.S.A., 1963.

[151] GROVE, W.; HUGHES, M. *Reexamining the Ecological Fallacy: a Study in which Aggregate Data are Critical in Investigating the Pathological Effect of Living Alone.* University of North Carolina, 1980.

[152] BEOBIDE, J. *La Soledad en la Gente de Mar.* Barcelona, 1993.

[153] SANTOS, F. *Ponencia sobre la familia del marino.* Málaga, 1995.

[154] SCHUTZ, A. *Estudios sobre teoría social. La vuelta al hogar.* Buenos Aires, 1974.

[155] Author's note: After my first voyage as a nautical apprentice, having been away nearly ten months travelling half way round the world, I returned home one night, late by then, and when after sharing a few hours with my family and celebrating my return I was once again alone in my bedroom, I had a very strange sensation. I felt almost depressed. It was a mixture of feelings. What made me feel worst was that I saw myself as a stranger, I couldn't recognise myself. At times I even thought of the ship, the cabin, my shipmates, and I wondered "What am I doing here?" It was a deflating feeling, which as the days passed became less acute, until I felt once again integrated into my "all-time family". Other seafaring colleagues have had similar experiences.

[156] See (155), p. 110.

[157] See (155), p. 110.

[158] See (155), p. 114.

[159] LARRAURI, F. *Psicología penitenciaria: observació y predicció de la conducta en permisos de sortida.* Barcelona, 1994.

[160] See (155), p. 115.

[161] HOHMAN, E. *Seamen ashore.* New Haven, 1952.

[162] See (139), and FORSYTH, C and BANKSTON, W.B.: The Social Psychological Consequence of Life at Sea: A Cause Model. Hants, 1984.

[163] KOZAK, S. *2nd International Workshop on human relations and conditions on board ships.* Rijeka, 1988.

[164] KOZAK, S.A *Personality Traits as Factor of Academic Success or Failure in Maritime Studies.* Gdynia, 1988.

[165] See (161).

[166] BORUCKI, Z. *Personality and Adaptability to the Profession of Seamen.* Gdansk, 1986.

[167] ARNAUTOVIC, D. *Psychological Selection of Applicants for Nautical Schools.* Rijeka, 1988.

[168] BOEHM, H. *The Social Climate on Board towards enhanced efficiency.* Opatija, 1982.

[169] ONKINA, T.A.; VINOGRADOV, S.A. *Psychological Selection of Ship's Specialists as the Factor of Prevention of Sea Ship Accidents.* Rijeka, 1988.

[170] CAVACO, F.A. *Leadership as a moderating factor of stress in the crews of Portuguese oil tankers.* Rijeka, 1988.

[171] See section 3.8.2.

[172] See (170).

[173] SCHAGER, B. *A new assessment for applicants.* Copenhagen, 1993.

[174] See (173).

[175] DYER-SMITH, M. *Enhancing Safety and Quality through focusing on the human factors in shipping.* London, 1993.

[176] FROESE, J. *More electronics - improved safety or more risk?* Surrey, 1994

[177] See (175).

[178] RIBERA ALSINA, J. *Bueques con tripulación reducida.* Barcelona, 1988. (Ships with reduced crews.)

[179] HERNÁNDEZ IZAL, S. *Buques con tripulación reducida.* Barcelona, 1988. (Ships with reduced crews.)

[180] FORSCHUNGSTELLE FÜR SCHIFFSBETRIEBSTECHNIK. *Sozialpsychologische Untersuchungen an Bord Deutscher Seeschiffe.* Flensburg, 1974.

[181] KLEMPERER, E. *Reduction of Ships' Crews. Factors to be considered.* Rijeka, 1988.

[182] See section 5.5.2.

[183] MUNK, T.; LAURITZEN, J. *Safety considerations in the design and operation of a six-man refrigerated vessel.* London, 1991.

[184] PUVOGEL, H. *Die letzte Fahrt der Scarabea.* Bremen, 1992.

[185] YEGOROV, Y.N.; KORMACHEV, V.V. *On personality traits conducive to successful performance and psychological compatibility of ship commanding personnel.* Leningrad, 1990.

www.ingramcontent.com/pod-product-compliance
Lightning Source LLC
Chambersburg PA
CBHW081214230426
43666CB00015B/2728